Transgender Marxism

'A terrific collection of essays – I couldn't put it down.'

—Kathi Weeks, author of *The Problem with Work*

'Is there a transgender Marxism? This pioneering collection shows that the answer is there are many – inspired by psychoanalysis, union organising, queer communities, Black struggles and more. Material realities matter, tremendously, in trans lives; and trans experiences can change our thinking about both capitalism and liberation.'

—Raewyn Connell, author of *Gender: In World Perspective*

'What lives and thinks on through the staggering failures of contemporary trans visibility and rights-based claims? This stunning collection answers in the collective form of a transgender Marxism. We find ourselves remade, hungrier and braver, in this book. Trans becomes in these pages the vibrant event of a historical materialism from below, intimate and urgent.'

—Jules-Gill Peterson, Associate Professor of English and Gender, Sexuality, and Women's Studies at the University of Pittsburgh and the author of *Histories of the Transgender Child*

'Powerful ... with stunning sophistication and insights, *Transgender Marxism* challenges capitalism's social foundations in gendered patterns of property, work, and entitlement to develop new forms of sociality beyond the family and its dyadic sexual division.'

—Petrus Liu, author of *Queer Marxism in Two Chinas*

'Brilliant, thoughtfully researched, and compelling. An immense contribution to the trans liberation struggle and to trans studies scholarship.'

—Dean Spade, Associate Professor of Law at Seattle University School of Law

Transgender Marxism

Edited by
Jules Joanne Gleeson and Elle O'Rourke

Afterword by Jordy Rosenberg

First published 2021 by Pluto Press
New Wing, Somerset House, Strand, London WC2R 1LA

www.plutobooks.com

British Library Cataloguing in Publication Data
A catalogue record for this book is available from the British Library

ISBN   978 0 7453 4165 1   Hardback
ISBN   978 0 7453 4166 8   Paperback
ISBN   978 1 78680 732 8   PDF
ISBN   978 1 78680 733 5   EPUB
ISBN   978 1 78680 734 2   Kindle

This book is printed on paper suitable for recycling and made from fully managed and sustained forest sources. Logging, pulping and manufacturing processes are expected to conform to the environmental standards of the country of origin.

Typeset by Stanford DTP Services, Northampton, England

Simultaneously printed in the United Kingdom and United States of America

Contents

Acknowledgements

First of all, we'd like to thank our contributors, and everyone who supported them in writing up their perspectives for this collection. You fulfilled all our hopes.

Producing a theoretical work from a stigmatised position (often reduced to a pathology by outsiders) will always be a trial. But equally, as editors we've found this process joyful. We're grateful for the generational work of solidarity and collaboration, that have allowed trans people both to survive our social conditions, and understand them. And for the freely shared goodwill and concrete support we found from transgender communists (and admirers) at every turn, while putting this all together. Thank you, thank you.

Kate Doyle Griffiths first suggested a collection of this kind, back in 2018. Completing it would not have been possible without the active support of Pluto Press, who greeted it with nothing but enthusiasm, and in particular from our primary editor David Shulman. Without David's consistent belief in this project, right from the beginning, this book would never have seen print.

We'd both like to thank all the members of Leftovers communist discussion group. Among many other topics, they provided a procession of insights on the interplay of Capital and gender, with chat ranging freely from the rigorous to the absurd.

Historical Materialism Conference (London and New York City) for providing a venue for many of these essays and ideas to receive a first airing, via our Leftovers Live sessions. Especially Paul Reynolds and Holly Lewis on the HM Sexuality and Political Economy stream, for arranging events including our plenary session in 2019, and book preview in 2020. MAMA (Zagreb), Salvage Quarterly, Death Panel podcast, Solidarity College, RS21, Plan C, the Centres for Global Political Economy and Sexual Dissidence at Sussex University, Hypocrite Reader, and New Socialist also provided invaluable platforms during harsh times.

Thanks to everyone at Homintern, Pinko Magazine, Invert Journal, and Lumpen. You revived some gnarled hobgoblins.

We would also like to extend our gratitude to our community readers, who read through draft chapters during the book's first round of copy editing. Each of them provided invaluable commentary and corrections, helping this collection take the best shape possible. Thanks to: Tom Lynch, Nathan Tankus, josie sparrow, Rowan Davis, Douglas Williams, Cara E. Hurtle, KJ Vincent, Rhys Jones, Mai G, Sylvia McCheyne, Kay Gabriel, Amelia Horgan, Greg Afinogenov, Maria, Ben Miller, Mel Mikhail, Michael Davin, David Hartery, Natalie TS, Matt Cull, Jo Zubrow, Purnima Tulsyan, Nina Taaffe, Charlie Powell, Amy De'Ath and Maya Andrea Gonzalez. And especially: Emrys Travis, who read every single draft with an infectious enthusiasm, and Jack Dragu for their invaluable assistance with Xandra Metcalfe's chapter.

To those passing through those twinned flames of stigmatisation and proletarianisation for the first time as they read this: we wish you the best, we know how you ache, and hope this collection will be of use to you.

* * *

Elle would like to thank her family, Jasbir, Laura, Ada, Eleanor, Ben, Toby, Caela, Phoebe, Natalie and Amber. Her friends at New Socialist, for their comradeship, solidarity and support, particularly Tom and josie. Everyone at QueerCare – for their assiduous commitment to uniting 'theory' and 'practice'. Greg Afinogenov, Owen Hatherley and Tim MacGabhann all offered generous assistance and kindness over this past year in ways that were greatly appreciated. Thank you, lads. Kyle Geraghty has been a consistent friend, particularly in encouraging her to pursue her academic interests, even when her health made that difficult. As has Griffin McCarthy Bur. Angela Mitropoulos' intellectual influence on the final text will be unmistakable. Thanks also to Erin & Sean, Tyler, Mo, Jools, Hassan E.T, Gavin M, Max A, Chuckie K, Nella Lou, Simon, Todd, Sean, Anna, Cate, Khan, Kyle, Matthijs, Tom P, Mairead, Aurora, Karen, Lauren G, Elka, Julie, Alex, Clancy, David, Esyld, Ronan, James C, James L, Cormac, Eugene, Frank, Louis, Críostóir, Chris L, Ash, Nicola and Lilith. Legends all.

The old Manchester Socialist Reading Group, John, Andrew and Ed, where many of her current interests and ideas were first cultivated. Friendships and conversations sparked on social media over many years, too innumerable to list but all deeply cherished. The Earthen Cat Tree, they know why. And, finally, Nelly, for everything. This book is for her.

Jules thanks Serafina, Zori, Daniel Massow, and Linda for getting her through the last year. Her sister Danielle, Barry, and all the books. Damon for 14 years of precious friendship. Alice, Squid, Denice, Denise, Marina, Magda, BJ and especially Mirah for making Vienna habitable. From its playful underground: Ju, Georgie, Penny, Svean, Zoe, Knorri, Andrea, Luka, Petra, Rheta, Nello, Carter, and her collaborator Ruby. Joss, Kirsten, Phoebe, Danny, Cedrik, Shabby, Sinead, Puck, Christina, Sophie, Allana, Dani, Tilly and Archie for hanging out, back in the day. Lyra, Naith, Vaughn, Jet and Valerie for inspiration during impressionable moments. Austria's intersex platform, VIMÖ and OII for all they've done. Elizabeth and Teddy. New Critical Approaches to the Byzantine World research network, BASIC, Lockdown Tarot Crew, and TFF. Avalon and Carmel. KDG, obviously. Nicole, Tingting and Julaika for the animals. Colin Beckett, Cedric Fauq and Tolerant Alice for the first break. Dr K. For bonds to grow from: Allison, Liv, Alyssa, and Merve. Laura Jung, for so much! Her therapist, JY. Her comrades and pals: Alex Vukovich, another Alex, Barms, Margarida, Kita, Jamie, Shenja, Hagen, Masha, Daniel Freithofer, Bea, Gabriel, the Gonan twins, Nick Evans, Nik, Barms, Ilya, Milinda, May, Sandy, Mia, Oelle, Matt Kinloch, Jose, Roxy, Bella, Nathan, Matthijs, Mariana, Kyle, Neil Braganza, Dylan, Taisie, Jo, Evan, Nykki, Kit, Grietje, Ankica, Emily Zhou, Eliana, Liz Cho, Izzy, Laurel, Emma Round, Rose-Anne, Stani, Jack Belloli, Aaron, Selin, Emily Muna. And Faeza, this is for you (моя кошка).

During this book's production Jules lost her brother, Laurence (1982–2019), an old friend who once named her, Madi (1992–2019), and her beloved confidant, Martina (1989–2020). They're missed every day, their wisdom and wit made this book possible, and their memories are a blessing. Rest In Peace.

Introduction

Jules Joanne Gleeson and Elle O'Rourke

Subcultures and separation

There seem to be more of us around, lately.

Trans aesthetics, stylings, and tastes have swollen well beyond the set of subcultures they spanned a handful of years ago. Transgender culture has popularised itself to an extent previous generations of Western gender subversives could have barely imagined. This blossoming form has expanded faster than even those most plunged into it can keep track of.

What had once been strictly clandestine – or otherwise associated with political radicalism – has now been embraced outside its niche constituency. Transgender culture has increasingly appeared as a *mass* culture. As such, we might expect to see a dwindling of trans politics as a subversive force. Instead, transgender communism has bloomed, with revolutionary movements around the world often enough being led by those whose lives have been reshaped around transition. Whether the struggle is liberation from prisons and policing, poverty and austerity, combating fascist street movements, or averting ecological collapse, trans people are found in disproportionate numbers, and full voice. Our unlikely prominence in revolutionary organisations and subversive circles is often as baffling to us as anyone else.

The role of this collection is not to birth a new perspective: clearly, Transgender Marxism exists already. For those minded to find it, marginal publications and private accounts have fostered this vein of thought for years. It does not fall to us to *bring into being* a coupling of transgender theory and Marxist politics.

Transgender Marxism is already a flourishing field, if one that has found itself confined to the most esoteric and fleeting outlets. This anthology collects theoretical perspectives by transgender writers that we had noticed spreading across ephemeral spaces: activist circles, book clubs, and social media, in zines and social media DMs.

Again and again, frameworks originating in the loose and meticulous tradition known as Marxism were to be found being brought to bear on questions around gender transition, or how gender nonconformity can survive in a capitalist context more generally. But how did the analysis of economic modes and historical epochs come to be so intuitively directed towards gender transitions, the most immediate and ethical of processes?

Let's begin with our cultural denigration, which remains a pervasive feature of our lives (popularisation of our experiences notwithstanding). Due to the stigma we still encounter so routinely, trans theorisation most often unfolds as a process of confiding and confessing. We speak about our own experiences more often than we attempt to speak more comprehensively. We gather audiences that are as much our confidants as our comrades. This style of publication has the blessing of the concrete, while also finding itself locked into inevitable repetition. Critical vocabularies for grasping (and one day defeating) transphobia are invented, then reinvented anew.[1] Commonalities between our epiphanies and attempts at repression result in extensive in-joking, moments of recognition that our most freakish features are also from another view quite easily predictable. Our struggles are at once life-or-death and laughable, unique and hackneyed. Slang comes into existence and becomes dated across seasons; gender positions that previously went unnamed are barely christened before becoming fuel for furtive in-joking. A resulting terminological churn threatens to become an end-in-itself, rather than an emancipatory tool.

This seems a revealing fate: our genders exist at once in normative and abstracted terms (women do this, men do that ...), and intimately concrete ones ('I have been on HRT for nine months now ...'). Transgender experiences straddle the conventional limits of political and private life, workplace and household. Transition is at once a procedure with far-reaching social ramifications, and an intimately personal matter.

But given this balance, why are so many transgender people apparently drawn to Marxism, and to revolutionary theory more generally? As workforces have been driven apart into ever more splintered formations, reduced in many instances to the casualised 'gig', why has systemic thought blossomed rather than contracted over the first decade of the twenty-first century? Most obviously, the same stigma that causes us to confine our thinking to private venues leads to our appearances in politics proving so eruptive. Transgender life is harsh enough that many are easily led to conclude that our conditions are beyond redemption; that no centre-left party or Third Sector trend can be relied upon to truly loosen the grip of oppression.

And so in recent years, for those introducing themselves to others in revolutionary circles, to hear 'trans' and 'communist' in the same breath has become quite routine. Again: we move between the freakish and outlandish to the predictable, the cliché.

Through collecting these essays as a mass-marketed book, we aim to capture the recent proliferation of gender-deviant Marxist thought in a more lasting and accessible form; to move us beyond the limits of ornate in-joking, and communal self-referentiality, and towards social revolution. Or at least to avoid unwitting repetition, and hopeless clashes of lingo, as divergent scenes and traditions come to the same conclusions using different terms.

Already, through this unsteady process of parallel analysis and reinvention, an array of trans people have deployed historical materialist approaches to gender. Our struggle for political emancipation has become understood as one progression within a broader process of class war, and our transitions as reshaping the demands of social reproduction.

We believe that the existing breakthroughs achieved by transgender Marxists will transform the scope for revolutionary action in the coming years. We were determined not to limit ourselves to the theorisation of trans lives available through traditional academic channels. What one faculty or another might deem sufficiently 'scholarly' could never be our standard. While we've held contributors to a high standard, fitting neatly into the existing division of intellectual labour is not one of our concerns. We aimed to include a global range of perspectives, without burdening any author with the role of serving as local 'representatives', or native informants.[2]

This collection will doubtless cause outrage in certain quarters *within* Marxism. Many have taken class politics as somehow in opposition to any consideration of gender minorities, who are framed as a sideshow to the simplicity and ordinary concerns of workers. What Eric Hobsbawm called 'vulgar Marxism' (the set of doctrines popularly associated with Marx's thought, but with a dubious foundation in his actual writings) has become a noisier trend in recent years.[3] Vulgar Marxists see class as a social division run out of uneven control of the means of production, and the deployment of labour required to keep these lopsided relations operative across generations. Strictly relating political struggles to a steadfast focus on this divide is taken to be the sole sound basis for a 'materialist' view of social relations. Middlebrow Marxists have increasingly come to juxtapose this rigid realism with the vagaries of 'identity politics'.

Yet, from Marx's earliest communist writings onwards, we see a sharp concern with questions of social particularity. From his writings on the American Civil War to the question of anti-Semitism, Marx refused to set aside the fate of minority groups from the structuring of society as a whole. In one of his earliest published works, 'On the Jewish Question', Marx introduces the distinctive operation of the state:

> The political annulment of private property not only fails to abolish private property but even presupposes it. The state abolishes, in its own way, distinctions of birth, social rank, education, occupation, when it declares that birth, social rank, education, occupation, are non-political distinctions. When the state proclaims – without regard to these distinctions – that every member of the nation is an equal participant in national sovereignty, when it treats all elements of the real life of the nation from the standpoint of the state. Nevertheless, the state allows private property, education, occupation, to act in their way – i.e., as private property, as education, as occupation, and to exert the influence of their special nature. Far from abolishing these real distinctions, the state only exists on the presupposition of their existence; it feels itself to be a political state and asserts its universality only in opposition to these elements of its being.

In other words, we find in Marx's writings and political concerns still of much relevance to our own struggles. If we are charged with operating outside of Marxism proper, we can only gladly assent and proudly take our place among 'improper Marxists', along with Marx himself.

The state that Marx described has not vanished. Still adopting a supposed impartiality, still supporting social oppression, the enmeshment of official civic identity and the communities which provide us lives worth surviving through continue to be confronted by successive generations of revolutionaries. Civic identity is always selectively extended in its official form (for instance, a migrant obliged to demonstrate herself as 'skilled' and well behaved in order to be given leave to remain) and then tacitly undermined by structural dispossession (a racialised minority of citizens may have equal rights in many respects from birth, yet still face oppression daily). This tension is one that confounded emancipatory movements of the twentieth century: formal emancipatory processes generated new constituencies willing to 'quit while they were ahead', and retire to private life, rather than press for more contentious 'structural' transformation, or through to social revolution. These same tensions are still struggled with in the present: participants in revolutionary political movements inevitably at once have to be minded with doing what they can to overturn the existing order, while fashioning a liveable life in the meantime. In much of Europe and the Anglophone world, the successes of generations of struggle for trans liberation are bringing victories which run aground in these terms. Granted official sanction approval for our shifting identities, trans people find ourselves drawing closer and closer to a formalised equality. Notable reversals have appeared in nations overtaken by right populism, such as Hungary and the United States under four years of Trump. Yet this simplification of bureaucratic processing has fallen far short of providing true relief from our everyday torments and humiliations.

The 'mainstream' of trans activism has focused on smoothing over the process of transition as it runs through institutions, including those belonging to the state. Our domination by state bureaucracy, by landlords and employers, is often enough treated as a given, to be reclad with sensitivity training workshops and pronoun go-rounds. In many national contexts, considerable breakthroughs have been won in affirming the doctrine of 'self-identification', as well as streamlining the process by which states validate legal sex changes. Although certain British feminist circles have reacted furiously against these breakthroughs – a backlash that has since metastasised into the wider liberal intelligentsia – this rainy backwater seems to be something of an outlier.[4] For the most part, left-wing circles and youth movements worldwide are coming to accept the call for 'trans rights' as a basic principle.

But what if the emancipation of trans people cannot be won through the securing of 'rights'? What if, however, smoothed-over the process of state validation were to become, a meaningful liberation remained out of view? What if even the most thoroughgoing political defeat of fascism would not be guaranteed to achieve our social liberation?

It's these questions which Transgender Marxism will begin to answer.

We offer our answer as a polyphony. There is no authoritative approach to Marx and his legacy, and nor have we sought to impose one. Marxism is a broad and living tradition, defined by its continual internal disputations, its vying schools, and its contested orthodoxies.

Each of these finds inspiration in a different facet of Marx's practice. For some, it is Marx the ur-sociologist with a voracious appetite for empirical research, huddled over a table awaiting deliveries from the archives in the British Library, steadily concocting a monumental achievement that still closely informs contemporary researchers' inquiries. Employment statistics, mainstream psychology and economic literature, journalism, workers' inquiry and testimony – the blue books of our age – are marshalled for our own purposes. Like Marx studying the political economists he sought to critique, we use this dry material to reveal the absurdities of our social system, in the terms of the very authorities who speak in its defence.

Others find consonance in Marx the philosopher, versed in the history of thought from Epicurus right up to the fevered esotericism of the German idealists of his day – a Marx who sought to apprehend the tangled relations of modernity, capitalism, colonialism, and the arrival of mass politics. Marx's mastery of philosophical terms of art left him at once working against their detachment, and embedded in their frames of reference. Marx responded to the output of these thinkers where it seemed relevant to his political concerns, while never being fully integrated into, or ingratiated with, any scholarly community – a common enough fate for transgender Marxist theorists today.

Still others take their cue from Marx the propagandist – a dedicated organiser, doggedly focused on developing autonomous power. A strategic monomaniac, involved almost exclusively with organisations founded by workers for the promotion of workers' interests. A rigid proponent of political struggle as the successive development of worker power who refused the fragmenting of politics into a series of 'issues', to be resolved by respective national parliaments, polite societies, and the intelligentsia. This aspect of Marx offers nothing less than a total break from what is conventionally considered 'political': it urges abstinence from the usual flurry of parliamentary gossip, earnest immersion in NGO reports, and reliance on sturdy electoral conventions which narrow the horizons of the possible. The grandiose chambers and stifling committees of national and global governance offer us only one dimension of the political. *Transgender Marxism* directs our attention towards the *power* on which any shop floor, building site or office truly relies.

But as much as any feature of Marx's life and work itself, what has surely drawn many trans theorists towards Marxism is frustration at what we might call the 'mainstream' of trans activism (as strange a notion as this may seem to many). From the reluctance of many organisations to either think beyond the state and the NGO complex, to those groups, self-styled as 'communities', that are clearly riven by the divided class positions and interests of its participants. Too often we have found ourselves expected to set aside questions of exploitation or modes of production, to quiet that part of us that might detect any differentiation within the commonality. The consequence is always the same: it will always require a dose of bad faith to maintain the conceit that all transgender people share precisely the same interests. For all the Global Right's panicked insistence that the state's willingness to tolerate our presence indicates a seismic rift in the course of history, in reality, whatever minor breakthroughs we win pose no threat to the much sturdier relations of exploitation on which society rests.

In this context, Marxism can offer explanations that prevent inevitable burnout from backsliding into mere cynicism. It can reorient us away from liberal optimism, and the predictable shocks that follow on from it. It directs us against the state, and the naturalisation of human exploitation. And, at times, it can direct us away from Marx himself. Marxism is, for us, a practice of immanent critique; that is, a practice of thinking with Marx in spirit rather than in letter. We think *with* him in order to think *against* and *beyond* his limits.

The old mole and the endocrine system

Transgender Marxism focuses wilfully on that which others might dismiss as vulgar, inappropriate, besides-the-political. It aims to provide a materialist account of the distinctive conditions of lack in which we find ourselves, and to help us wriggle free through unlikely means.

Political economist and pornographer Georges Bataille, writing between the wars, distinguished between the work of earlier revolutionaries and Marx's baser materialism. Whereas previous generations had sought out a transcendent principle as a means of drawing 'above' the grisly realities of imperialism, Marx, Bataille argued, chose a humbler metaphor:

> The eagle's hooked beak, which cuts all that enters into competition with it and cannot be cut, suggests its sovereign virility...Politically the eagle is identified with imperialism, that is with the unconstrained development of individual authoritarian power, triumphant over all obstacles ... Revolutionary idealism tends to make of the revolution an eagle above eagles, a *supereagle* striking down authoritarian imperialism. An idea as radiant as an adolescent eloquently seizing power for the benefit of utopian enlightenment. This detour naturally leads to the failure of the revolution and, with the help of military fascism, the satisfaction of the elevated need for idealism.
>
> Meanwhile, brought back to the subterranean action of economic facts, the 'old-mole' revolution hollows out chambers in a decomposed soil repugnant to the delicate nose of the utopians. 'Old mole', Marx's resounding expression for the complete satisfaction of the revolutionary outburst of the masses, must be understood in relation to the notion of a geological uprising as expressed in the *Communist Manifesto*. Marx's point of departure has nothing to do with the heavens, preferred station of the imperialist eagle as of Christian or revolutionary utopias. He begins with the bowels of the earth, as in the materialist bowels of proletarians.[5]

Following the mole's tracks, Transgender Marxism unearths the base needs of trans proles and brings them above ground, into clearer view.

Much work remains to be done expanding the earthy, intestinal visions of Marx and his successors outwards, moving from the bowels towards the glands and receptors that make up our endocrine system. Transition, too, must come to be understood by revolutionaries as a response to its own form of *hunger*. The longings that drive so many to reforge lives for ourselves that leave us thoroughly proletarianised, or cast out, rendered surplus. Those cravings and cavings-in that clinicians have long attempted to desiccate under the catch-all term 'dysphoria'. In truth, our moments of euphoric coping are enmeshed with the moments in which we are struck dumb by gut-churning dread. These are the moments that define our everyday lives. The restless energies that produce for us new needs; needs that can be difficult even to describe. Transphobic strands of 'revolutionary' thought would rather these yearnings be set aside, left unspoken; to be repressed (at least in the political arena), or perhaps to be exterminated altogether.

Too often, what passes for revolutionary thought on sex has done little better: endocrinology is reduced to a corporate plot. Just another opportunity for polluting human bodies in pursuit of profits. For us, the flows of hormones which can condemn or revive us are no more natural than capitalism, and no more sinister than filling our bellies with food. Our needs bury themselves measurably through our blood-stream, then define our contentment on levels still not possible to fully isolate, or reliably record.[6]

We do not recognise readings of Marx which see him as unconcerned with matters of physicality and bodily involvement in exploitation. Contemporary Marxist scholars, including Keston Sutherland and Maya Gonzalez, have drawn attention to Marx's definition of labour as consisting of 'a productive expenditure of human brains, muscles, nerves, hands etc.'.[7] And Marx was certainly not oblivious to the ways in which the forces of production determine what counts as an acceptable or a useful body.[8] We follow in this tradition closely, understanding that our physical forms are reshaped first and foremost by the demands of capital. From muscle mass to skin, skeletons to hair follicles, our forms take shape in the face of history. But transitions never *belong* to capitalism. Even as they are always routed through it, they also run against it. The transgender revolutionary is one who can neither deny their cravings, nor curse themselves for their untoward identity. We resent the society that birthed us, just as we refuse to set aside the tools it has offered us. We find ourselves at once immersed and resistant.

Key to our agenda is ensuring that trans life *itself* comes clearly into view: we are opposed to the entrenchment of a transcendent principle of 'trans' that comes to obscure the particular struggles of trans people to survive in the face of capitalism (or indeed, other modes of production). The false promise of transcendence is that our experiences can soar in the manner of Bataille's eagle, offering a view of worldly affairs from such a distance that the grime and stretch marks are out of sight. We reject this approach. Our struggle is one that must be understood as intimate, concrete, and particular; just as it restlessly casts shadows over more universal questions, upsets attempted settlements between classes, and erodes otherwise tidy attempts at systemic thought. Transition is not a dive into unbounded expansiveness, but a mess that a thousand failed attempts at comprehensive sociology have tried to push out of view. A persistent irritant, disturbing the smoothness of grand narratives.

We are forced to hide ourselves, while pinned in clear view. We are human refuse or exotic delicacies, depending on the website. To see us clearly evokes cringes and trembling, yet we are driven onto the streets.

True to this nature, trans people occupy an awkward space in social theory and Marxist politics. When not actively vilified, or included as a polite footnote, many assume an interest in trans people thanks to our *marginalisation*. As we are more likely to experience poverty, destitution, engage in sex work, experience abuse and mistreatment by wider society, and the police and the criminal justice system, we tend to be more radical than the general population, and thus a source of special interest. By dint of our positionality, this argument runs, we are readymade comrades.

In particular, because we occupy a 'liminal' and 'ambiguous' space in the gender order, we are taken to embody (or at least provoke) a space of subversion and rebellion. One that can, perhaps, shake existing society out of its complacency vis-à-vis sex and gender – a gender vanguardism of sorts. The upshot is that trans people are perhaps a useful source of recruits, or a fashionable cause to follow – and, *sotto voce*, bearers of a special responsibility.

We might call this the 'auxiliary' move: transgender workers are cast as playing a prominent role within a shared struggle due to the extent of their proletarianised condition. The upshot is that trans people and trans struggles are taken as being relevant *only in so far* as they boost struggles in which socialist groups are already participants, or in which they wish to participate. This runs at odds to drawing from the obvious questions thrown up by the lived experiences of trans workers. From sex work to 'trans in tech', the fields most stereotypically associated with trans people are generally also those notoriously resistant to unionisation, to strikes, and other standard fare for workerist organising.

As an account of trans and queer life this 'auxiliary' argument is precisely *negative*. We are of note due to our suffering, and by dint of our stigmatisation and its travails. In short, we serve the cause as exemplary proletarians. Little space is left for the actual substance of trans life, the experiences of surviving in the context of separation that we already share among ourselves, and the resultant insights for a broader and refreshed view of capitalism's reproduction.

But while ever more popular, this is hardly a new move. Emma Heaney has shown that throughout modern history trans women find themselves and their experiences always represented as an allegory for *something else*. Rather than being treated on their own terms, trans women serve to ground the universality of cis experience.[9] Literary modernism is replete with examples of trans women as metaphorical figures for the destabilisation of inherited gender traditions. We are stand-ins for broader destabilisations brought about by urbanisation, suffrage, and women entering new roles in the workforce, and with that, attendant anxieties over masculine self-assurance and patriarchal entitlement. In other accounts, transgender experiences serve as an example of the dizzying achievements of techno-scientific modernity. In Freud's hands, we appear as a degraded figure who is, nevertheless, a critical allegory for the unconscious that clarifies his theory of same-sex desire as inversion and castration anxiety. Here, wilful feminisation is a looming threat of egoic injury, clarifying the operation and universality of *cis-sex*.[10]

Yet here we find a double bind: in so far as the transgender woman is seen to be speaking of herself, she is taken to be trafficking in mere particularity. She appears as a marginal concern of no wider import, easily corralled. But in so far as she is taken to be speaking on a more general, more universal register, she effaces her very particularity. As she is brought to bear on all topics of social weight, she instrumentalises herself – trans as condition, as a way of being, as a mode of life – and is made to bear the burden of the entire gendered order. Whatever she is, the trans woman is always not herself; she is a representation of gender trouble writ large. Her own account can only be received with suspicion, yet much is demanded from her. Not only must she offer an account for her gender, but for yours as well.

The figure of the trans woman interloper, disrupting otherwise stable and harmonious relations within the community of women, functions to relieve radical feminism of the indignity of acknowledging the incoherence of the radical feminist project as such.[11] Conveniently, the trans woman as pest distracts from long-running doubts around radical feminism's claimed ability to speak for, represent, and defend the sanctity of women-in-general: women's rights, women's interests, women's spaces and women's knowledge. Here, the grit of trans women is abraded into the pearl of a rear-guard defence of female universalism. What the earlier feminist movement had sought to destabilise now becomes anxiously reasserted. If one is inclined to wonder how successfully the predominantly white, professionally-trained, and well-off ladies who have always dominated feminist 'leadership' might serve in that role, those self-appointed representatives find themselves with a readymade riposte: 'Well, we will at least do a better job than males'. By 'males', of course, they mean trans women.

Our answer to this is simple enough. Rather than a second-order modality of feminine embodiment, we insist that trans women face down the same imperatives of capitalist exploitation, exacerbated by patriarchal relations, as anyone else.

But something else is elided here. What about trans men? Thus far, the distinctive struggles and joys of transmasculine life have been downplayed to the point of being disappeared in much revolutionary theory. The question of how a proletarian manhood, or something like it, can be forged in the face of separation is a fraught one; like many such questions, it is too often avoided altogether. Most relevant revolutionary thought in the Anglophone context has been articulated under the label 'transfeminism', a designation which often seems to relegate trans male activists to a secondary standing.[12] This tendency self-perpetuates through a cycle of reaction, as transphobes take particular offence at the notion of trans womanhood, meaning attempted rebuttals of their bigotry tend to centre around a defence of trans women. The consequence is that the particular position and distinctive struggles faced by those transitioning to male are unthinkingly downplayed. We have little time for analysis which weighs up diligently who ranks as most oppressed among the oppressed. Let's move beyond this dead-end evaluation, and towards the shared emancipation which can only be achieved by comrades. Scholarly attempts to do so have featured freewheeling endocrino-romanticism (Paul Preciado), tenuous comparison (Maggie Nelson), and academic phenomenology (Gayle Salamon). Transgender Marxism offers a different approach.

Marx in transition

So how can we develop a theory which views trans politics as neither figural nor instrumental, but an account of self-knowledge? One generative of its own theoretical conclusions?

The beginnings of an answer appear in Marx and his critique of value. The categories Marx presents in *Capital* – commodity, capital, money – are performatives. While Marx attempts what he terms a 'scientific' approach to grasping capitalism, this is always a partial science. To accept Marx's view of value unsettles the naturalisation that ideology coats earlier accounts of capitalism (as well as more schools that rose to prominence in the wake of Marxism, particularly marginalism.) Marx's presentation of these categories is intensely parodic and deconstructive, in intent and effect. He operates with the gaze of a critical anthropologist, bringing in one character after another, before disassembling their roles in reproducing an emergent assemblage called capitalism.[13]

As a text, the structure of *Capital* bears more of an ironic resemblance to a play, or to the thrilling arc of Alexandre Dumas' *The Count of Monte Cristo* than to François Quesnay's *Tableau économique* or David Ricardo's *On the Principles of Political Economy and Taxation*. Marx's point is that beneath the reified social spheres of 'markets' and 'commerce' as objects of knowledge for the ascendent social science of political economy is a historically-bounded, emergent form of social organisation. One deeply invested in regulating the behaviours, bodily comportments, and affective dispositions of its subjects – and one whose underlying logics had heretofore escaped the attention of a genre of political economy that imagines itself to be a science of mechanistic social laws.

What was thought to be an abiding substance, *value*, is in fact the result of contingent social practices. Rather than being natural or reliable, value is revealed to be processual and relational. And rather than appearing obviously, value's origins mean it will always remain unstable and subject to continual change and transformation.[14]

It's true enough to say that capitalism dominates gender relations. But once the above aspects of Marx's view of value are grasped, we can see too how the varied experiences of sexuation are churned out by the course of history. This view of value as at once binding and decisive, yet endlessly supple and historically contingent, distinguishes political economy drawing from Marx's critique as uniquely useful for our purposes.[15] It mutes any hope of understanding capital's logic as one 'system' plugged into another. We cannot set capitalism on one side, as a fixed and dependable feature, with gender on the other as a 'cultural' set of norms and identifications. The two admix at every turn, developing and shifting more quickly than we can easily keep track. Our gendered experiences are dominated by capital, yes, but capitalism's relation to gender is one of mutual dependence.

For this reason, gender's temporal dynamics are not static, but constantly revolutionised by transformations in how we organise society collectively.[16] This is constantly denied by any number of research fields, from sexology to evolutionary psychology, committed to 'peeling away' gender until we reach a sturdier and more fixed core of 'sex'. Yet these efforts are continuously outstripped by the efforts of trans culture. Trans people have taken a more practical approach of continuous adjustments, using the understandings of the natural sciences as a point of departure, rather than a final word.

So having observed this practical process, how do we think through an explicitly transgender Marxist politics and social analysis?

Clinician, consumer, and capitalist household

Let's ditch a narrow understanding of trans subjectivity, tidily shorn of its messier, harsher edges. Our lives have already been cosily packaged up for dissemination in cinema, television, and popular culture. In other words, the transgender experience has been recast as readily amenable to our integration as properly subjectified market citizens. This liberal bargain is a live option for only a very narrow group of people – and always contingent on hecatombs of dispossession. Even those who enthusiastically embrace it come to exist in a tenuous balance between their implicit rejection of the accepted order, and their conscious efforts to reassert those norms.

Let's accept that the clinic is not only a sinister force, but an absurdity. The pathological view of transition has never provided a true remedy for it. We have neither been cured, nor suppressed. Where clinicians have refused to proffer treatment, communities have provided for each other. And so we must turn to transgender life as it threatens private households.

There is no thoroughly anti-capitalist politics that does not include a critique of the household as a social unit of capitalist governance. There is no critique of value that succeeds without becoming queer. Household and mode of production are never segregated: their motion grinds us between workplace and homestead. But if our gender experiences are not outside the grandiose processes of political economy, where are they located within them?

Through Marx's critique, we can develop an understanding of the interconnection between the loftier abstractions of political economy and the often brutal demands of transition. Between the seemingly abstract operations of risk, value, speculation, psychologisticly driven changes in the market value of assets in money prices, the movement of wages, unemployment, growth rates, and gross domestic product (usually apprehended in the dry statistics of national income accounts) – and with the violence, prejudice, and exclusion we experience on a grinding, day-to-day level. Capital and its mediating categories do not just *direct* distribution of a social surplus. They are actively *productive* of the ways of understanding and behaving towards which it leads us. The motions of capital link subjectivity with objectivity, form with content, abstract with concrete, universal with particular.

They do this through the racialised and gendered processes of making demands on time and surplus labour, organising speculative operations into contractual bonds, underwriting the differential extension of credit and life chances to various classes and strata, apportioning labour between sectors and households, and demarcating certain modes of comportment and expression as socially valorised and compensated – or as demonised, excluded and open to intense forms of socially-validated violence.

In states where the formal processes of emancipation have clearly run aground, we can clearly see the ways that the ruling classes can benefit from popular transphobia. Even in this context, the oppression of trans people remains unmistakably capitalist. For instance, mass evictions of trans and gender-nonconforming street workers in Turkey have been supported *ad hoc* by a predictable alliance of nationalists, the police, the local state, and neighbourhood associations alike.[17] The transphobic animus of the popular classes finds itself routed through the blunt self-interest of the rentier.

But this protean feature of capitalism means that moments of resistance also appear in varied forms. Both those challenging and empowering processes required by capitalism's continual expansion may not address it explicitly. The Black Lives Matter campaign across the United States was overtly a movement against police violence. But over the past three years, this movement has also come closer to challenging the foundations of property rights than any other political moment in living memory. Equally, reactionaries minded to protect capitalism express their racism in terms of sustaining 'law and order' against the Antifa mob. This is not simply a ploy by the right to veil their true politics: empowering the police *does* protect property rights, which reinforces continuing processes of racialisation. It is this rich interconnection that allowed BLM, after a string of murders and attacks on Black trans people, to rapidly popularise the slogan 'Black Trans Lives Matter'.[18] Throughout the summer of 2020, people around the world demonstrated around this straightforward slogan, most notably in New York City where one Brooklyn rally sent 15,000 to the streets with only the briefest organisation.[19] Where many social theorists have struggled with their apportioned task of 'squaring the circle' of structural intersections, fussing over gender-race-class as the so-called Holy Trinity, this street movement did not even hesitate.

Triumphalist accounts of capitalism as an indifferent, frictionless coordination mechanism, where the multiplicity of human wants and needs can find their ready satisfaction on the market, meet their obverse in anti-capitalist critiques that imagine capitalism merely as a force for the dissolution of social bonds. These horror-fiction infused accounts present capitalism as a sinister squid-like entity, intent on the generation of 'anomie', restless in efforts to devour out any scrap of comfort. Or perhaps it is a heartless machine that tears apart homes, communities, received patterns of custom, gender, family life – all that is precious for human flourishing is dissolved remorselessly in the 'icy water of egotistical calculation'.

But this is, at best, just one moment in the motion of capital. Less well appreciated are the ways in which capitalism constantly renews its social foundations. Rather than merely destructive, capitalism is simultaneously productive of affects, attachments, fierce passions, commitments, and hatreds. Each of these passions provides sources of legitimacy and social assent for the continued organisation of production and exploitation. In missing these intense affective bonds and sources of renewal, 'class first' leftists misunderstand the real dynamics of the forces they wish to oppose. The denial of capitalism's 'positive face' does not result in a stricter anti-capitalism, but one clad in blinkers.

That capitalism does us harm is to be assumed; what must be explained is how it survives through us. And how, despite this wounding and bitterness required at each turn, it endures over generations. In this way, accounts that attempt to 'dry out' social relations miss the deeper roots of capitalism's continued history. They do not equip us to anticipate capitalism's persistent tendency towards reinvention and revival, and its apparent entrenchment, even long after its supposed 'sell-by-date'. The problem with so-called class-reductionist perspectives is that to reduce to class often enough means a failure to explain how class divisions arise historically, or are sustained.

Due to the ever-shifting, continuously-adjusted faces of value, political actions often do not explicate themselves precisely in the terms upon which they impact. They follow indirect operations that either challenge or reaffirm the underlying basis of the intergenerational continuance of exploitation.

But what does the value-form have to do with sex?

The history of sexual difference is inextricably a history of contracts. These contracts might be entirely formal, informal but explicit, or they may barely even register within conscious thought. They are forged with yourself, your family, your doctors, your school, your employers, and with the state. What other accounts of transgender lives have identified as a transition in epistemic regimes in the social, scientific, and medical understanding of gender; we would identify as the weighty historical corollary of a transition in property regimes, working patterns, unwaged labour, family structures, and domestic life. Transition requires an eruption in all of these. We cannot settle for grasping how knowledge was organised and reorganised – we have to develop an account of *why*, and to what ends. Transgender lives, no more than any other, are not always lived for our own purposes, or towards our own ends. To live in any capitalist society is to make the best one can of alienation, of having one's will twisted through a logic that can never fully belong to us.

In other words, to speak meaningfully of any mode of production requires appreciating its subdivision into the private household. This division requires processes that extend well beyond the individual actor. Nobody is free of an upbringing. So to grasp capitalism as it plays out in our lives is to grasp the *oikos* (household) as it shapes history – as households replenish themselves, our personal histories mingle with the fate of our governing mode of production.

Capitalist society turns on what Angela Mitropoulos has analysed as the organisation of a predictable *oikonomic* and genealogical ordering – 'the nexus of race, gender, class, sexuality and nation constituted through the premise of the properly productive household'.[20] While this is a truly tangled and mutable arrangement, it is always imagined as a natural order. Here, appeals to underlying

fundamental value is a euphemism for the more-or-less stable capitalist futurity, and this is a future premised on the persistence – or as the case may be, restoration – of genealogical composition and lines of inheritance, or more broadly put: on the orderly transmission and transfer of property, debt and authority across time.[21]

Oikonomia here operates as a critique of economic discourse and its limits in apprehending social reality – including Marxist attempts that hypostatise capitalist society at the point of production, at the locus of exchange, and in the form of the wage.

To grasp the process at work, we cannot set aside questions of convention. The *salto mortale* – that aleatory leap across contingency that is necessary for the valorisation of capital – finds its unavoidable foundations in the assertion, formalisation, and contractualisation of genealogical ties of dependence, and the norms, laws, conventions, epistemological claims, and moral philosophies that naturalise them. Those social practices that serve to transform contingent possible futures into an inescapable deadlock of the present.

From Aristotle to Ricardo, Malthus to Polanyi, Smith to Hayek, the annals of political economy recurrently constitute the ideal market citizen through a series of racialised, gendered and sexualised exclusions. This citizen arrives at the marketplace always-already bounded as the sovereign and rights-bearing master of his patriarchal estate, and always circumscribed by a theory of laws, norms, standards, and foundations that presuppose his arrival.

Against those perspectives that stress the abstract market citizen, the dissolution of ties, and with it, the progressive expansion of relative freedoms, we would emphasise that every moment of flight sees a corresponding reversal – the moment of restoration.

In times of crisis, we see this underappreciated dynamic burst to the fore. During capitalism's periodic harrowing phases, politicians and economists become intensely concerned not just with the reproduction and recovery of the towering juggernauts of industry, commerce and finance, but *also and always* the household and its received patterns of family life. 'Traditional' ideas about the 'moral economy', of the family and gender, are not only to do with the provision of comfort and shelter. They also aim to internalise the harsh costs of adjustment and austerity against the vicissitudes of the market. This includes additional demands for uncompensated feminised labour, romanticised as a freely given 'gift'.[22]

It's no coincidence that, exactly when standards of living are ravaged and proletarian households reach their breaking point, the Global Right takes a moral turn – extolling the family as a unique safe haven against sinister plotting and alien forces. For these traditionalist voices, only the *oikos* exists beyond the rapacious squid's tentacles. But in truth, the family's delicacy rests exactly in its total immersion in the reproduction of capitalist relations.

Capitalist families are never the answer to the separation to which proletarians are subject. They are exactly the means by which this alienation persists, one generation after the next.

All moral-economic parables of sound money, productive capital, productive bodies, and the (re)productive heterosexual family unit necessitate unrelenting disciplinary violence directed towards 'irrational' speculation, unproductive Capital, unproductive consumption, and unproductive desires. It's upon this repressed underside to the pristine rationality of economics we unflinchingly train our gaze.

So-called 'post-Fordist' life sees the household and reproductive labour articulated in new forms – not just the sphere of wages and the sphere of domestic labour, but the broader reproduction of families as managed consumers of financial services, servicers of debt, and, crucially, as beneficiaries (or not) of a financialised dynamic of rapidly appreciating household wealth, where intergenerational wealth transfers acquire an increasingly distinctive role in contemporary class formation.[23] Households are increasingly elicited to internalise the calculative rationality that they are 'businesses' of a kind, to manage themselves as but one nexus in a series of interlocking balance sheets of cash-inflows and cash-outflows, assets and liabilities.

This elevated role of the household as a consumer unit is matched in the shift in the analytical primacy of progressive discourse from concerns about *unemployment* to concerns about *inequality* – what we might call a transition from Keynes and downside risk to Minsky and upside risk.[24] It's through securitisation, which turns mortgages, credit card debt, student, and car loans into readily tradable liquid assets, with an expectation of their future returns being grounded in the continuity of properly productive heterosexual American families, that contemporary capitalist society has organised a deeply hierarchical and unstable monetary order. From the early 1990s onwards, this process steadily gathered apace and purported to 'diversify' itself. Groups that had previously been excluded from access to finance as a matter of course – African-Americans, Latinas, female heads-of-household – found themselves aggressively targeted for lending under predatory and adverse terms. This was required to satisfy the voracious appetite of institutional investors for asset-backed securities.[25] Instead of this development leading to a promised democratisation of consumption — the basis for a great levelling of inequalities — this expanded subsumption of ever more groups to the calculative logics of financial life enforced their steady continuity. When the sub-prime crisis hit in 2007, these groups found themselves worst hit by the ensuing fallout.[26]

Rather than an innocent throwback to gentler and less alienated times, the family has served as an increasingly important cornerstone of US dollar liquidity — and with it liquidity to global markets and the international capitalist order as a whole. Such financial deepening has increased the capacity of the US imperial state to govern through debt dramatically, but is contingent on the ability of ordinary households to continue serving as a source of securitised asset-backed debt, on their capacity and willingness as consumers to assume ever-higher levels of indebtedness by diverting ever greater shares of their income to the disciplinary constraints of repayment schedules. If central banks serve as the 'liquidity providers of last resort', ordinary households are increasingly exhorted to act as 'risk absorbers of last resort', expected to honour payment obligations long past the point of rational sustainability. This burden directly links the micro-politics of domestic space to the macro-dynamics of international finance in new and novel forms.[27] It's in this fraught context that violence which appears 'traditional' in form in fact shores up an entirely contemporary dynamic of twenty-first-century capitalism.

Put another way: when examined closely, there is no way to segregate the *economic* order inaugurated by the New Right and their successors from the pre-eminent role families played as the *means* of dispersing previous generations' hopes of a social-democratic settlement. The retrenchment of the family was exactly how the debt, deprivation, and division was made to seem obvious, rather than arbitrary.

This deepening of dependency on debt, access to credit, and the financial intermediation of social reproduction has meant public provision is increasingly abdicated ever more to the differential fortunes of privatised households, and domestic life and labour are ever more attuned to the survival constraint of promises-to-pay falling due.[28]

This has been concurrent with a brutal reorganisation of labour, social life, and public space. Let's consider the hidden abode of discourses surrounding supposedly immaterial labour.

Recent decades have seen global working patterns and labour politics reshaped dramatically, both by automation and by the move by leading firms in imperialist countries to 'peripheralise' large sectors of industrial employment. Manufacturing has been relegated to 'developing countries', where lower wages and more lax labour protections, as well as a much greater readiness of many local states to provision infrastructure, have allowed for better profit-making prospects for trans-national firms. This has continued even as the broad-based gains that were supposed to follow from industrial development and 'hooking in' to global supply chains have failed to materialise for all but a few. We have not seen the convergence and flattening of hierarchies of wealth within and between nations, but their sturdy resilience.[29]

In turn, the supposed sureties of Fordist employment (a bargain offered to a select minority) have been superseded by casualisation, flexible or temporary working arrangements, workfare, and a growing demand for the feminised skills of caring and service labour. These measures have expanded to encompass ever more sectors, as each step seems to proceed without countervailing the leverage that once existed in the form of the global workers' movement. On the one hand, the casualisation of labour has made it less likely that any given trans person will require a singular 'professional persona', to last their whole working lifetime. On the other, this same process also guts the institutions which might previously have been called upon to offer some semblance of protection from employer prejudices. Casualisation places us at risk of disposability for any number of the commonplace reasons that trans people frequently encounter.

It's at this point that trans people often find themselves viewed askance, excluded from broad sectors of monetised economic activity by virtue of a stigmatised identity, and often out of step with heterosexual society's expectations of their birth kin. Reactionaries have cast the rise of Transgender Marxism as one hydra of a beast named 'gender ideology'. A malign force of delusion, confusing the youth and gutting previously sturdy norms. But in truth, gender has come to be a topic of such attention, and explicit confusion, thanks to a disintegration of material circumstances – one inaugurated by the right and since officiated by liberals of every possible orientation. The family was supposed to play a dominating role in the stabilisation of capitalism, which in the event exposed its underbelly. Now, many fear, one generation will not follow so easily from the next.

Life beyond the clinic

The weaknesses of the abstract materialism of natural science, a materialism which excludes the historical process, are immediately evident from the abstract and ideological conceptions expressed by its spokesmen whenever they venture beyond the bounds of their own speciality.[30]

Transgender Marxism holds that the struggles of living one's life transgender must be threaded, rather than dispersed into distinguishable 'spheres'. From the rejection most trans people still find in the private households that reared them to the jeers and curious stares encountered on the street, in buses, bars, online, from passing cars. From encounters where one like form makes another's plight feel shared rather than freakish, for a night, to the sweat sticking unfamiliar clothes to the seat in the year's first job interview. From the debuts of looks and names at dubious house parties, to squinting bureaucrats fussing over forms, verifying a shifting existence glimpsed from a definitive filing-cabinet's-eye view. Getting used to street work, webcams, online pharmacies. Rubber-stamping procedures that pass from seeming intractable hassles to clearly marked in a fashion which feels unique in a life otherwise scattered with mixed apprehensions and divergent readings. Itching skin, pinching fabric. Rare communities offering directory boards, old-timers' tips, solace. Moments you aren't sure *why* you're getting stared at. Life-transforming provisions of shared experience and procedural hand-holding that can seem by turns dependable and bitterly fleeting. These experiences never occur in their own 'worlds'; they find their context in the same mode of production that now dominates the planet. Each of us struggles to pass through the eye of the state, to subsist as best we can.

But it's in our confrontation with the clinic and medical science that the narratives of and about our lives have generally been understood in popular consumption. Medicalisation organises transgender possibility as defined by our interactions with medical science. In the aetiology of clinical life, transsexuality is understood as deviation, excess to or deficient from an otherwise desirable state of embodiment. While possible to manage and mitigate, 'transsexuality' in this sense remains a pathological diagnosis, a defect within one individual's psychological development that can never be allowed to challenge the norm of sex itself.

The chaos of gender nonconformity is reconceived and swept under the organising logic of a racialised, normatively teleological binary transition. The origin and endpoint of trans possibility, where our identities are justified, legitimated, and consolidated in-and-through their journey down a narrow pathway of surgery, hormones, and 'living in the *role*'.[31]

This is not restricted to the treatment of adult trans patients. Interventions into the lives of intersex infants and children take a symmetrical form: surgeries and hormonal treatments justified primarily by how well they will serve to sustain an approximation of dyadic sexual division. Yet this professional set of imperatives has not discouraged trans communities from continuing to produce a rich array of terms and monikers to describe our ways of moving through the world. The main solace we can offer is that trans culture seems set to produce subject positions faster than clinicians can update their disapproval.

Trans historian Jules Gill-Peterson notes how contemporary discussions of 'gender identity' largely efface its origins as a conservative response intended to suture over the epistemic crisis of sex as a clinical category. Rather than appearing through an emancipatory concern, 'gender' in this sense served as a sexological speculation, ushered in by eugenic experiments on trans and intersex children and adults.[32] To their evident horror, clinicians discovered that neither genotype, gonads, hormones, genitals, internal organs, nor secondary anatomical features proved decisive. No one isolatable feature could provide the foundational, determining, and unambiguous influence on which binary sexuation could depend. As such, frameworks ranging from pathological reduction of transsexual experiences to the sensual impact of 'dysphoria', to the later framework of 'Disorders of Sex Development' to account for intersex variations, formed a rear-guard reaction to sustain a conceptual binary. Gill-Peterson uses these histories to mount a critique of both popular cultural prejudices and the prevailing academic narratives of gender, which frequently pivots twentieth-century trans history around the rise of the gender identity clinic. These would-be canonical accounts pinpoint as a decisive factor the medicalisation of transition ushered in most famously by Stanford University and Johns Hopkins from the 1950s onward.[33] As Gill-Peterson's revisionist account ably demonstrates, trans life did not begin with the clinic, and it does not end there either.

We can begin to see how the clinic functions as an *oikonomic* institution. At the clinic, stewarding patient wellbeing is a subordinate concern to the propertarian interest of the state in administering and managing sexual difference itself. The clinic's remit and operations are a site of continual contestation between the state, patients, clinicians, and wider social attitudes – between, on the one hand, gendered difference as it is actually lived, practised, and experienced, and, always on the other, the state and capital's attempts to organise, constrain, and manage the effects of gendered difference. As ever, the state constructs an orderly and reliable pattern of commitments and obligations – of domination and exploitation – across space, time, and lines of inheritance. It's for *this* reason that trans people increasingly find themselves in receipt not (solely) of denial, but of a highly conditional validation from state authorities.

Where trans life cannot be eradicated or driven underground, it can at least be normalised and disciplined into prevailing understandings of gendered behaviour and expectations. For the transphobic moderate, transition is understood as a possibility only in light of individuals with personal histories matching up to a clinical ideal. But our realities have always been complex. Not every trans life fits the teleological model of 'binary transition'; in fact, very few ever do. Nor should our account of transition have to be straightforward in order to receive formal validation. In abdicating and surrendering our self-understandings to those very institutions that, throughout their histories, have sought to suffocate trans life – to render it unthinkable, unknowable, unredeemable – we suffocate ourselves in turn.

To experience alienation is to live towards the ends of another. To transition requires one to assert one's own terms of living, in whatever way appears practical. Our response in the face of a division of labour intent on verifying, monitoring, and delimiting us will decide more than only our own fate.

From panic to revolt

The guiding thread of this book is that 'transgender' is not a staid ontology, or an abstract, regulative identity imposed from without, but a practical truth. Our every identification is realised by the conscious, patient, and collective action of intentional communities which ground and give meaning to it.

Capitalism as a mode of production requires circuits of circulation, consumption, and social reproduction. Far from a marginal concern, the regulation of gender and sexuality must be understood as integral to capitalism as it survives across time. The wrath 'trans ideology' triggers among reactionaries is not simply mindless contempt. It is not reducible to psychodrama. Instead, capitalism's right wing treats apparent breaches of continuity in the operation of its private households for good reason. This open contempt will not be quieted, however skilfully the left wing of capitalism offers hollow promises of accommodation, of an ever more encompassing bourgeoisie featuring reformed households, modernised subjectivities, and gender enlightened oppressors.

Transgender Marxism means the refusal of this seemingly ferocious disagreement. Transgender rights provide a hollow target. Civic emancipation is a pyrrhic victory. Private households and workplaces alike offer a continual churn of oppression and developmental damage. This wounding across generations will not find itself mitigated through any institutional shift, or any movement that falls short of the commune. To emancipate trans people requires, above all else, overturning class divisions, reversing our separation from the means of production, and developing new forms for nurture beyond the family.

Transgender Marxism offers not only an account of our experiences as *differentiated* from the norm, but an analysis of how the state and capital turn these ascriptive distinctions into a material force. Gender is not merely a site of expressive potential – of self-realisation and self-fashioning – but also, and equally, a site bounded by property relations. Property appears as natural through patterns of ownership and entitlement, both of which are simultaneously deeply gendered and racialised. And so it is that those abdicating their expected role for new, self-fashioned positions are read as a mortal threat to the continuity of capitalism. To transition is to renege on agreements that were previously assumed, albeit never actually signed for.

Let's sum up: the convulsive rise of the Global Right has placed the transitioner alongside the migrant as a key symptom and agent of 'cultural degeneracy'. The situation is best summarised in the term innovated in response to a legal defence frequently mounted by murderers in the United States whose justification for their violence is that their heterosexuality was undermined by their attraction to a woman who turned out to be trans: 'trans panic'. This panic appears on a grand scale, as well as in these singular episodes: the right determines us a threat to all fixity and normality, justifying both bursts of explosive, extrajudicial violence, and the systemic deprivation of rights and basic dignity from state officials.

Once, a binary conception of the world was imposed worldwide by British, French, Spanish, and Portuguese colonialism; as much through colonial law-making as massacres by European explorers.[34] Now the 'West' of the imperial core has become synonymous with gender pluralism, and this progression has been gladly and symbolically instrumentalised by Global Right regimes. Nationalist parties such as United Russia,[35] Hungary's Fidesz,[36] and Brazil's Social Liberal Party[37] each depict 'trans ideology' as a globalist contamination, a foreign plot seeded by scheming NGOs, depraved academics, and George Soros.

The dissonance between these simultaneously surging forces cannot be answered by left-liberal proposals for 'trans rights', nor even the busted flush of social democracy, which has time and again offered the illusory prospect of thrashing the right and installing economic equity via the ballot box.[38] With stakes this high, a much more drastic intervention into world history is needed, and a much sharper theory for grasping our social conditions is demanded than we yet have to hand. Our circumstances demand more than one simple answer to a complex series of questions.[39]

This is where a *specifically* Transgender Marxism is required. Transgender Marxism presents trans life as it is lived. Neither figural nor instrumental, but unadorned. Not for the sake of fidelity, or 'representation' to others. For ourselves, and to best remake the circumstances faced down by workforces worldwide, as well as the ever-swelling 'industrial reserve army'. For the sake of a proletarian autonomy that does not demand we strip our lives bare of our existing means of survival. For a movement that does not demand, we set aside our needs and cravings as distractions from a higher and more righteous cause.

Capitalism and the struggles against it are both matters of history. Imposing new limits, pressing new cruelties, just as it offers new spaces for expressive potentials, joys, solidarities, and transformations. Transgender Marxism provides a bleak hope for those surveying this process.

Transgender Marxism leads us not to deny the joys, or ourselves, while equally never allowing ourselves to be deterred from the path of internationalist revolution. Our end is not just a more rigorous under-standing of our social afflictions, but fuel for the abolition of what has long been intolerable. What we have suffered was logical, but never necessary. What has been made can be unmade.

Notes

1. Much like the inconsistent and unsteady theorising of 'patriarchy' in the earlier women's movement, this produces infinite terms of art, and an ever-shifting mélange of idiom which often enough define the limits of 'in-groups' more than living movements.
2. One of our contributors from the Global South has opted to do so without reference to their name, gender position, or national origins. In many contexts, trans politics remains a clandestine affair.
3. More recently, Ashley Bohrer has referred to this as the 'orthodox story' peddled by those Marxists most well acquainted with *Capital Vol I*.
4. For a more detailed overview of this particularly British affliction, see Sylv, M. (March 2018). You Are More Oppressive Than Our Oppressors: Transphobia and Transmisogyny in the British Left. *New Socialist*, https://newsocialist.org.uk/you-are-more-oppressive-than-our-oppressors-transphobia-and-transmisogyny-in-the-british-left/.
5. Bataille, G. (1985). The Old Mole and the Prefix Sur in the Worlds Surhomme and Surrealist. In *Visions of Excess*. Minneapolis, MN: University Of Minnesota Press, p. 34.
6. Blood plasma levels measure sex hormone levels fairly reliable: in pg/ml or p/mol for estrogens, and ng/ml for testosterone and progesterone. However the impact these levels will have on any physique is dependent on hormone receptor sensitivity, and hormones are further stored in adipose tissue (fat) resulting in variations from person-to-person much harder to monitor among the living. Between these factors and still more complex genetic variations, not to mention divergent means of delivery (from injections, to gels, to creams, to pills taken either swallowed or interguinal, to implant pellets), the measurable levels at which any given trans person might achieve either visible 'results', or relief from dysphoric sentiments more generally, is truly unpredictable.
7. Quoted in Sutherland, K. (2008). Marx in Jargon. *World Picture Journal*, 1.
8. See Sayer, D. (1987). *The Violence of Abstraction*. Oxford: Basil Blackwell; Sayer quotes Marx:

> Under the present system, if a crooked spine, twisted limbs, a one-sided development and strengthening of certain muscles, etc., makes you

more capable of working (more productive), then your crooked spine, your twisted limbs, your one-sided muscular movement are a productive force. If your intellectual vacuity is more productive than your abundant intellectual activity, then your intellectual vacuity is a productive force, etc. etc. If the monotony of an occupation makes you better suited for that occupation, then monotony is a productive force.

9. Heaney, E. (2017). *The New Woman: Literary Modernism, Queer Theory, and the Trans-Feminine Allegory*. Evanston, Illinois: Northwestern University Press. Heaney traces this case across late nineteenth- and twentieth-century representations of trans-femininity, including in sexology literature, modernist fiction and social theory.

10. See Freud, S. (1905). *Three Essays on Sexuality*. London: Hogarth. Where Freud negates with one motion, in his critique of the reduction of gendered psychic identity to genital configuration, he retrieves with another. Following Heaney, one could say that a spectre is haunting classic Freudian psychoanalysis – the spectre of the trans lesbian. She who embraces her feminine identity, and affirms it by having sex with other women. See Xandra Metcalfe's essay for a fuller exploration of this.

11. This view was developed in dialogue with Marxist theorist Sophie Lewis' many immanent readings of radfem foundationalism, including her 2017 essay: Lewis, S. (6 February 2017). SERF and TERF: Notes on Bad Materialism, *Salvage Journal*, and further developed in her forthcoming *Bad Feminisms*.

12. This does not seem to hold nearly so true in the Spanish and Italian speaking contexts, where trans women make up a clear minority of many trans feminist circles. Here the term typically signals primarily a rejection of foundationalism, just as with 'queerfeminism' in German speaking contexts. The situation in Brazil is still more complex, see: Kaas, H. (2016). Birth of Transfeminism in Brazil: Between Alliances and Backlashes. *TSQ*, 3(1–2), 146–149.

13. Our reading of Marx here is indebted to Pepperell, N. (2010). *Disassembling Capital*, PhD Thesis, RMIT University.

14. Here we echo certain value-form theory approaches in understanding value not as abiding-social-substance, but as *social form*. This approach stresses considerations of how value conditions individuals subject to its determining pressures. As with so many features of Transgender Marxism, we not being truly original in twinning value-form theory and questions of transgender experience. We are especially indebted to *Invert Journal*, and particularly from their first issue the essays: Gabriel, K. (2019). Gender as Accumulation Strategy, *Invert Journal*, 1, and Cohen, J. A. (2019). The Eradication of 'Talmudic Abstractions': Antisemitism, Transmisogyny and the National Socialist Project, *Invert Journal*, 1, and the editorial team's introduction.

15. Doyle Griffiths, K. (2020). Labor Valorization and Social Reproduction: What is Valuable about the Labor Theory of Value? *CLCWeb: Comparative Literature and Culture*, 22.2, https://doi.org/10.7771/1481-4374.3839.

16. A comparison of Karl Marx and Judith Butler's approach to gender's temporal face can be found in Arruza, C. (2015). Gender as Social Temporality: Butler (and Marx). *Historical Materialism*, 23.4. See Rosa Lee's essay in this book for a transgender Marxist view on this question.

17. Güler, E. (27 July 2020). Trans Sex Workers' Collective Struggle in Urban Turkey. *Focaal Blog*, https://www.focaalblog.com/2020/07/27/ezgi-guler-trans-sex-workers-collective-struggle-in-urban-turkey/. Bayramoğlu, Y. (2013). Media Discourse on Transgender People As Subjects of Gentrification in Istanbul. In Fraser, V. (Ed.), *Queer Sexualities: Diversifying Queer, Queering Diversity*. Oxford: Inter-Disciplinary Press, p. 41–48. Engin, C. (2018). Sex work in Turkey: Experiences of transwomen. Nuttbrock, L. (Ed.), *Transgender Sex Work and Society*. New York, NY: Harrington Park Press, pp. 196–213.

18. These murders followed a long legacy of violence directed towards black transgender proletarians across America. Treva Ellison explored this running conflict in US labour history in their 2017 Barnard College lecture, Ellsison, T. (2017). Black Trans Reproductive Labor, https://www.youtube.com/watch?v=4n1uqggrVPs.

19. Patil, A. (15 June 2020). How a March for Black Trans Lives Became a Huge Event. *New York Times*, https://www.nytimes.com/2020/06/15/nyregion/brooklyn-black-trans-parade.html.

20. Mitropoulos, A. (2012). *Contract and Contagion: From Biopolitics to Oikonomia*. London: Minor Compositions, p. 28.

21. Ibid., p. 185.

22. For a recent history of neoliberal social policy through the prism of the family see Cooper, M. (2017). *Family Values: Between Neoliberalism and the New Social Conservatism*. Cambridge, MA: MIT Press.

23. See Adkins, L., Cooper, M., & M. Konings (9 September 2019). Class in the 21st Century: Asset Inflation and the New Logic of Inequality. *Environment and Planning A: Economy and Space* for a recent analyses of this understated dynamic and a critique of the limits of employment-based class taxonomies in grasping its implications.

24. A historical irony of note given that Minsky himself was also concerned not just with the vicissitudes of systemic financial instability but, first and foremost, with unemployment.

25. In conservative circles, this development was understood as a proximate cause of the crisis and one understood in explicitly racial terms – the politically driven, 'unsustainable' extension of credit to racially undeserving groups, who could not help but default. For a critique of the most academically respectable form of this argument, see Konzcal, M. (n.d.). Guest Post: A Review of Fragile by Design, *Roosevelt Institute*, accessed 2 February 2020.

26. Roberts, Adrienne (1 February 2013). Financing Social Reproduction: The Gendered Relations of Debt and Mortgage Finance in Twenty-First-Century America. *New Political Economy*, 18(1), 21–42, https://doi.org/10.1080/13563467.2012.662951.
Allon, F. (2 January 2014). The Feminisation of Finance: Gender, Labour and the Limits of Inclusion. *Australian Feminist Studies*, 29(79) 12–30, https://doi.org/10.1080/08164649.2014.901279.
Wyly, E., Moos, M., Hammel, D., & Kabahizi, E. (June 2009). Cartographies of Race and Class: Mapping the Class-Monopoly Rents of American Subprime Mortgage Capital. *International Journal of Urban and Regional Research*, 33(2), 332–354, https://doi.org/10.1111/j.1468-2427.2009.00870.x.
27. Bryan, D., Rafferty, M., & Tinel, B. (2016). Households at the Frontiers of Monetary Development. Accessed 3 October 2020, https://freidok.uni-freiburg.de/data/11523.
28. The account of financialisation developed here is focused on the US, but is applicable in many respects to the UK, Canada, and Australia.
29. Suwandi, I. (March 2019). Monthly Review | Global Commodity Chains and the New Imperialism. *Monthly Review*, 70.10, https://monthlyreview.org/2019/03/01/global-commodity-chains-and-the-new-imperialism/.
New Left Review (May–June 2014). Sean Starrs, The Chimera of Global Convergence. *NLR*, 87, https://newleftreview.org/issues/II87/articles/sean-starrs-the-chimera-of-global-convergence.
30. Marx, K. (1990). *Capital: A Critique of Political Economy, Volume I*, Chapter 15, footnote. London: Penguin.
31. Ruth Pearce documents a 2009 gathering of Gender Clinicians in the UK, where one clinician reports a growing issue – many patients are choosing not to 'fully' transition medically, while living for all social and legal respects as females. The doctor reporting this was unsatisfied that many of what he called 'she-men' were perfectly content without genital surgery. For the clinicians, this is a suboptimal outcome, explicitly against the intention of their clinical practice, and threatens to redefine what it might mean to be a woman or a man. Unsurprisingly, for the clinicians this was treated as an inadvertent problem, with these trans women an accident of poorly conceived institutional practices, to be spoken of in casual and derogatory terms. Typical to conventional prejudices, the still larger proportion of trans men who opt for hormones but not SRS was apparently not identified as a concern. It seems inevitable that now much the same attitude is taken towards the growing number of non-binary people seeking healthcare via the NHS. And then will be equally true of more novel subject positions such as femboys, or T-microdosers, as soon as these conservative-minded medical staff become aware of them. Pearce, R. (2018). *Understanding Trans Health: Discourse, Power and Possibility*. London: Policy Press, pp. 104–105.

32. To this day, most visibly intersex infants are subject to aggressive interventions. The earlier doctrines of sexology have been replaced by more sophisticated pretexts to continue mutilating surgeries into the 21st century. See Black feminist philosopher Catherine Clune-Taylor on how these clinical protocols have survived under the new framework of 'disorders of sex development', or DSDs: Clune-Taylor, C. (2019). Securing Cisgendered Futures: Intersex Management under the 'Disorders of Sex Development' Treatment Model. *Hypatia*, 34.4.

33. Gill Peterson, J. (2018). *Histories of the Transgender Child*. Minneapolis, MN: University of Minnesota Press.

34. For an account tracing just one part of this juridical process, the rendering of Indian hijra into a criminalised population, see: Hinchy, Jessica (2020). Governing Gender and Sexuality in Colonial India The Hijra, c.1850–1900. Cambridge: Cambridge University Press.

35. For an overview of resistance from Russian trans revolutionaries, see: Kirey-Sitnikova, Y. (1 May 2016). The Emergence of Transfeminism in Russia: Opposition from Cisnormative Feminists and Trans* People. *TSQ*, 3.1–2, 165–174.

36. Gál, H. (25 May 2020). Trans Rights and 'Gender Ideology' in Hungary. *RS21*, https://www.rs21.org.uk/2020/05/25/trans-rights-and-gender-ideology-in-hungary/

37. Treated in more detail in our contribution by Virginia Guitzel.

38. On the long history of social democracy's structural hostility towards trans life, see: O'Brien, M. (2019). To Abolish the Family: The Working-Class Family and Gender Liberation in Capitalist Development. *Endnotes*, 5 (The Passions and the Interests), 360–417.

39. Mamedov, G., & Shatalova, O. (18 August 2017). Against Simple Answers: The Queer-Communist Theory of Evald Ilyenkov and Alexander Suvorov. *ArtsEverywhere*, https://artseverywhere.ca/2017/08/17/against-simple-answers/.

1

Social Reproduction and Social Cognition: Theorizing (Trans)gender Identity Development in Community Context

Noah Zazanis

The questions of agency that arise with gender transition present a challenge to feminist theories of socialisation. If gender exists as a structure imposed onto its subjects, what does it mean to 'change' genders while remaining subjected to that structure? Many liberal trans-affirmative arguments have relied on essentialisms (biological or otherwise) to justify the necessity of transition, and the validity of trans identity.[1] But if trans identification is not determined by our biology, neither is it an uncomplicated product of early socialisation. Transgender identification is not inherent, or even necessarily constant. Instead, trans identities are formed responsive to their social context. We transition through the exercise of individual and collective agency. This occurs in community with other trans people, and through everyday acts of reproduction – each of which influences social cognition. To understand how trans identities are formed, it is necessary to examine the social relations produced and reproduced by trans people. It is these continuously developing contexts which allow for transitions to occur and identities to emerge.

The discussion of socialisation into specific gender roles originated in the radical feminist canon, but has since been mainstreamed within both popular feminist movement politics and the academic study of gender. One of the earliest theorisations of 'gender socialisation' in feminist theory is found in Catharine MacKinnon's 'Feminism, Method, Marxism and the State'.[2] MacKinnon presents socialisation theory as a radical feminist intervention into socialist feminism, which she argued had until that point located gender in the labour of (biological) reproduction, presenting sexuality as neutral/natural while ignoring men's exploitation of women through (hetero)sexual relations. 'Gender socialization', she writes, 'is the process through which women come to identify themselves as sexual beings, as beings which exist for men. It is that process through which women internalise (make their own) a male image of their sexuality *as* their identity as women'.[3] Womanhood, to MacKinnon, is defined through coercion into heterosexuality.[4] In this view, *the* defining characteristic of women's shared subjectivity is powerlessness at the hands of men, as reinforced through sexual objectification.

MacKinnon's radical feminist analysis spoke (and speaks) truth to many women's experiences of male domination and traumatisation at the hands of men. For these women, to be female is to exist as object and victim; gender socialisation is a unidirectional and non-agentic process, to be resisted through feminist organising but with little potential for subversion from within. So while trans-inclusive radical feminisms have existed since its advent, and MacKinnon herself has expressed support for trans women's self-identification,[5] many of the underlying assumptions of radical feminist socialisation theory lend themselves readily to transantagonistic conclusions when applied outside the realm of cisgender experience. If womanhood is defined by forcible sexual submission, what positive content could trans women see that draws them towards a female identification? And if trans men have experienced sexual assault at the hands of men – as most of us have[6] – do these experiences forever mark us as, in some sense, female? Without an understanding of agency, and of gendering as a multidirectional process, there is little room for trans people to legibly exist outside of our initial assignment. According to this 'old school' perspective, female-assigned trans people will always be seen as victims of our socialisation, and male-assigned trans people will forever benefit from theirs – at least until gender is abolished.

The more classically feminist varieties of trans-exclusive radical feminists (TERFs) often point to such 'socialisation' arguments to suggest that trans people's self-identification as our genders could not possibly reflect 'material reality'. While these arguments may not seem to dignify a response, it's worth reproducing an example to illustrate the tenor of the current debate within feminism. Referring to

Shon Faye, a UK-based trans woman and activist, Canadian feminist Meghan Murphy writes:

> Faye has only been living as a self-defined transwoman for two years, meaning that for 27 years, he [sic] was socialised as a male, and offered all the power and privilege men are under patriarchy. He [sic] has no idea what it feels like to fear pregnancy, to be talked down to or over, to be discriminated against in the workplace, to live in fear of rape or abuse in private and in public, from the time he [sic] was a child.[7]

This is, of course, both empirically and experientially false. For instance, trans women experience sexual violence and intimate partner violence at rates higher than those typical for cis women.[8] Likewise, while trans men's relationships to male power are hardly straightforward, many of us can describe instances in which being read and treated 'as a man' has resulted in privileges granted that were previously denied.[9]

Similarly, trans-exclusive feminists have pointed to essentialisms within trans politics and rhetoric in order to argue that trans identity is necessarily bioessentialist, and therefore both misogynistic and scientifically questionable. In her review of the controversy surrounding J. Michael Bailey's *The Man Who Would Be Queen*, Alice Dreger attributes trans criticisms of the homosexuality/autogynephilia typology of transsexualism to a 'feminine essence' theory of transness, which relies on a belief in innate gender identity to justify transition.[10] It's certainly true that there are some strands of contemporary trans discourse which do appeal to a certain bioessentialism, in order to argue for the validity of trans experiences, presenting transgender neurochemistry as an uncomplicated 'point of fact'.[11] These 'trans liberal' arguments attempt to establish trans people as just another natural fact. These assertions are both scientifically contested and politically questionable, but adjudicating this dispute is not my main concern here. It will suffice to say here that these views by no means represent the *totality* of trans understandings of gender. While many trans people hold essentialist understandings of gender identity, one could equally say that so do the majority of cis people. In order to challenge this mischaracterisation of trans politics, however, it is necessary to conceptualise exactly how trans identities *are* formed socially.

One key component missing from socialisation theory, which is necessary to understanding identity formation, involves the role of *agency* in gender identity development. Radical feminist accounts claim to offer a thoroughgoing explanation of why societies produce gendered subject positions or identities. However, they provide no explanation for the conditions in which a certain socialisation may *fail* to be internalised by a subject; why any person, trans or cis, may choose to reject the prescriptive roles into which they are socialised through transition, feminist resistance, or gender nonconformity of any sort. This silence raises the question: To what extent is socialisation theory 'social'? The dialectical relationship between structure and agency poses a paradox for socialisation theory; if genders cannot be transformed except through their wholesale abolition, how can *anyone* step out of their gender roles enough to incite such transformation?

In comparison, Marx himself stresses the importance of human agency to alter the conditions of our existence. As he notes in the *Eighteenth Brumaire*:

> Men make their own history, but they do not make it as they please; they do not make it under self-selected circumstances, but under the circumstances existing already, given and transmitted from the past. The tradition of all dead generations weighs like a nightmare on the brains of the living.[12]

Building upon Marx, social reproduction theorists have emphasised the extent to which often-naturalised categories such as gender and the family are themselves socially contingent upon practices of reproductive labour. As such, social reproduction theory (SRT) allows room for agentic behaviour through new practices of reproduction – both within economic systems and as a necessary precursor to economic transformation.

In an article for *Viewpoint Magazine*, Fulvia Serra emphasises the importance of nurturance and emotional intimacy as modes of reproduction necessary for creating and sustaining revolutionary movements. Intimacy, she says, has been increasingly enclosed into the private household – or channelled into value-producing activities. Serra rejects liberal feminisms that pursue women's liberation through their inclusion in male-dominated workforces. Serra argues that the so-called breakthrough of liberal feminism have resulted in for-warding the burden of care work onto more vulnerable, marginalised women for little pay, while not causing significant shifts in the basic structure of the family relation. Liberal feminisms have not mean-ingfully challenged the capitalist mode of production. Instead, citing Silvia Federici, Serra pushes for changes in the fundamental mode of reproduction through the collectivisation of care labour, so as to undo the 'hierarchy and domination' inherent in the division of repro-ductive labour across gendered lines. She especially emphasises how the failure to successfully transform internal relations of reproduc-tion has harmed revolutionary movements. Overlooking reproductive questions can cause the replication of destructive power dynamics, as exemplified through the experiences of women in the Black Panther Party. At the same time, she stops just short of describing a path forward – or of illuminating reproductive practices that could prove transformative within radical communities.[13]

So far, most writing available on transformative practices of repro-duction has come directly from queer and trans scholars writing on their own conditions of daily living. In 'Transition and Abolition: Notes on Marxism and Trans Politics', Jules Joanne Gleeson high-lights the often unacknowledged practices of reproduction which have laid the foundation for the so-called 'transgender moment'.[14] While she notes that trans social reproduction is not necessarily revolutionary, it is through these reproductive practices that trans people produce the means for our survival – a prerequisite for any revolutionary activity. Additionally, in her later work, Gleeson begins to depict the processes through which trans people produce and reproduce our own identities, through our relationships and social spheres. While transition is often framed as a process of shifting encounters with cisgender expectations, she clarifies that it is equally a process of active community cultiva-tion, and sustenance of trans identity. Through 'support, mentoring, and reciprocal recognition', as well as the curation and dissemination of 'shared knowledge' and 'practical wisdom', trans people ourselves facilitate the development of transgender identities in community with one another.[15]

Taking Gleeson's cue, we should examine the specific processes and practices through which trans social reproduction occurs – and transgender identity formation is facilitated – more closely. These endeavours are instances of informal, unpaid labour for which a Marxist analysis is particularly well-suited. At the same time, they are also social-psychological processes of human development, with implications for individual consciousness and enacted experience. As such, mainstream psychological science offers valuable insights into how gender identities are formed. In conjunction with analysis of the conditions of reproduction which facilitate this formation, we can provide a detailed depiction of how trans community self-activity facilitates individual self-recognition, and eventual transition.

As of yet, there is no scientific consensus on how gender identity development occurs in cases of cisgenderism, much less on the particularities of transgender identity formation. Nonetheless, psychological researchers have developed several theories as to how these processes function. Kay Bussey and Albert Bandura provide one particularly compelling explanation of gender identity development.[16] Social cognitive theory (SCT) incorporates both psychological and socio-structural determinants of gender, and allows for a wide range of sources of social influence. This complicates traditional ideas of socialisation by accounting for the possibility of multiple, competing gender influences. It also takes a life-course perspective on gender identity development, rather than just focusing on early childhood. This makes more room for fluidity and agency in gender identity development – rather than insisting that one's positionality is determined by early-life socialisation.

According to social cognition theory, processes of gender identity construction rely on a reciprocal relationship between personal, behavioural, and environmental factors, called 'triadic reciprocal causation'.[17] Socio-structural constraints determine the extent to which each factor influences gender, i.e. societies with rigid gender roles will rely less on personal factors and more on environmental influences. Notably, SCT holds that individuals have the agency to choose their environments (to varying extents) and play a role in constructing their social environments. It is through processes of social reproduction that trans people construct our social environments, and make space for trans identities to flourish.

Social cognition theory delineates three modes of environmental influence: modelling, enactive experience, and direct tuition.[18] For both cis and trans people, family, peers, and mass media provide models for appropriate gendered behaviour, beginning in early childhood and extending through the life course. Learning through enactive experience occurs as individuals engage in gendered behaviour, observe how others respond, and adjust their behaviour accordingly. Early-life punishment for gender nonconformity is often regarded as a characteristically trans experience. In reality, however, not only do cis people share similar enacted experiences, but successful discouragement from gender transgression constitutes much of the cisgender phenomenon. The third mode through which the social environment regulates gendered behaviour is direct tuition. Through tuition of more-or-less formal kinds, individuals are provided with explicit instructions for appropriate gender conduct. This, too, is present in its normative form throughout the lives of both cis and trans individuals.

Whereas 'socialisation' theories tend to struggle at extending themselves beyond the individual, and often fall short of explaining their complex interactions while facing down 'society', social cognition theory concerns itself with the threefold processes that we must pass through to cultivate any meaningful identity.

Using social reproduction theory, we can examine how these three modes of influence are manifested through the everyday reproductive labour of cisgender subjects.[19] Models, enacted experiences, and instances of direct tuition do not occur spontaneously – cisgender norms cannot be treated as a given. They are reproduced daily in the household, the school, the medical facility, etc. by human action, with varying degrees of intention attached. What's more, they are enforced through the violent regulatory practices of the state, which *literally* polices gender through the criminalisation of sex work and through targeted police violence against and incarceration of Black and Brown trans people.[20] Together this helps construct a powerful normative gendering: to consciously reject such gendering requires both individual agentic decision making and strong networks of community counter-reproduction.

Unlike many theories of gendering, social cognitive theory goes beyond normative forms, instead centring the role of agency in gender identity formation. People have the ability to choose their social influences. Would-be trans people shape their experiences of gender by seeking out trans community. This process often begins well before conscious realisation of one's own transgender inclinations. What leads people to seek out trans community is beyond the scope of this chapter, as is analysis of the 'roots' of gender dysphoria. What is relevant is that once a trans community is found, alternative social influences are available. These hooks of transformative relationality appear in the form of new models, enacted experiences, and sources of tuition. These influences, too, do not arise out of nowhere, but are reproduced through the everyday labour of trans individuals in community with one another.

While trans social reproduction occurs in community, there exists no one trans community to be neatly summarised or 'represented'. Jules Joanne Gleeson explains:

> Communities are never to be assumed as unified, or taken for granted. Trans communities, like any other kind, always have to be actively cultivated, and sustained actively across time. Communities of this kind are the product of careful development in less than ideal circumstances by trans people, and can never be treated as a given.[21]

In lieu of communities, she proposes an analysis of multiple overlapping 'trans circles', each a site of reproduction in its own way. Here, we'll examine the processes of social reproduction influencing cognition in a few such circles, and compare the reality of these practices to rhetoric around social influence and 'contagion' coming from anti-trans critics.

In a series of qualitative interviews, Sally Hines[22] explored practices of care in four UK transgender support groups. One of the key functions of trans support groups, according to Paul (a 34-year-old 'FtM' respondent)[23] was to provide models of successful transition. He is quoted: 'I always go to the FtM Network get together every year, because it was really important to me. It was quite sort of pivotal in convincing me that I could do it … if these guys can look like this so can I'.[24] While internalisation of cisgender modelling serves a regulatory function, the availability of trans models serves to build an internal sense of self-efficacy around transition. Social cognitive theory tells us that gender transgression, and human agency more generally, relies on perceived self-efficacy: 'Unless people believe they can produce desired effects by their actions', write Bussey and Bandura, 'they have little incentive to act or to persevere in the face of difficulties'.[25] To the extent that models of trans existence are presented at all in conventional society, they're most often treated as laughable or tragic – an outcome to be avoided at all costs. In contrast, the modelling available within the trans support group (and in other forms of trans community) proves that transition[26] *is* possible, and *can* produce desired effects. In this way, trans people actively participate in the reproduction of trans identity – through serving as models to new generations of transitioners.

Increasingly, however, burgeoning trans identities are nurtured through practices of reproduction occurring primarily or entirely virtually. The internet serves as a source of both modelling and enacted experience. Most notably, however, it opens up instances of social influence to trans people who, due to closets, physical location, or limitations of autonomy, lack access to offline sites of social reproduction such as support groups. In the early days of the trans internet, this tuition occurred in fora and in plain-text passing guides (such as *Hudson's FTM Resource Guide*, which still exists today). Today, however, mostly due to changes in the structure of the internet as a whole, the majority of online trans social reproduction occurs through social media. On YouTube, a prospective transitioner can access thousands of videos where trans people document their transitions step-by-step, answering questions and providing advice.[27] These videos most commonly serve as a mixture of modelling and direct tuition. For example, a trans woman YouTuber may share her experience with voice training, while also providing voice training techniques for other trans women to use.

Direct tuition also occurs through explicit norms-setting on outlets including Twitter, Tiktok, and Discord. Just as cisgender society provides direct instructions for 'appropriate' gender conduct, trans circles provide instructions on how to be trans. These instructions vary depending on the online trans circle in question. A group of 'transmedicalists' may circulate a post about how dysphoria is a requirement for trans identity, and a group of trans people with different ideals may 'quote-tweet' or 'reblog' that post to make the opposite claim. None of these claimants to authoritative definitions can truly claim the last word. There is no singular aetiology of the trans experience, or a singular understanding of what being trans *means* to those concerned. The particular inputs that a trans person receives serve an integral role in reproducing their trans identity. But as this process is reciprocal, each trans person also maintains the agency to select their environments and choose which inputs to integrate.

Lastly, through engagement with others like us, online or in physical proximity, trans people are able to build self-efficacy through enacted experiences that starkly contrast those provided by cis-assuming norms of society. As has been mentioned previously, many trans people hold early-life experiences of punishment or discouragement from gender nonconformity. This tension is only heightened upon coming out. Most, if not all, trans people will at some point in our lives experience some form of harassment, unsolicited commentary, mockery and/or pity targeting their identity or presentation. In the face of common-place rejection, trans people turn to our interactions with other trans people for a more-or-less reliable source of the positive enacted experiences we need to maintain the self-efficacy to transgress.

This process looks different across race and class lines, due to the historical and present segregation of trans circles and the ways in which racialisation and political economy structure gendered experience. In the nonprofit model of a support group, where social reproduction takes a primarily therapeutic form, intentional acts of affirmation and 'validation' serve to reassure each other that we are what we say we are (and have every right to be). For working-class trans people of colour, however, community identity development is most often necessarily inextricable from the reproduction of everyday life. Largely without the access to funding and medicalised legitimacy held by white-led NGOs, trans people of colour (particularly Black and Brown trans women) have developed extensive grassroots mutual aid networks and chosen familial structures. Trans-led organisations such as No Justice No Pride in Washington, DC and GLITS in New York City provide physical subsistence in the form of housing, medical accompaniment, and harm/risk reduction practices for survival sex work. From there, they can then facilitate the development of individual and collective self-efficacy through balls, organising trainings, and the formation of kinship ties. As friendships and organising relationships overlap with shared housing, and housemates work together and accompany each other on outcalls, community practices of identity formation in these settings are necessarily inseparable from other forms of unpaid care work and paid reproductive labour.

In discussing the practices of social reproduction which manifest trans identities, we see a clear path through which trans people assist other trans people in the development of our identities. This allows for a degree of agency unrecognised by certain trans essentialisms. It further opens up some risk by acknowledging that trans people's identities are often contingent upon our interaction with others in the trans community. To recognise this can be loaded, as career journalists and TERF activists frequently turn to exaggerated claims of 'social contagion'. Proponents of this moral panic claim that so-called 'gender ideology' grooms helpless (usually female-assigned) gender nonconforming children for recruitment into the trans cult. In a 2018 study of 250 *parents* of trans children recruited from an anti-trans message board, Lisa Littman refers to 'Rapid Onset Gender Dysphoria', which she claims can arise from exposure to transgender group dynamics and transition-related advice, particularly online through social media.[28] This, combined with parental claims regarding previous mental illness or experiences of violence, is used to claim that youth transition is a harmful coping mechanism akin to self-harm or alcohol/drug abuse.

In truth, trans community influence must be considered in the full context of the many social influences dedicated to grooming children for cisgenderism, and depicting transition as the worst of all possible outcomes. While many trans people have experienced instances of interpersonal violence, the structure of gender under capitalism is formed through violence *in all cases*. Trans people are not distinguished by our victimhood. It is in cases of cisgender identification that this coercion has been most effective. Through internalisation of cisgender models, enacted experiences, and lessons learned through direct tuition, all gendered subjects establish internal standards for social behaviour. Everyone attached to a given gender has learned to police themselves according to those standards. It is through an (often intentional) change of influences, and specifically through the reproductive practices that generate that influence, that individuals make room for a change in internal standards. For trans people, this provides a much-needed intervention against cisgender standards. For us, these have proven painfully repressive, and potentially impossible to meet.[29]

As such, trans practices of reproduction generate modes of influence that make possible alternate modes of living. They open new conditions of possibility for trans people's self-realisation. This facilitates the process of transgender identity formation, and makes opportunities for transition possible – opportunities that cis society would otherwise cruelly foreclose. This represents a manifestation of agency on the part of both would-be transitioners (who seek out a trans community) and already-established trans people (who choose to reproduce trans possibilities rather than cisgender standards and norms.) By foregrounding conscious acts of reproduction in the formation of trans identities, we can bypass both trans essentialisms and cis feminist social determinisms. We can then move forward towards a historical materialism capable of thoroughly conceptualising trans existence and resistance.

Notes

1. Raha, N. (21 September 2015). The Limits of Trans Liberalism. *Verso Books Blog*, https://www.versobooks.com/blogs/2245-the-limits-of-trans-liberalism-by-nat-raha.
2. MacKinnon, C. (1982). Feminism, Marxism, Method, and the State: An Agenda for Theory. *Signs*, 7(3), 515–544.
3. Ibid., p. 531.
4. Ibid., p. 533.
5. Williams, C. (27 November 2015). Sex, Gender, and Sexuality: An Interview With Catharine A. MacKinnon. *The Conversations Project*, radfem.transadvocate.com/sex-gender-and-sexuality-an-interview-with-catharine-a-mackinnon/.
6. James, S. E., Herman, J. L., Rankin, S., Keisling, M., Mottet, L., & Anafi, M. (2016). *The Report of the 2015 U.S. Transgender Survey*. Washington, DC: National Center for Transgender Equality.
7. Murphy, M. (28 November 2017). If Trans Activists Truly Cared about Feminism, They Would Respect Women's Spaces. *Feminist Current*, www.feministcurrent.com/2017/11/23/trans-activists-truly-cared-feminism-respect-womens-spaces/.
8. James et al., *The Report of the 2015 U.S. Transgender Survey*.
9. The late transgender neuroscientist Ben Barres is known to have recounted a story in which a fellow faculty member, not knowing he had recently transitioned, opined that 'Ben Barres gave a great seminar today, but then his work is much better than his sister's'.
   Yong, E. (3 January 2018). The Transgender Scientist Who Changed Our Understanding of the Brain. *The Atlantic*, www.theatlantic.com/science/archive/2018/01/remembering-the-transgender-scientist-who-changed-our-understanding-of-the-brain/549458/.
10. Dreger, A. (2008). The Controversy Surrounding *The Man Who Would Be Queen*: A Case Study of the Politics of Science, Identity, and Sex in the Internet Age. *Archives of Sexual Behavior*, 37(3), 366–421.

11. For example, in the foundational trans theory text *Whipping Girl*, biologist Julia Serano refers to notions of 'brain sex' in order to refute arguments that trans women are irrevocably 'biologically male'; Serano, J. (2007). *Whipping Girl: a Transsexual Woman on Sexism and the Scapegoating of Femininity*. Emeryville, CA: Seal Press.

12. Marx, K. & De Leon, D. (1898). *The Eighteenth Brumaire of Louis Bonaparte*. New York, NY: International Pub. Co.

13. Serra, F. (23 September 2018). 'Reproducing the Struggle: A New Feminist Perspective on the Concept of Social Reproduction'. *Viewpoint Magazine*, www.viewpointmag.com/2015/10/31/reproducing-the-struggle-a-new-feminist-perspective-on-the-concept-of-social-reproduction/.

14. Gleeson, J. (2017). Transition and Abolition: Notes on Marxism and Trans Politics. *Viewpoint Magazine*, https://www.viewpointmag.com/2017/07/19/transition-and-abolition-notes-on-marxism-and-trans-politics/.

15. Gleeson, J. (2018). *How do Gender Transitions Happen? Encounters and Communities*. London: Pluto Press, https://www.plutobooks.com/blog/how-gender-transitions-happen/.

16. Bussey, K. & Bandura, B. (1999). Social Cognitive Theory of Gender Development and Differentiation. *Psychological Review*, 106(4), 676–713.

17. Ibid., p. 685.

18. Ibid.

19. At the time of writing, openly transgender people have increasingly been able to take part in the cisgendering of future generations through participation in nuclear families and assignment of gender to offspring. Such assimilation occurs for many reasons, both practical and ideological, and individuals who participate in these structures are no 'less trans' for doing so. Regardless, while the subject of trans family-making warrants future discussion, this paper will maintain its focus on distinctly queer and trans processes of extrafamilial social reproduction.

20. Stanley, E. A. & Smith, N. (Eds.) (2011). *Captive Genders: Trans Embodiment and the Prison Industrial Complex*. Edinburgh: AK Press.

21. Gleeson, *How do Gender Transitions Happen?*

22. Hines, S. (2007). Transgendering Care: Practices of Care Within Transgender Communities. *Critical Social Policy*, 27(4), 462–486.

23. The term 'FtM', or female-to-male, is controversial today within some trans spaces, though it remains the term used by many medical professionals. The term 'trans man' or 'transmasculine person' currently stands as the generally-preferred alternative.

24. Ibid., p. 480.

25. Bussey & Bandura, Social Cognitive Theory, p. 691.

26. In using 'transition', I am including all means of medical *and* social transition, including changing names and pronouns, or simply coming out as trans.

27. Horak, L. (2014). Trans on YouTube: Intimacy, Visibility, Temporality. *TSQ*, 1.4 (December 2014), 572–585.
28. Littman, L. L. (2018). Rapid Onset Gender Dysphoria In Adolescents And Young Adults: A Study of Parental Reports. *PLoS One*, 13(8), e0202330.
29. Why else would we have embarked on the arduous and often personally endangering process of transition at all?

2

Trans Work: Employment Trajectories, Labour Discipline and Gender Freedom

Michelle O'Brien

Introduction

Carolyn grew up in a difficult working-class Irish-American family in Brooklyn in the 1970s.[1] Years before she came out as a woman, Carolyn's dysphoria led her to make some difficult choices about how to present her gender. In 1986 she graduated from high school, and had been growing her hair to chest-length for two years. She refused to cut her hair, for reasons not yet fully evident to her. 'My gender dysphoria – I didn't think of it that way back then – I could not cut my hair. I could not mentally do that'. Her long hair was extremely disruptive to how others experienced her as otherwise presenting as a young man. People were hostile and threatening to Carolyn on a daily basis. She recounts, 'from a work perspective, I was *completely* unemployable', before listing a series of working-class positions she was offered – contingent on her cutting her hair. Instead, she turned to substantial and chaotic drug use, and dived into the 1980s metal scene of Brooklyn. Among metal fans, men having long hair was socially acceptable. She cobbled together precarious and temporary jobs from scattered family members. After spending the 1990s organising with anarchists, Carolyn eventually found work as an out trans woman, working at a Manhattan sex toy shop called Babeland. Babeland was lesbian-owned, marketing itself as a feminist and pro-queer store where sex-knowledgeable staff could answer difficult questions. Hiring a trans woman fit broadly into their self-conception as progressive-minded business owners. At the time, it was one of the only formal wage labour jobs where Carolyn could be out as trans. Long after she left Babeland, the workers there

47

unionised, led in part by the many trans people on the staff furious over the gendered harassment they suffered on the job. Today, Carolyn teaches others how to rock climb, and lives in the Hudson Valley north of New York City.

In Carolyn's story, we see broader themes that trans people face concerning work. Trans people usually have a hard time finding work, get treated poorly in most of our jobs, and consequently end up poor. Carolyn, like many trans people, felt a deep and strong commitment to expressing her gender, even in the initial step of growing her hair long. This gendered choice sharply constrained her employability, contributing to a period of habitual drug use and social marginality. Even as she regained stability in her life, Carolyn's employment options were sharply limited. The retail job she was able to find was accessible because of subtle gendered expectations. These factors enabled trans people to eventually gain an employment niche there, where they were able to wage a collective struggle as trans workers.

Here I am concerned with trans people's experiences of work. Some trans people pass as cis at their jobs, then face the problem of how to manage their resumes and mismatch with the narratives of former employers, or the risk of discovery. This chapter focuses on the experiences of trans people *unable* to pass much at all at their jobs, particularly trans women. The experience of being a gender deviant needing work, and how trans people fight for their economic survival, has much to say about gender freedom for all.

Writing on queer work and trans precarity

On the passenger ocean liners of the 1930s, male workers undertook tasks otherwise considered women's work when done in the home: cooking and serving food to the passengers, laundry, and janitorial work. On some boats, African-American men were hired for these reproductive service tasks, much like their contemporaries working as railroad porters. On other lines, Chinese men took up this work. Under the white supremacist cultural logic of the US, Black and Chinese men were already considered feminine and appropriate for women's work. But some of the ocean liner companies prided themselves on maintaining a white workforce, offering an elite experience to a white and racist clientele. Few white men, however, would demean themselves by doing such feminised work. Their employers already considered this type of work somehow 'queer'. It is here that white gender-nonconforming effeminate men managed to get a foothold in the industry. These stewards found a solidarity and support among fellow queens, coming to incorporate drag parties, homoeroticism, and soon a defence of gay rights into their work life. Over workplace struggles through the 1930s, ocean liner service workers formed the Marine Cooks and Stewards Union, bridging these feminised Black men, Chinese men, and white queer men into a Communist-Party-allied militant labour union. These militant workers organised under the slogan 'No Race-Baiting, Red-Baiting, or Queer-Baiting!'

Alan Bérubé's study of the Marine Cooks and Stewards Union inaugurated the growing historical and current literature on what he calls 'queer work' – professions and industries where queer people helped each other get jobs, found some space to express their non-normative genders at work, reduced the risks of homophobic attack, and in some cases were favoured by employers. These jobs are those often associated with stereotyped gender roles of one's opposite gender – specifically blue-collar labour for women, and activities like cooking, service, laundry, and food service for men. Following Bérubé, researchers have traced the history of queer people working as flight attendants[2] and in department stores,[3] and in blue-collar industries like steel manufacturing and trucking.[4] These studies enrich a growing literature about queer people in the labour movement.[5] What makes these jobs *queer* is not really about sexual object choice, but about gender expectations. Employers, customers, and co-workers have assumptions about the gendered nature of the work itself, allowing gender-nonconforming queer people to find a limited and difficult niche. Deviant or non-normative gender expressions exclude queer people from work, constrain the industries where we can find work, and make experience at work contentious and dangerous. This research on queer work gives us a framework for thinking about trans people's experiences with formal employment.

We don't actually know much systematically about the range of trans experiences with work. The national surveys that provide statisticians with representative data don't include any means of identifying trans people. Queer researchers generally lack the resources for rigorous empirical investigations. The most systematic report on trans

Americans available comes from a 2011 survey by the National Center for Transgender Equality, including 6500 respondents.[6] The data on employment was dire: 28% of African-American trans respondents report being unemployed, and 12% of white trans people, compared to 7% of the general population; 15% of all trans respondents were living in extreme poverty, with incomes below $10,000 a year, four times the rate for the general population. When excluded from stable employment, trans people turn to whatever means they have available to survive. Over a quarter of respondents had participated in the underground economy: 44% of African-American trans women reported experiences in sex work, and 28% of Latinx trans people. No law protects trans people against discrimination in 34 American states. An uneven patchwork of US anti-discrimination law protects trans people against overt and explicit employment discrimination. A majority of American employers can openly fire someone on the basis of them being trans.

This confirms what many trans activists already know: most trans people face serious problems with work. The severity of these problems vary based on race – and hence likely by education and class backgrounds. For a substantial number of trans people, difficulties with work add up to living in extreme and severe poverty and economic deprivation. Facing the indignity of exclusion and mistreatment at work both unites many trans people, and makes clear the challenges we face in organising across the considerable variations in our work life. Communists and Marxists have long recognised that the kinds of work we do shapes not only the kind of misery we face, but also how we are able to organise. Workplaces determine where we are able to exert power through disruption, and the kinds of relationships of support and solidarity we are able to build with each other. How we work shapes how we can engage in class struggle.

Trajectories in trans work

Given the lack of comprehensive statistics, we can turn to the stories and experiences reported by trans people themselves. In trans activism, trans writing, and discussion within trans communities there is much reflection about people's experiences with work. Here – using the NYC Trans Oral History Project – I identify stories that reflect broad and common trends found across many different interviews. These cases are all trans women of colour who are relatively out as trans or gender non-binary in their work; all faced discrimination and anguish in their work – but the differences in their stories reveal a lot about trans work trajectories. In all three trajectories I consider here, key elements of trans work experience shape the form of class struggle and the gender rights movement waged by trans people in New York City.

Naomi is one of the more professionally successful trans women in the archive. Naomi grew up in a middle-class family in Seattle, Washington. Her mom was Japanese-American and a social worker; her dad was white and an academic. When she was 11 years old, Naomi lived in Japan for a few years, and immersed herself in the local nerd subcultures. Popular anime TV plotlines featured outrageous and extravagant gender transitions woven into science fiction and fantasy settings. Following education at an elite university, Naomi developed programming skills, and ended up working in the tech industry during the dot-com boom in web design. She began to discuss with her friends the possibility of transitioning. She was terrified, believing transitioning would bar her from gaining any employment. Her friend reassured her that she could get a job *somewhere*, suggesting she could become a janitor at the Gay Center – a comforting thought at the time.

Though her web-design department was dominated by queer 'art and design weirdos', the firm included many 'misogynist programmers', and she expected difficulties if she stayed there. After coming out as trans, she found work managing the website of a major LGBT advocacy organisation in New York. Naomi was radicalised, both through NYC trans organising and in a vibrant online discussion community of queer and trans people Naomi helped build called *Strap-On*. She found the advocacy group where she worked politically dissatisfying, eventually coming back to more fulfilling work in game design, secured through her social networks of tech geeks. Naomi worked in game design for some years before suddenly finding herself among an exploding community of other queer and trans women:

In 2012 there were like a kajillion trans women working in games, and I had never met any trans people making games before that. All of a sudden there was this gigantic wave of, you know, what's kind of being called the Queer Games Movement ... then there were all these younger trans people being like, 'Oh my gosh! You've been here this whole time? Who are you?' again [laughter] and I'm just like 'Yeah I'm just me, you know, I've been just plodding along working, finding what work I can, working as a freelancer'.

Today, she is a professor of game design at NYU.

Many dimensions of Naomi's story reflect broad patterns that have shaped emerging trans communities. Many white and Asian-American trans women have found long-term employment in tech, internet, and gaming firms. It is one of the first stable professional employment niches open to substantial numbers of trans women beyond nightlife entertainment and social work. Despite her elite education, Naomi saw herself as needing to be willing to entirely sacrifice her class-standing and professional future in order to transition, basing this assessment on the horrors many other middle-class trans women faced in their professional fields. She was able to find her way back to her chosen professional field, but through a circuitous route via gay advocacy nonprofits.

Many trans women in tech, like Naomi, found early community online – including a rapidly evolving landscape of trans-centred online discussion and networking. Naomi not only reflected this trajectory, but did much to help create it – through *Strap-On*, through supporting the many queer and trans women who entered game design, and through the online battles over gender and sexuality within gaming that came to be known as 'Gamergate'. Many recent fights in tech, including Gamergate, are simultaneously about the working conditions of tech workers, the balance of power between them and their employers, the dominance of misogyny and transphobia in the industry, and dynamics of gender freedom for tech workers.[7] Like many recent class struggles, workers in tech have fought over work in part through fighting over gender. Naomi helped make tech an industry of 'trans work', much as scholars have identified other sectors of queer work. Like many other professional trans women working in tech, Naomi's relative economic stability did not lead her into political conservatism. Instead, she was radicalised in these online networks, and continues to be very politically active. Naomi's life and work helped open the space for the hundreds of trans women turning to communist politics and queer theory on social media today.

While 'trans in tech' is a relatively well-known labour phenomenon, other avenues for workplace life during adult transition have received less attention. Many working-class trans New Yorkers are able to find wage labour jobs in retail and customer service. The attention to fashion and style that circulates in many communities of trans and queer people of colour makes them appealing as sales floor staff at apparel retail stores. In gay neighbourhoods many young trans people work as baristas, in bars, or as waiting staff. Trans people are especially well represented in the sexualised retail and service industries. As with Carolyn, this often includes sex toy shops.

For workers in low-wage retail, class and gender struggle are also profoundly interwoven. Workers at Babeland and the Pleasure Chest, two sex toy retail businesses, fought for union representation that would defend them both as workers and gender-nonconforming people. Their workforce was nearly all queer, and trans people played leading and central roles in the organising efforts. Selling sex toys as gender nonconforming people subjected them to frequent harassment and the risk of gendered violence from customers. Staff faced routine misogynistic prank phone calls, drunken aggressive groups of men entering the stores late at night, reactive and charged homophobia and transphobia from customers, and other gendered risks in their jobs. These served as primary motivations in trying to unionise. The owners of these businesses, gay or lesbian identified, both wanted to understand themselves as progressive and queer-inclusive. But they were uninterested in taking any substantial steps to actually address the safety concerns of their staff, and actively resisted unionisation. As of January 2020, workers at Babeland are nearly three years into their first successful contract. They have remained unusually militant, at one point acting collectively to successfully get a manager fired for misgendering workers. Workers at the Pleasure Chest also won a collective bargaining agreement in August 2019.

Nico is a sex-educator and salesperson at the Pleasure Chest. She grew up in West Texas, Houston and Oklahoma to a 'middle-class aspiring' Mexican-American family. Nico was a gender nonconforming child, frequently told by adults that she was 'creative', and that people would 'get her' if she moved to New York. Not able to find retail work in Texas, she moved to New York City to work in advertising, television, and fashion. She met many other trans women of colour trying to pursue careers in fashion. She worked for a high-profile queer fashion designer, and grew to hate the industry. The work was intensely exploitative, and rarely paid. She found her first stable job at Babeland through a queer employment mutual aid Facebook group. At Babeland, she encountered a new level of discussion and reflectivity about queerness and gender. She moved onto working at the Pleasure Chest just before the unionisation got going at Babeland.

Informed by theories of Black feminism, queer theory, and Afro-Pessimism, Nico was extremely conscious of the power dynamics of anti-Black racism, misogyny, transphobia, and transmisogynoir at the Pleasure Chest. In listing forms of mistreatment of staff at the Pleasure Chest, she highlighted the singling out of trans women in enforcing dress codes, also a major theme in interviews with Babeland workers. Nico recognised how abuse by management staff, dress codes, and other day-to-day employment conditions were rooted in broader dynamics of domination. At Babeland, several workers politicised by the unionisation campaign became involved in a theory-heavy, communist, feminist organisation through a project organising queer workers. Nico similarly joined a broader left movement through her workplace by organising the Pleasure Chest, speaking on trans worker struggles at the 2018 NYC International Women's Strike mobilisation, and then at the Labor Notes Conference for left union militants in Chicago.

For Nico, and many other queer and trans retail workers involved in workplace organising drives in NYC, her experiences of race, sexuality, gender and transmisogyny profoundly inform how she understands herself as a worker. The work process of retail draws on and markets her cultural and gender savviness to link hipness to her employer's sales campaigns, while insulting and abusing Black and trans workers. Nico, like many other queer workers involved in retail organising campaigns in NYC, weaves sophisticated identity-based politics with workplace solidarity. Rather than identity politics and workplace organising being counterposed, Nico understands they can profoundly enrich each other.

As a third trajectory, there are many African-American and Latina trans women who have survived through criminalised sex work. Though few current sex workers feel the safety and openness to be able to share a public and non-anonymous interview about their work

experience with the NYC Trans Oral History Project, many former
sex workers still involved in sex worker communities have contributed
their stories. No doubt many current sex workers have been inter-
viewed, and chose to avoid discussion of their job. Three interviews
reflect in depth on experiences with sex work, followed by the narrator
moving into significantly lower-paid, but more stable, work in HIV
and AIDS services.

Paris was born in Atlanta. Her mother raised Paris and her two
brothers alone by working a series of jobs, including work as a home
health aide, a nurse, and at a car dealership. Paris became involved in a
circle of mostly other African-American trans women while working
a series of low-level administrative jobs at universities in the region.
Her trans communities faced heavy, chaotic drug use and frequent
incarceration, and engaged in paid sex work. Paris understood sex
work in a broader context of criminalised hustles trans women used to
survive, describing in detail the mechanics of scams including identity
theft, 'bank pulls', or the 'fiddler scam'. She engaged in sex work, 'like
everyone else', recognising it was much more lucrative than any paid
work options. She discussed the stratification between sex workers,
the separation between those who worked the streets and those who
found their customers online:

> The ones that I were hanging out with, that were doing sex work,
> they were strictly online. At that time, it was like a stark difference
> between the online girl and the – you know, the young lady in the
> street. Yeah. It was like a caste system, I guess, like a difference in
> class. It was like, 'Oh, you know – oh, she walks the street', kind
> of thing.

In contrast to street-based sex work, online work required 'the look,
personality and just the manner', what she acknowledged as a certain
class status. Trans sex workers who found customers online were able
to more carefully screen clients, knew more about HIV risk, and were
less likely to find themselves exposed to law enforcement. Paris ended
up deciding to leave sex work when she wanted to go back to school.
She found a job as a case manager at a large HIV service agency in
Brooklyn. Despite receiving much lower pay than she had from sex
work, she found the work fulfilling. She particularly appreciated the

opportunity to be of help and support to those going through experiences similar to Paris' own.

Both sex work and HIV services constitute major sites of class struggle for trans women of colour. Black and Latinx trans communities have been extensively and well organised in major eastern US cities since at least the early 1960s. Here sex work and nightlife entertainment financially sustained strata of otherwise socially marginal trans women of colour. Though they were almost entirely excluded from wage labour and were largely unable to access urban social welfare programmes, Black and Latinx queer and trans communities were able to build out extensive networks of mutual aid practices. Sometimes these networks centred around the competitive dance countercultural scenes known as balls or the house scene. These scenes operated under the crushing violence of criminalisation, incarceration, extreme poverty, police violence, or their internal contradictions of competition and drama. Whatever their limits, these networks were sufficient to support many young transfeminine people to come out and transition much earlier in life than many of their middle-class and white counterparts. These networks of trans women of colour constitute forms of self-activity and survival-struggle among the lumpenproletariat. At times, this organising took an overtly political form, such as the 1970s Street Transvestite Action Revolution (STAR) organised by Sylvia Rivera and Marsha P. Johnson. Trans women of colour have long been among the most militant and confrontational segments within LGBTQ organising movements. Trans women of colour continue to play major roles in sex worker organising today in New York City, most recently against the passage of FOSTA/SESTA, federal legislation that criminalised websites that hosted online networking and advertising of sex work services, significantly eroding the spaces of self-organisation and resistance by sex workers.

HIV services constitute one of the few viable employment exits for trans women of colour trying to leave sex work. Transfeminine people of colour face extremely high rates of HIV infection, due to poverty, sex work, and exposure to violence. According to several urban needs assessment surveys in major US cities, HIV infection among trans women of colour exceeded 80%. HIV service agencies centred on high-risk communities and the skills of hustling and social networking among trans women of colour forged one of the only stable employment niches available in the early 2000s. HIV/AIDS services are generally among the only employers to whom a sex worker can disclose their actual work history. HIV services continue to be the major mode for trans women of colour organising and advocacy, including battling with trans-oblivious gay rights activists.

These constitute three distinct trajectories available to substantial numbers of trans people, particularly trans women, into forms of trans work and trans class struggle: from geek culture into tech and game design and online political communities, from culture industries into retail employment and identity-savvy workplace organising, and from sex work into HIV social services. In all cases, these forms of work constitute around them major dimensions of class struggle and politicisation for trans people.

Gender discipline and the labour process

The experience of trans people in work has much to offer in how we understand gender freedom and gender oppression in the lives of working-class people. Trans people have so much trouble finding work because work itself imposes gendered expectations on everyone. Trans people's experience of work – not being able to find it, getting a foothold in only a handful of industries, being subject to harassment and the risk of violence on the job – makes it clear that all working-class people are subject in their jobs to various forms of gender discipline and regulation.

For the many people forced to try to get by on wage labour or criminalised informal employment, the experience of work is central to our day-to-day quality of life and wellbeing. Working-class insurgent movements have long documented the many horrors and abuses of so much work: unsafe working conditions and risk of death, abusive and cruel bosses, crushing boredom or desperate competition, or just the despair of being subject to a process antagonistic to our humanity. Gender discipline is an underappreciated and major dimension to this daily misery for proletarians. All work imposes some varying forms of expectations for gender expression and gendered behaviour. Gender takes many forms in the labour process: masculine toughness expected in the face of the dangers in many industrial manufacturing jobs, the gracious feminising and racialised subservience expected by service staff, the highly gendered professional dress codes of white-collar employment, the pervasiveness of sexual harassment and sexual coercion in most industries, or the maternal activities of teaching, nursing, and childcare.

The almost complete power of employers over hiring and firing, particularly in 'at-will' employment in the US or 'zero-hour' contracts in Europe, where employers can fire a non-unionised employee without reason, allows employers to impose any arbitrary bigotry without apology. For the majority of American workers without access to a union or collective bargaining agreements, there are few mechanisms for contesting employer power – besides high-risk and criminalised disruptive protest. Further, employers expect and impose these gendered expectations as how they observe and define compe-tence in the job. Behaviours that fall outside of gendered expectations of behaviour not only violate an employer's homophobia or misogyny, but also their understanding of what the work requires.

Under the tyranny of employers, all workers face day-to-day gendered expectations that constrain how we are able to embody and express our genders. The room available for working people to explore and experiment with our genders, and the opportunity for trans people to transition or find employment in the first place, are constrained as one feature of this broader regime of class rule. Like many people's experience of the family, employment is an institution of gender violence and everyday coercion.

Gender freedom and the future of trans work struggles

The many forms of how trans people wage class struggle have much to offer for a broader vision of gender freedom against capitalist society. For trans people in tech, this class struggle is in the strong solidar-ity between cis queer women and trans women in their battle against gender fascists in Gamergate, or against institutionally-sanctioned misogynistic sexual harassment at Google. For trans workers in sexu-alised low-wage service retail like at Babeland, this class struggle can take the form of fighting for unions fit for our purposes – that is, for worker organisations that place gender safety and the right to gender expression as central concerns, and which accept trans leadership. For the trans people excluded from employment – mostly poor trans women of colour – collective action is in sex worker organising, in the highly organised systems of mutual aid in the ball scenes, and in the dense social networks through which people survive and support each other. For trans social movements broadly, many of the major policy battles of recent years include a substantial attention to the conditions of unemployment and hardship with work faced by trans people: in opposing sex worker criminalisation; in fighting to ban open discrimination against employees on the basis of gender expression; in calling on LGBTQ service and advocacy organisations to employ more trans people and treat the trans people they employ well.

As trans people make headway in these struggles over access to work and transforming the gendered expectations of work, this opens onto a potentially broad struggle of working-class people over rights to self-determine one's body, to express oneself with dignity and joy, to find pleasure and love with each other. Workplace indignities which appear in distinctly gendered ways are hardly limited to trans people. Kate Doyle Griffiths documents the teacher's strike in West Virginia in 2018, and the central concern of many workers over a new health-care monitoring practice of forcing them to wear Fitbits and be subject to regular medical testing, and to fine them if they fail to exercise sufficiently or don't lose weight or meet other health targets.[8] Teachers understandably found this level of coercive surveillance and disciplining of their bodies to be outrageous and unacceptable, in ways remarkably close to why trans people are willing to be fired rather than not transition on the job. Even the struggles of trans sex workers open onto broader questions of how unwaged and unhoused people survive against mass incarceration and criminalisation, against coercive social service regimes, for the need to forge non-work strategies of getting by. Trans people fighting for dignity in formal employment, and the right to survive outside of work, are the leading edge for working-class people to discover the power and pleasure in refusing the gender expectations imposed on everyone.

Trans work struggles, and what they offer to the broader gender freedom of the working class, break open the relationship between identity liberation and class struggle. Rather than identity politics being arbitrarily opposed to labour struggles, in trans-work organising they are inseparable. In trans work fights, the possibility is that of a deeper and fuller freedom than further subjugation to work: dependency on labour markets constrains the ability of all working-class people to fully express their potential, self-development, and self-expression in the world. Gender expression is central to human fulfilment, to our creativity and our dignity, to express beauty, and to experience pleasure. Trans people – whatever the limits or costs – show a remarkable and rare commitment to courageously following nonconforming yet fulfilling self-expression. Trans people waging struggles for economic survival offer a means of imagining a class politics that pursues the potential for full human development.

Notes

1. Throughout, all names and individuals referred to here are real people, who contributed their life stories in the NYC Trans Oral History Project, an online and public archive hosted by the New York Public Library, http://oralhistory.nypl.org/neighborhoods/trans-history. The author is a significant contributor, organiser, and part-time member of staff working on the project.

   Last names are omitted, to reduce the immediate likelihood of this chapter appearing in internet searches. But their original interviews, with transcripts, are accessible through the archive, and easily matched with their names here.
2. See Tiemeyer, P. (2013). *Plane Queer: Labor, Sexuality, and AIDS in the History of Male Flight Attendants*. Berkeley, CA: University of California Press; Murphy, R. (2010). *On Our Own: Flight Attendant Activism and the Family Values Economy*. Minneapolis, MN: University of Minnesota.
3. Ross, A. (2001). Strike a Pose for Justice: The Barneys Union Campaign. In Krupat, K. & McCreery, P. (Eds.), *Out at Work: Building a Gay-labor Alliance*, pp. 78–91. Minneapolis, MN: University of Minnesota Press.
4. Balay, A. (2014). *Steel Closets: Voices of Gay, Lesbian, and Transgender Steelworkers*. Chapel Hill, NC: University of North Carolina Press Books.
5. Frank, M. (2014). *Out in the Union: A Labor History of Queer America*. Philadelphia, PA: Temple University Press.
6. National Center for Transgender Equality (2012). *National Transgender Discrimination Survey: Full Report*, https://transequality.org/issues/resources/national-transgender-discrimination-survey-full-report.
7. I am thinking here of several events over 2017 and 2018, including the unionisation campaign among programmers at Lanetix, the growth of the Tech Workers Coalition nationally, and the protests at Google and Microsoft. In all cases, gender has played an underappreciated and central role. The impetus for the unionisation campaign at Lanetix, for example, centred around discrimination against a worker for her pregnancy. At

---

Google, a major walk out was prompted by revelations of how their employer had responded to sexual harassment by executive staff.

8. Doyle Griffiths, K. (2018). Crossroads and Country Roads: Wildcat West Virginia and the Possibilities of a Working Class Offensive. *Viewpoint Magazine*, https://www.viewpointmag.com/2018/03/13/crossroads-and-country-roads-wildcat-west-virginia-and-the-possibilities-of-a-working-class-offensive/.

3

Judith Butler's Scientific Revolution: Foundations for a Transsexual Marxism

Rosa Lee

I've subtitled my piece 'Foundations for a transsexual Marxism', a choice of words I know may cause a stir for many readers who've opened this collection. Many see 'transsexual' as a term best left in the twentieth century (a point of view I will return to). And many Marxists see Marxism as a universally applicable science, which should be kept free from the contamination of 'identity politics'. But I want to return to this term, now out of fashion, because I think that appending 'transsexual' to 'Marxism' allows us to think Marxism differently, to refocus Marxism in a way that 'transgender', as a much broader umbrella, does not enable so precisely. Transsexual Marxism does not simply imply 'trans people doing Marxism' or 'Marxist analysis of trans people's lives'. Rather, 'transsexual Marxism' suggests a transformed Marxism, a Marxism which has been in some way transsexualised. A Marxism which has undergone or is embarking on a process of transition, if you will.

In short, my suggestion is that if Marxist feminism is Marxist analysis refracted through the analysis of gender, transsexual Marxism is Marxist analysis but refracted through the analysis of gender and sex transition.

In order to undertake this transformation, to make Marxism as a field of scientific theory adequate to the practice of class struggle, we must transsexualise our Marxism by making it methodologically accountable to trans struggle and the experience of gender/sex transition. And to bridge the gap, so to speak, between gender/sex transition and the transition to communism, we will have to begin our scientific study with the paradigm shift in feminist analysis inaugurated by Judith Butler's theory of gender performativity.

The term 'paradigm shift', though these days invoked fairly colloquially, was first introduced as a technical term by the historian of science Thomas Kuhn in his 1962 book *The Structure of Scientific Revolutions*.[1] According to Kuhn, the day-to-day activity of scientific research is always structured by a broader, shared institutional and methodological paradigm. When scientific study simply tests and explores this paradigm, it is called 'normal science'. However, every once in a while, circumstances cause this normal science to push at the edges of the paradigm, to disrupt the tacit background assumptions that the model depends on for theoretical and practical coherence. In this account, a paradigm shift, or scientific revolution, can occur when a new paradigm is generated which can better account for the anomalous results thrown up by the practice of normal science.

So what is a scientific paradigm? Donna Haraway, in her 1976 book *Crystals, Fabrics, and Fields*, argues that the central characteristic of a paradigm is the reliance on a shared metaphor.[2] According to Haraway, what she calls 'paradigm as disciplinary matrix' involves shared 'symbolic generalizations that give points of attachment for ... logical and mathematical techniques', shared 'belief in the appropriateness of particular models', and shared 'exemplars or concrete typical solutions'.[3] In this sense, we might talk about the Copernican revolution as the shift in metaphor from a geocentric model of the solar system to a heliocentric one, opening up new possibilities of the scientific study of the heavens. Similarly, we might talk about Marxism as a scientific paradigm structured by the mode of production as a central metaphor, on the basis of which a whole series of analyses and investigations are made thinkable. It is these analyses and investigations that are often referred to as the field of historical materialism.

Now, what I want to argue is that with her 1990 book *Gender Trouble*, Judith Butler inaugurated, or at least consolidated and proposed, a scientific paradigm shift in the analysis of gender, a shift analogous to the shifts inaugurated by Copernicus and Marx.[4] This will open through to exploring both the limits of Butler's formulation, and the ways in which it may still be useful to the project of a transsexual Marxism.

When Butler wrote *Gender Trouble*, they was primarily confronting what we might call a radical feminist paradigm. This is a paradigm

that is alive and well today – not only in the forms of contemporary radical feminism that exist in large part as the theoretical basis
for anti-trans political practice (i.e. TERFism) but also in the mainstream of contemporary liberal feminism. This paradigm, one we
might today call 'feminism as identity politics', is what Butler calls
'the construction of the category of women as a coherent and stable
subject'. This 'coherent and stable subject' forms the theoretical basis
for a broad set of political practices – whether they be the feminist
'consciousness-raising' of the 1970s, the support for female politicians
called upon by contemporary liberal feminism, or the attacks on trans
women engaged in by contemporary TERFs.

Butler's central intervention is the consolidation of a reconceptu-
alisation of gender away from this 'coherent and stable subject', based
on what they call 'the metaphysics of substance'.[5] In her analysis, the
radical feminist view of womanhood follows from an ontological
metaphor in which gender is taken to be something which one simply
is. Butler seeks to replace this view with one that treats gender not as
a monolithic substance, but as something processual and relational, as
what they call a 'constituted *social temporality*'.[6] Instead of describing
gender through the metaphor of *being*, they suggest that it be understood through the metaphor of linguistic performativity, what they call
the 'stylized repetition of acts',[7] which in citing a supposedly authoritative identity actually comes to constitute that identity as such.

Gender presents itself as obvious, inevitable. Butler's argument
is that, in order to critique it, one must realise that it is exactly this
conceit which leaves gender ever-contested, ever-shifting.

Cinzia Arruzza has argued, quite persuasively, for the Marxist res-
onances of this framing of gender as 'constituted social temporality'.[8]
As she points out, this formulation neatly describes Marx's analysis of
capital as something always-in-motion and always-contingent, which
comes to appear as its own substantive, original, and authoritative
subject. As Arruzza quotes Marx:

Capital, as self-valorizing value, does not just comprise class
relations, a definite social character that depends on the existence
of labour as wage labour. It is a movement, a circulatory process
through different stages, which itself in turn includes three different

forms of the circulatory process. Hence it can only be grasped as a movement, and not as a static thing.[9]

In other words, what gender regimes share with capitalism is that they are *naturalised*: gender regimes appear as 'ever thus', in just the same way that capitalism's specificity as a system is obscured by just-so stories that anachronistically extend distinctively modern practices and institutions onto the pre-capitalist past. Indeed, Butler points to this analogy, writing that they share with Marx the aim of exposing 'the contingent acts that create the appearance of naturalistic necessity'.

It may be noted that Butler was not the first person to talk about gender being constructed. Indeed, they cite quite heavily Simone de Beauvoir's famous claim that 'one is not for a woman, but rather becomes one'. However, in shifting from the metaphysics of substance to constituted social temporality, Butler goes further than simply asserting that gender is socially constructed. For many of her contemporaries, following Beauvoir's assertion, biological sex was taken to be the raw material which society shaped into gender; thus, females were not born women but made into them. For Butler, however, this was insufficient. Her argument, in *Gender Trouble* and especially in her follow-up *Bodies That Matter*, was precisely that the assumption of the sexed body as unchangeable material substrate limited the analysis of gender construction by reinstating a metaphysics of substance. Thus, Butler writes:

> Gender ought not to be conceived merely as the cultural inscription of meaning on a pregiven sex (a juridical conception); gender must also designate the very apparatus of production whereby the sexes themselves are established. As a result, gender is not *just* to culture as sex is to nature. Gender is also the discursive/cultural means by which 'sexed nature' or 'a natural sex' is produced and established as 'prediscursive', prior to culture, a politically neutral surface *on which* culture acts.[10]

And so this is why, for a project of a transsexual Marxism, Butler is so central. Because it is her materialist assertion that not only gender but the sexed body itself is social rather than natural, that gender and sex, as constituted social temporality, are not permanent but change-able, mutable, and impermanent. This opens up the possibility of us seriously thinking through both gender and sex transition on a personal level – and the possibility of collective transition to communism as a process of undoing, remaking, or even substantively abolishing gender.

Now, one of the main obstacles to the taking up of this new paradigm by Marxists has been that it coincided with a period of retreat from science in critical theory. Others, particularly Rosemary Hennessy, have written eloquently and incisively about the retreat from the radical political imaginary of the 1960s which coincided with the neoliberal ruling class offensive of the 1980s and 1990s.[11] As Hennessy argues, this was an easy context for Butler to engage with historical materialism selectively, drawing out a flavourful insight from Marx, without full engagement with, or extension of, historical mate-rialism more generally. This era saw the deradicalisation of Marxist, feminist, and anti-racist theory which had been forged in the heat of a prior cycle of struggle. 'Critique' became increasingly academised and distanced from working-class struggle. In her own way, Butler sought to resist these circumstances. But her work was unable, at the time, to escape its context.

And so Butler's scientific breakthrough coincided with what is often called 'the linguistic turn' – the ontologisation of language and the evacuation of other considerations from social analysis. This timing defined her own work, as well as in its reception. Indeed, part of what this meant was that linguistic performativity in Butler's work was not understood simply as a metaphor but as a direct description. The process of gendering that Butler described was understood to be a linguistic process. At its worst, this trajectory reduced gendering to a process of pure signification in which questions of division of labour, social reproduction, and class domination and struggle were obscured. This wasn't simply a misunderstanding of Butler's own work by others, though certainly that was very much at play. Rather, Butler herself goes so far as to claim in *Gender Trouble* that 'the juridical structures of language and politics constitute the contemporary field of power'.[12] In large part this turn in Butler is legitimated by a characteristically Anglophone misreading of Foucault.[13] This defanged Foucault (espe-cially desiccated in terms of his class politics) contrasts glaringly with the more recent accounts offered by queer Marxist theorists, such as Chris Chitty.[14]

Nonetheless, my contention is that by remembering the metaphorical character of any scientific model, we can draw out the insights of the theory of performativity while putting it into conversation with our other Marxist metaphors. And performativity is especially useful for those theories which have animated the exciting advances in Marxist feminism in recent years – both contemporary analyses of the terrain of social reproduction and of the structural separation of spheres, as put forward by Maya Gonzalez and Jeanne Neton in The Logic of Gender.[15]

To return to our starting point, then, let us go back to the question of transsexual Marxism. Now, as I pointed out, the term 'transsexual' here appears as somewhat archaic; these days, 'transgender', or simply 'trans', with or without an asterisk, have become much more popular. However, I find the term useful because I think it names something specific, something crucial, which is often lost in the use of those terms. Generally speaking, 'transgender' and 'trans' both circulate as broad umbrella terms, indicating some sort of deviation, in presentation, lifestyle, or personal identity, from the sex people have been normatively assigned at birth. However, in conjuring an earlier, medicalised and at times pathologised framing, 'transsexual' on the other hand highlights the centrality for many trans people of a process of *transition*.

Often transitions are framed in biological or medical terms – hormone replacement, surgeries, etc. – but at their core transition in this sense refers to a process of remaking the self, of wilful self-transformation. For trans people, transition denotes a set of self-fashioning practices that are crucial to the way that many of us live, practices which occur in our experiences as part of a process. Far from being the solitary resolution of a pathology through clinical treatment, transition as a process can be considered a glimpse of the forging of new forms of solidarity that might breach a new mode of production. For this end, I think Butler's theory, which highlights the constructedness and malleability of sex, is a crucial point of departure for trans Marxists. We must bring into view the social and temporal nature not only of gender, but also of the sexed body. We must incorporate our intimate understandings of this kind of self-transformation, this work of the self, into our theory. Social theory cannot exist segregated from the practical struggles, affinity circles and unlikely alliances we so often rely on. In a different era, Marxists spoke of the construction of a 'new socialist man' as a crucial task in the broader process of socialist construction. Today, in a time of both rising fascism and an emergent socialist movement, our challenge is transsexualising our Marxism. We should think the project of transition to communism in our time – communisation – as including the transition to new communist selves, new ways of being and relating to one another.

Notes

1. Kuhn, T. (1962). *The Structure of Scientific Revolutions*. Chicago, IL: University of Chicago Press.
2. Haraway, D. (1976). *Crystals, Fabrics, and Fields: Metaphors of Organicism in Twentieth-Century Developmental Biology*. New Haven, CT: Yale University Press.
3. Ibid., 4.
4. Butler, J. (2006). *Gender Trouble: Feminism and the Subversion of Identity*. London: Routledge Classics.
5. Ibid., 34.
6. Ibid., 191.
7. Ibid.
8. Arruzza, C. (2015). Gender as Social Temporality: Butler (and Marx). *Historical Materialism*, 23, 28–52.
9. Marx, K. (1978). *Capital: A Critique of Political Economy. Volume II*. Fernbach, D. (Trans.). Harmondsworth: Penguin, p. 185.
10. Ibid., 10.
11. Hennessy, R. (2000). The Material of Sex. In *Profit and Pleasure: Sexual Identities in Late Capitalism*. London: Routledge.
12. Butler, *Gender Trouble*, p. 7.
13. The Anglophone reception of French Theory in the 1980s and 1990s grouped together a variety of different theorists, who often had little to do with each other in method, interests or approach, under the body of 'French Theory' – whilst this sent a shockwave through the academy, and was enormously generative of whole new fields of study and subjects, it did so at the cost of intellectual reductionism, obscuring many of the thinkers' own problematics, influences and concerns. For an intellectual history of the moment of 'French Theory' see Cusset, F. (2008). *French Theory: How Foucault, Derrida, Deleuze, & Co. Transformed the Intellectual Life of the United States*. Minneapolis, MN: University of Minnesota.
14. Chitty, C. (2012).Towards a Socialist Art of Government: Michel Foucault's 'The Mesh of Power'. *Viewpoint Magazine*, https://www.

viewpointmag.com/2012/09/12/towards-a-socialist-art-of-government-michel-foucaults-the-mesh-of-power/; and Chitty, C. (2017). Reassessing Foucault: Modern Sexuality and the Transition to Capitalism. *Viewpoint Magazine*, https://www.viewpointmag.com/2017/04/20/reassessing-foucault-modern-sexuality-and-the-transition-to-capitalism/.

15. Gonzalez, M. and Neton, J. (2013). The Logic of Gender: On the Separation of Spheres and the Process of Abjection. *Endnotes*, 3, https://endnotes.org.uk/issues/3/en/endnotes-the-logic-of-gender.

4

How Do Gender Transitions Happen?

Jules Joanne Gleeson

When confronting this question, we must first set aside *why* questions. Focusing on how transitions unfold is a concern distinct from what Julia Serano has termed the 'etiological' fixation of writing on trans issues: the fascination around why it is certain people *become* transgender. (This speculation is one cis thinkers seem to be especially prone to). On the ubiquitous 'why?' questions so often asked of trans people, Serano wrote:

> Eventually, I realized that it is a pointless question – the fact is that I am transsexual and I exist, and there is no legitimate reason why I should feel inferior to a cissexual [i.e. a nontranssexual] because of that. Once I accepted my own transsexuality, then it became obvious to me that the question 'Why do transsexuals exist?' is not a matter of pure curiosity, but rather an act of non-acceptance, as it invariably occurs in the absence of asking the reciprocal question: 'Why do cissexuals exist?' The unceasing search to uncover the cause of transsexuality is designed to keep transsexual gender identities in a perpetually questionable state, thereby ensuring that cissexual gender identities continue to be unquestionable.[1]

This 'etiological imperative' is often pushed onto trans writers, burdening us with an expectation that we account for why it is we deviated from the cisgender norm, preferably garnished with vivid childhood memories, and the all-important moment of dramatic revelation.

Another line of inquiry is whether transitions can be considered legitimate at all, with an increasingly vocal minority of Anglophone feminist philosophy attempting to undermine the case that trans people (and for various reasons, trans women in particular) ever have a valid claim to our gender.[2] Trans lesbians in particular have faced the charge that their coupling of trans status and sapphic sexuality is harmful, 'erasing' cisgender lesbians.[3] Let us set aside these questions for something more interesting.

For the purposes of this essay, I take it as a given that transition between genders is, indeed, possible. Referencing mostly the writings of other trans people, I will distinguish between two commonplace understandings of how transitions unfold: one that centres transitions as the consequence of trans people overcoming an array of hurdles on a personal level. And another that centres the work of trans communities in the realisation of our genders, and our quite particular pursuit of human flourishing.

These two conceptions are not rivals, nor strictly speaking opposing views. I suspect that most trans people have alternated between dependence on one or the other – perhaps daily, and certainly across the course of transition. Both have their uses for trans people, both as individuals and as a group, passing through the world. With that said, these views can be distinguished as follows:

- Firstly, transition as purposefully varying 'the encounter' between the individual and society's gendered expectations. This view identifies 'determining' qualities, which taken as a whole amount to an 'overdetermination': a certain number of 'tells' might make one perceived as a woman, or a man, or as something unclearly in-between. Trans people struggle with mastering the way they in particular will be perceived, and mastery over this moment of encounter (the aleatory exchange) through exercises, affectations, and physical changes is the focus of transitioning.
- Secondly, a view focusing on *trans communities*, which perform the central work of reciprocal recognition. This view frames identities as arising out of formative relationships and processes within those bonds. These loose collectives provide a context or 'space' for the articulation of new language, lifestyle developments, and culture. This view foregrounds the circles that trans identities have tended to arise out of, and which offer support and resources, which only this kind of affinity-based grouping can.

View 1: transition as mastery over the encounter

The first view of transition is an analytic one: it considers gender recognition to be a process that unfolds socially, and which trans people are tasked with doing their best to take command of, using hormones, surgeries, training in posture or speech, their wardrobes, and formal changes to identity documents. It focuses on the evaluative moments trans people go through in considering themselves, and preparing themselves, and in their encounters with the broader world.

To provide a simple example: nail polish alone might not do the job in getting a transitioning woman seen as she wishes to be, but nail polish together with long hair, a certain posture, five sessions of laser hair removal, and six months of HRT might very well. Transition consists of amassing a medley of decisive features, which inform the public at large of how you expect to be read, both overtly and on an intuitive level.

This approach to transition is exemplified by the focus on 'passing': the ideal state for many trans people, and the focus of a considerable amount of energy, is passing through the world being mistaken for their cisgender target gender. The focus of those pursuing 'passing' is both their own form (body, attire, voice, mannerism, word choice), but also interactions with an observer (assumed usually to be cis, and perhaps relatively uninformed on gender affairs). Perfecting this art requires not only a purely self-directed transformation, but a new orientation to the cis majority: would-be passers usually speak of the importance of 'blending' (appearing among a group of cisgender people of one's target gender, without any apparent mismatch). One ideal endpoint sought by some who pass is 'deep stealth': transgender people who've reached this lofty goal have only a select few friends, lovers, and physicians they have disclosed their transition to. (In most cases of adult transition this would, of course, require some form of radical relocation.)

Passing has been 'problematised' many times by some critically minded trans people, who are prone to opposing it on political grounds as assimilationist: a transition calculated to cause no disruption to the prevailing cisgender order. Yet passing remains a commonplace concern both for those transitioning, and those considering it. For as long as the apprehension of cis people that trans people encounter has a substantial impact on the wellbeing of those embarking transition, with the threat of violence ever suspended over those who are visibly transgender, passing (on an at least an everyday level) will remain a conscious priority for many.

Most recently, this perspective of transition-as-modified-encounter was expressed very clearly in a chain of tweets by Natalie Wynn, best known for her YouTube channel Contra Points. Accounting, and tacitly justifying, her desire for Facial Feminisation Surgery, Wynn introduces her transition in the following terms:

> What I really want is not for people to call me a woman because they pity me, sympathize with me, or respect me. It's better than them calling me a man, but only as a last resort. Really, I want them to call me a woman because it feels natural to do so, because I just seem like a woman to them. This is not something I can just demand, so a lot of the burden is on me. I have to change my appearance, my voice, my mannerisms not with the aim of becoming a woman in some metaphysical sense (a nonsensical idea) but of becoming a woman socially by appearing & interacting 'like a woman' with other people.
>
> But subjective isn't the same as unpredictable. There is a lot of intersubjective agreement about what sorts of things make a person seem manly or womanly. And the point of transitioning is largely to present female to that collective perception.[4]

In this view, transition appears as a reconciliatory move, a burden which for the most part lands on Wynn's shoulders. Shifting not only how one is addressed by one's friends and confidants, but also how one is intuitively understood by a passer-by, postman, or ticket collector; the burden of transition is at once an intimate one and yet involves the entirety of society, as its 'other', or on-looker: those undergoing transition must prepare themselves for encounters with strangers, through whatever changes are required to get them 'read' correctly. However, Wynn's account is not altogether downbeat:

> A year ago very few people thought of me as a woman. Now a majority of people probably do. My goal is to push that trend as far as I can, look back on my progress and one day say, 'You know what?

Good enough'. Hair, makeup, surgery, voice training, mannerisms – each of these is only a small part of a general effort to change how I'm perceived, how I'm treated by others, how I interact with others. It's the net effect of these things – my acquired social position as a woman – that makes it philosophically sound to call me a woman. The minutiae of how I achieve that end are not particularly relevant … The goal of my transition is merely to conform *enough* to elicit that mysterious 'seems like a woman' perception.

This view of transition as a gathering together of a medley of determining features can prove especially compelling to those still in the early stages of embarking on transition (or contemplating such a move, a process that can stretch out for years, or even decades).

While Wynn (as a self-described 'Wittgenstein gal') was doing her best to avoid taking a metaphysical stance in making this case; this account is highly reminiscent of the emphasis on 'the encounter' developed throughout French philosopher Louis Althusser's career. Later terming this position 'aleatory materialism',[5] Althusser presented human interactions as drawing subjects into being through encounters, as they confronted institutions which demanded them to identify themselves. The 'collective perception' described by Wynn follows this line in its rejection of any underlying truth: she wishes to be taken as a woman and (in her words) being read as such is the only philosophically sound basis for her being considered one.

Much the same approach to discerning womanhood appears in C. J. Hale's classic response to Monique Wittig: 'Are Lesbians Women?'[6] Taking Wittig's provocation (that lesbians are not) quite seriously, Hale draws from a rich selection of social science research to identify the features most probable to cause someone to be identified as a woman. In this form of account, being apprehended as a given gender is an apprehension triggered by a medley of cultural markers, each of which determine the evaluation given by those who encounter the person in question.

Gendered traits can cause a considerable degree of anxiety during the transition process (just as cisgendered men might worry that wearing too much pink attire makes them seem 'unmanly', or a cis woman could be concerned a short haircut would leave her face appearing 'mannish'). However, in most cases trans people will encounter immutable features they are unlikely to be able to do anything much to alter (the hip bones of trans men who transition post-puberty or the ribcages of trans women are two common examples). Between these fixed and immutable features, much attention and energy can be expended on weighing up one's prospects of encountering the outside world as one would desire. In a short film made by Wynn, entitled *Gender Dysphoria* (since removed from public view), she conveys the tortured internal dialogue confronting many who are considering the process of transition, a process of self-examination that at its worst can leave trans people trapped in their homes for extended periods of time.

Taking up this outlook, many trans people have grown near obsessively astute in noticing, and itemising, gendered features of everyday presentation. Few of society's arbitrary sexed associations or gender expectations today escape the discerning eye of anxious transsexuals. The contents of many 'how to' guides are intended to exactly instruct putative transitioners, with their more seasoned authors revealing the tricks and tips they have accumulated to achieve the desired outcome of passing through the world seamlessly.

This perspective is notable for matching very closely to the perspective of the state: for instance, to satisfy the British Passport Office that your gender change is permanent enough for a corrected 'sex' entry, one currently needs the following: an assessment by a relevantly qualified medical professional, a letter from an employer or local authority confirming that your new identity is in use with them, and a completed deed poll. In certain US states further measures such as taking out an advert in a local newspaper announcing the transitioners name change is required. This reliance on a 'checkbox list' rather demands those wishing to update their official bureaucratic records pass through transition as a process of completing successive tasks, at least on this paperwork level. In many cases compliance with this occurs on an obviously bad-faith basis: trans people passing through Gender Identity Clinics often wear more overtly gender-coded clothes than they would on a day-to-day basis, and provide an account of their daily lives and gender histories which they know to match the preferred model of 'transsexuality', in order to ensure access to hormones. Given the many indignities and 'second-guessing' games required of trans people by the state, and medical profession, it seems inevitable that many adopt much the same view for surveying their basic lived experiences.

'Transition as preparations for an encounter with the world' is ultimately both most useful and least theoretically satisfying for its steadfast focus on the individual, and those around them. The greatest risk of this line of thinking is reducing transition to simply one process which takes place in an overall condition of atomism. Social influence only emerges analytically as a block or constraint on easy transition requiring individualised responses. Recognising the much broader role social relations play requires a different theoretical approach. This brings us to another view of transition, which centres the role trans communities play in cultivating the very transitioning subjectivity that this first perspective takes not as socially engendered, but as a given.

View 2: transition as founded in community action

When turning to trans communities, I should first clarify that what I have in mind is not any one entity called 'the transgender community'. The notion of a unified community is one mostly appealing to career politicians, who are fond of imagining they might be able to interact with an entire tier of potential voters, through taking a single 'representative' out for lunch. In reality, trans people are prised apart and mutually alienated in much the same way as any other group: differences in class, race or ethnicity, and gender position still ensure that even a pair of trans people in the same city might be unlikely on various grounds to even meet. (With this said, the likelihood of prolonged unemployment, and dispossession from one's family, make the life experiences of trans people significantly more likely to converge, and severe mental health problems are pervasive among trans people of whatever demographic station.)

Communities are never to be assumed as unified, or taken for granted. Trans communities, like any other kind, always have to be actively cultivated, and sustained, across time. Communities of this kind are the product of careful development in less than ideal circumstances by trans people, and can never be treated as a given. For the commonality between trans people to become a true affinity, a more profound engagement is required, and in most cases these groups will consist of those with both trans status and other significant social commonalities (with an exception for clearly structured online communities such as /r/AskTransgender, which as its name suggests is intended exclusively for Q&A threads).

As such there is not, has never been, and could never be one 'trans community', and it's better to think in terms of trans circles. These groupings might be founded around support groups, book clubs, club nights, youth centres, web forums, social media constellations, WhatsApp group chats, flatshares, and community potlucks. These 'trans circles' have become easier to establish across time, both because of mass access to advances in communication technology and a certain self-perpetuating cycle of access to potential mentors.

These circles are often not strictly exclusive to trans people: many cis people also find themselves developing an affinity with trans circles, and boundaries can often become porous in queer scenes. Such groupings of affinity can arise spontaneously, or they can be the product of purposeful development, also known as 'community organising'. Sometimes sites for the celebration and mutual development of trans identities can arise in unlikely places. Even often hostile online outlets like 4chan seem to have fostered distinctive non-binary identities.[7]

Immediately, considering transition in these terms presents a rather different view to splitting that process into gendered determinations. Whereas the focus on the 'encounter' trans people must master in order to move through the world can tell us much, it's not only interactions with strangers that form the core of self-realisation for many undergoing transition. Trans people most often draw strength from interacting with other souls like-minded enough (often, but not exclusively, trans themselves) who are able to offer them the specific support, mentoring, and reciprocal recognition that identity formation requires.

Beyond the personal level (what trans circles offer the individuals who make them up), there is also a collective progression brought about by the shared pool of expertise and experience built up by lasting bonds between those developing a shared approach to life, and developing ties of affinity. On the level of community, trans people are collectively able to build up a considerable base of shared knowledge. This is especially urgent in a context in which much of the medical profession remains wedded to pathologising conceptualisations of trans people, and often deploys outmoded medical practices.

One indispensable service offered by trans communities to newcomers is presenting them with the fact that much of what they had considered their most freakish features are, within trans circles, so familiar as to be articles of cliché.

An example of this 'practical wisdom' in action can be found in Imogen Binnie's first novel, *Nevada*. Here the protagonist, Maria, several years deep into her transition and soon after encountering another trans character deeply in denial, has her approach to online trans activism recounted:

> There's a thing Maria is used to doing on the internet. It came from the older practice of telling everybody who thought they might be trans that they must be absolutely certain that they were trans before they even considered buying some clothes or starting a testosterone blocker ... Trans women on the internet looked around and were like, well, maybe surviving for the first part of your life in the role of a cis dude is an adaptive strategy ...
>
> For a while they were like, 'You must be entirely certain'. Then they were like, 'I dunno man, it sounds like you're probably trans, you should explore that'. Then, eventually, when Maria and the trans women of the internet couldn't help but notice that they were 100% accurate in their message board diagnoses, they started just saying, 'Welp, you are definitely trans'.
>
> Because even on the off chance that somebody finding a trans community to talk to about these things was not, actually, trans ... maybe hearing somebody say, like, 'You are trans', would spur some useful thinking. Like, if you're going to decide on your gender for the rest of your life based on what a couple of idiots on the internet tell you, you probably have problems beyond a false diagnosis of transsexuality.[8]

It's notable here that the group reaching these conclusions is 'Maria and the trans women of the internet', a collective who are described here as having moved through both a stage of theorisation and experimentation, before concluding with a 'best practice' of encouraging potential transitioners with affirmation. Through their shared experiences and observations, those who had already embarked upon transition established a 'bridge' between their own conditions, and the conditions of those still weighing up the prospect of committing to changing their gender.

What this passage reveals is the rather pragmatic character expectations and theorisations we can expect from communities of affinity. Needless to say, the maxim 'If you're asking whether or not you're trans ... You're trans!' is a gender normative statement of its own kind. However, the relevant capacity for coercion is entirely missing: as Binnie wryly implies, 'trans women on the internet' are unlikely to wield the power available to doctors at Johns Hopkins, and anyone susceptible to their advice was likely encountering uncertainty around their gender for sound reasons.

Prior to writing this novel, Binnie had spent years as a leading trans activist, with her protagonist clearly informed by her own experiences as a politically engaged New Yorker (the novel is obviously and unabashedly self-satirising throughout). In other words, *Nevada's* success was based on many years, and innumerable conversations, distilling experiences of transgender life into a single narrative account.

In addition to the mentoring and enculturation of younger trans people by 'old hands', there are also direct and ongoing ways in which trans (or trans celebratory queer) circles enrich and fulfil the lives of those involved.

Communities with a sense of affinity for each other are able to build up their own language for describing experiences and bodies. This can ultimately allow for a thoroughgoing rewriting of terms which trans people apply to their own physical forms. Another piece by C. J. Hale focuses on the variations in sexuality, gender, and embodiment allowed for in the S&M practices explored by 'Leatherdyke' communities (many of whose participants have since transitioned to men). Predecessors of today's queer and trans scenes served to provide frameworks for shifting gendered embodiment, in a way that today's trans communities offer on a more conceptual level. In 'Leatherboys and their Daddies: How to Have Sex Without Women or Men',[9] Hale writes:

Leatherdyke genderplay enables a phenomenon sometimes called 'retooling' or 'recoding' our bodies in trans community discourse. Sexual interactions, along with public restrooms and medical settings, are some of the sites at which dominant cultural connections between genitals and gender are the tightest, so many transpeople must remap the sexualized zones of our bodies if we are to be sexually active ...

One such phenomenon is that inanimate objects – dildoes – sometimes take on some of the phenomenological characteristics of erogenous body parts ... Sometimes leatherdykes resignify sexed bodily zones. Among some leatherdyke faggots, an important desideratum is to keep masculinity as seamless as possible during scenes, and gay leathermen's masculinities often provide the paradigms of masculinity here. Thus, if the body part a leatherdyke daddy is fisting is that which a physician would unequivocally deem a 'vagina', it may be resignified so that its use for erotic pleasure is consistent with male masculinity. It may become a 'hole', 'fuckhole', 'manhole', 'boyhole', 'asshole', or 'butthole', and a leatherdyke boy pleading, 'Please, Daddy, fuck my butt!' may be asking daddy to fuck the same orifice into which a physician would insert a speculum to perform a pap smear. Of course, this resignification may prove painful if this boy's daddy does not understand it.[10]

While these practices were not exclusively explored by those who were later to transition, Hale makes clear that for many involved they provided a means of breaching the normative associations with their physical forms which had previously stifled them.[11]

This 21-year-old account of directly transformative practices, native to a particular community with its own understandings for terms suitable for those immersed in it, still speaks to the sexual practices developed by trans people today. A poem by Gabe Moses entitled 'How to Make Love to a Trans Person' relates much the same process of semantic rearticulation, and conceptual re-imagining:

Forget the images you've learned to attach
To words like cock and clit,
Chest and breasts.
Break those words open
Like a paramedic cracking ribs
To pump blood through a failing heart ...

Get rid of the old words altogether.
Make up new words.
Call it a click or a ditto.
Call it the sound he makes
When you brush your hand against it through his jeans,
When you can hear his heart knocking on the back of his teeth[12]

These pieces of writing record the processes of transformation collectively enabled by the communities of affinity which have enabled and celebrated transition. This would seem to point in quite a different direction to the process of identification and elimination of stray misleading features presented in the first view of transition. Whereas much of the attention of trans people, especially early into transition, is drawn towards the 'moment of encounter', the subjectivity robust enough to weather such a storm is provided in large part by this 'underground' body of community-built resources.

The prominent role played by communities in substantiating transitions can be understood in a few ways. Julia Serano's view of transition constituting an 'intrinsic inclination' on the part of trans people would suggest that these communities serve as an underground means to achieve the expression that certain cultures have more institutionally established outlets for. By contrast, Susan Stryker's account of identity realisation in *Transgender History*[13] is considerably more complex and historicist. Stryker traces how new identities arose in particular contexts, both informed by the perceptions of cisgendered physicians and challenging them at every turn. A third perspective, and the one that I'm most interested in developing, is that trans communities (like all others) serve as the basis for the shared development of ethical standards, an Aristotelian view advanced by Mijke van der Drift.[14]

Individual and communal progressions

The two views outlined here are not directly at odds, and can be thought of as two differing 'registers' for understanding the process of transition.

Neither can account fully for transition as it exists today: there are those who eschew community as far as possible, treating their transition as a solitary affair (although it seems unlikely that many would not rely at least to some extent on information gleaned from the auton-omously stockpiled resources by trans communities). And there are those who report limited concern with the need to eliminate undesir-able features, or affirm themselves through encounters with strangers.

A strange quirk of today's internet resources is that a trans person could easily draw heavily on community compiled resources, while still in direct terms treating their transition as a solitary, personal project. Nevertheless, for political purposes, it can be especially helpful to consider the autonomous sources of strength, and forms of organ-isation, which have promoted the current growth in the prevalence of trans people around the world. While transition can still worsen the isolation and exacerbation already prevalent in modern life, the continual work of trans collectives must be appreciated when consid-ering why so many are opting to embark on transitions at all.

From communities to communism

But can either of these views – individual wriggling in the face of interpellation or community working up their own normative bedrock – ever be fully accepted, for our purposes?

While they have been my primary interest, my intention here has not been to laud the workings of communities. Organisation between ourselves as peers has achieved breakthrough after breakthrough in the pre-political labours required for forming and sustaining ourselves. But keeping one another alive cannot be collapsed with revolutionary change. We have made the best of our proletarianised existence, but we have yet to escape it.

For as long as trans people operate in the face of a capitalist state, we will break in two directions: atomised struggle and the fashioning of a trans-specific mode of 'Civil Society'. Trans people oscillate not only out of their atomised state but often enough back into it: many of our worst traumas are inflicted by other trans people, many drop out of activism with an embittered set of scare quotes placed around the words 'trans community'. Every petty corruption, frustration and normativity-enforcing eccentricity finds itself empowered by the raw necessity of communal work to avoid trans life becoming heterony-mous to the whims and outdated protocols of state provision. In other words, to exist on our own terms immediately follows through into ferocious rows about exactly who 'we' are.

The result is that trans communities are despised and relied upon by trans people in equal measure, and for the exact same reason. These ever imperfect and *ad hoc* circles of shared interest are the best (and worst) stopgap against the total immiseration provided by the existing capitalist division of labour.

Surpassing this divide requires a new movement, which we so far have only the haziest picture of. An anti-capitalist struggle fully responsive to, and in part growing *out of*, the existing struggles waged to secure our basic subsistence.

Notes

1. Serano, J. (n.d.). On the Etiology of Transsexuality, http://www.juliaserano.com/TSetiology.html#TSetiology.
2. For a response to this tendency, see Jaffe, A. (7 June 2018). How Not To Debate Gender. *Verso Books Blog*, https://www.versobooks.com/blogs/3868-cis-fears-and-transphobia-how-not-to-debate-gender.
3. For more than anyone could want to read on this, see my earlier immanent essay: Gleeson, J. (19 July 2018). Lesbians Going Their Own Way, *New Socialist*, https://newsocialist.org.uk/lesbians-going-their-own-way/.
4. This thread is preserved here, while the original tweets have since been deleted: https://threader.app/thread/1006648025148723200.
5. Althusser, L. (2005). Du matérialisme aléatoire. 11 Juillet 1986. *Multitudes*, 2005/2(21), 179–194. doi: 10.3917/mult.021.0179; https://www.cairn.info/revue-multitudes-2005-2-page-179.htm.
6. Hale, C. J. (1996). Are Lesbians Women? *Hypatia*, 11, 94–121.
7. I explored the 'femboy' here in 2017, although since then they have proliferated on social media sites beyond 4Chan: Gleeson, J. (3 February 2018). An Anatomy of the Soyboy. *New Socialist*, https://newsocialist.org.uk/an-anatomy-of-the-soy-boy/.
8. Binnie, I. (2013). *Nevada*. New York, NY: Topside Press, pp. 194–195.
9. Hale, C. J. (1997). Leatherdyke Boys and Their Daddies: How to Have Sex without Women or Men. *Social Text*, 52/53, 223–236.
10. Ibid., p. 230.
11. Hale: 'For some FtMs who used to be leatherdykes, our abilities to rechart our bodies – I would even say to change our embodiments without changing our bodies, that is, to change the personal and social meanings of our sexualized bodies-began in the queer resignifying practices available to us in leatherdyke cultures' (ibid. p. 230).

12. Moses, G. (26 March 2012). How To Make Love To a Transperson, https://indian2006.wordpress.com/2012/03/26/poetry-how-to-make-love-to-a-transperson-by-gabe-moses/.

13. Stryker, S. (2008). *Transgender History*. Berkeley, CA: Seal Press.

14. Pearce, R., Moon, I., Gupta, K., & Steinberg, D. (Eds.) (2020). *The Emergence of Trans*. London: Routledge.

5

A Queer Marxist Transfeminism: Queer and Trans Social Reproduction

Nat Raha

*'Wages Due Lesbians' and the emotional
work of queer life under Thatcher*

Wages Due Lesbians was an international organisation connected to the International Wages For Housework movement.[1] On 24 October 1986, the London chapter of the group published a three and a half-page list of forms of emotional labour expected of lesbians issued as part of the first *Time Off Day* (part of the international *Time Off For Women* campaign[2]), where they argued for the recognition, counting of, and pay for 'the particular physical and emotional housework of surviving as lesbian women in a hostile and prejudiced society'.[3] More than a historical curio, the pamphlet advances a significant queer, theoretical perspective on Marxist feminism. In subsequent years, this is an outlook that has been marginalised within the Marxist feminist canon. The document highlights many facets of the emotional work demanded of lesbian or bisexual women within Thatcher's Britain, illustrating the difference in the group's position from the stifling mainline of Marxist feminist groups. This document's concerns are far from bygone, remain largely unresolved, and are worth quoting at length:

- Pretending to be 'straight' to get some of a man's wage …
- Coping with the fear of losing children, jobs, homes, respect, or respectability in your community if you come out as lesbian …
- Coming out – a continuous process of working out when, where, how, to whom, on what occasions …
- Wanting to be with women and with men and having to choose in order to fit in somewhere …

- Being told you have to be 'butch' or 'femme' and not wanting to be either
- Wanting to be 'butch' or 'femme' and being told you can't
- Being called a 'pervert', 'sick', 'disgusting', 'weird', 'dirty', 'abnormal', 'nymphomaniac'
- Wanting to be accepted but not wanting to be normal ...
- Undergoing family visits and recovering afterwards
- Facing deportation because you have left a man and so have lost your right to stay in Britain, or because your relationship isn't acknowledged as 'real' ...
- Challenging Black separatists who say it's not 'Black' or 'Third World' to be lesbian and that being lesbian is a white/European contamination or disease
- Challenging/coping with racism, ageism, class prejudice and disability racism (sic) in your relationships with lovers
- Being silenced about violence in relationships with women because speaking out would make us all more vulnerable
- Having to invent lesbian lives ...
- Having to get by on low women's wages or poverty-line benefits ...
- Having to settle for limited places to meet other lesbian women ...
- Being an unemployed lesbian woman working on the game and having to hide the money when people don't know how you get it ...
- Doing emotional and physical work for lovers, friends, family ... but never being acknowledged for doing it because your relationships are not 'real' ...
- Bringing up children in a hostile society, constantly threatened with having them taken away from us because we're classed as 'bad' or 'unfit' mothers ...
- Fighting anti-lesbian prejudice in housing, social services, the health system, colleges, schools, employment ...
- Being told that being lesbian means liberation and wondering why you're still poor, overworked and not happy all the time ...[4]

The list highlights the risks of asserting one's sexual and gender difference in 1980s Britain. The devaluation of the reproductive labour sustaining lesbian relationships is highlighted, but so too are struggles we would today call 'intersectional' – being a lesbian might mean fighting for one's right to remain in the UK (and one's children as well), challenging homophobia, racism, ableism, and classism in a variety of contexts – on the street, in domestic, familial spaces, while accessing public services, engaging with the state, and in one's workplace. The list draws out how the emotional work of lesbian life varies across the different social and material positions inhabited by lesbians and bi women. Rather than homogenising the experience of queer women, the group aimed to make visible the variety of demands for labour made by society upon them for survival, amid a lack of recognition that such work was even taking place at all.

Given that access to the basic means to sustain oneself was a fundamental precondition for lesbian self-expression, Wages Due Lesbians argued that wages for lesbian emotional work would provide queer women 'the economic power to afford sexual choices and [such that we] can come out in millions',[5] building a life away from the heterosexual family. In 1989–1990, the group supported the Time Off For Women campaign's Counting Women's Unremunerated Work Bill, which was introduced into the UK Parliament in April 1989 by Mildred Gordon MP. The Bill was introduced in a period marked by the Conservative Government's Section 28, alongside protests and riots against the Poll Tax. It connected the enormous amount of unremunerated labour undertaken by women around the world to the small share of income they actually receive, and with it to the global ownership of assets, and demanded that 'All government departments and other public bodies shall include in the production of statistics relating to the gross domestic product, a calculation of the contribution of women's unremunerated work to the formal and informal sectors of the economy'.[6] In her speech presenting the Bill, Gordon argued that, by counting this unremunerated work undertaken by women in GDP, 'no one will be able to continue to ignore the extent of dependence of the mighty institutions of the state, industry, commerce and every social organisation throughout the United Kingdom on women's voluntary and involuntary unwaged work'.[7]

The group's work and connection to the Counting Women's Unremunerated Work Bill implies that lesbian emotional work is already *productive* labour – an unrecognised contribution to GDP. The theoretical advance made by Wages Due was to make visible the fact that, on the one hand, the unpaid work of queer women keeping themselves and their lovers alive (and in the country) contributes to an essential part of the economy – including, but not limited to, the reproduction of labour power. On the other hand, they documented how proscriptions on lesbian, gay, bisexual, transgender, and queer (LGBTQ) sexualities, relationality, and life also put particular pressures on queer women, placing them in precarious and surveilled positions within the labour market, heteronormative society, and even within queer subcultures.

Wages Due also produced a detailed analysis of the economic and social impact of Section 28 of the UK's Local Government Act (1988), which banned promoting 'the acceptability of homosexuality as a pretend family relationship' in schools,[8] theorising the wider implications of the law for diverse groups of lesbian women. They argued that Section 28 would 'increase lesbian mothers' unwaged emotional housework' and the burden of 'constant suspicion and scrutiny' lesbian mothers faced; put a strain on parental relations; increase neighbourhood surveillance and policing; potentially lead to the forced sterilisation of lesbian women deemed 'unfit mothers', as had been inflicted on disabled women; and potentially force gay and lesbian groups and subcultural spaces to close under economic pressure.[9] The group's reading of the material impact of Section 28, beyond the immediate pedagogical impact of the policy's sanctioning of homophobia, biphobia, and transphobia in schools, highlighted the interrelation between homophobic and whorephobic state policies. The group was already savvy to the affective work groups and communities of queer women undertake to support each other and survive.[10]

Contemporary Marxist feminism and queer reproductive labour

Despite the recent resurgence of Marxist feminism and social reproduction theory,[11] the social reproduction of LGBTQ lives still remain under-theorised. Marxist feminism has yet to bring into view the caring, domestic, and emotional labour, which is the precondition to our survival. In Barbara Leslett and Johanna Brenner's often cited definition, social reproduction describes '[the] activities and attitudes, behaviours and emotions, responsibilities and relationships directly involved in the maintenance of life on a daily basis'.[12] Marxist feminism

conceptualises socially reproductive labour as the work that reproduces both workers as living human entities *and* their labour power
under capitalism. In this view, the latter form of labour is exchanged
either directly or indirectly with capitalist employers for wages.[13] The
relationship between socially reproductive labour and Marx's value
theory has been a source of contestation since the 1970s, primarily
around the question of whether domestic labour is 'integral' to capitalist production by directly or indirectly reproducing surplus-value,
or if it is 'unproductive' in an economic sense in that it does not create
surplus-value.[14] Arguing for wages for housework from the former
position, Mariarosa Dalla Costa and Selma James argue that domestic
labour is 'extracted' through the site of the 'social factory' – primarily
through the (heteronormative) nuclear family and undertaken mainly
by women (and/or migrant women and/or women of colour). In the
1975 Wages against Housework manifesto, Silvia Federici emphasises the political importance of wages for housework *as a demand* in
the direct struggle against the 'social role' of women under capitalism.
Demanding wages serves to demystify and make visible the gendered
character of housework ('our femininity as work').[15] 'To say that we
want wages for housework is to expose the fact that housework is
already money or capital, that capital has made and makes money out
of our cooking, smiling, fucking'.[16]

The more recent work of Sara Farris and other Marxist feminists
has also highlighted that the gendered, racialised division of labour
within Western European societies is reproduced on a global scale,
across the supposed 'divide' of nation-state borders. Women and
feminised workers from the Global South (that is, workers of colour)
are often responsible for the social reproduction of people in or from
the Global North.[17]

Considering heterosexuality as a product of labour and the work
of social reproduction has long been a staple of Marxist feminist
analysis.[18] Nevertheless, the existing canon of Marxist feminism
has side-lined the material implications of this for queer sexualities,
including the arguments made by Wages Due Lesbians.[19] The declaration of the Wages Against Housework manifesto cannot be easily
understood except as an analysis of work: '*Homosexuality and heterosexuality are both working conditions ... but homosexuality is the workers'
control of production*', alongside the more cautious questions of its pen-

ultimate paragraph 'can we *afford* gay relations? *Are we willing to pay the price of isolation and exclusion?*'[20] Despite this, the theoretical implications of queer positionality within, or more often than not exclusion from, the social factory of capitalist society remain absent. Correcting this would require the recognition of the particular burdens of socially reproductive labour placed upon queer and trans life.[21]

Contemporary queer femme and trans cultures have addressed how the reproductive labour necessary for queer and trans communal survival falls disproportionately on certain femme/feminised, trans, poor, disabled people, sex workers, and/or people of colour. Writing in A Modest Proposal for a Fair Trade Emotional Labour Economy (Centred by Disabled, Femme of Colour, Working-Class/Poor Genius), Leah Lakshmi Piepzna-Samarasinha highlights both the importance of this emotional labour *as a form of work*, and its necessity in helping each other survive. This work occurs in the absence of institutions for social support and alongside the 'harm [of] misogynist ideas about care labour, where endless free emotional labour is simply the role our communities have for femme and feminine people'.[22] Linking femmephobia, transmisogyny, and sexism more broadly to the lack of respect given to femmes, Piepzna-Samarasinha emphasises that poor, of colour, sick, disabled, parenting, sex worker and/or rural femmes still 'hold it the fuck down':

> [Y]our life as a working class or poor and/or sex working and/or disabled and/or Black or brown femme person has taught you that the only damn way you or anybody survives is by helping each other. No institutions exist to help us survive – we survive because of each other. Your life is maintained by a complex, non-monetary economy of shared, reciprocal care …
>
> We organize miracles – from complex political actions to the life support work of making sure people are fed, don't die, don't get evicted – on no sleep and low spoons and a quarter tank of gas. Our organizing skills in these departments are incredible, and often not respected as much as masculine leaders, or indeed seen as skills. Far too often, the emotional labour we do isn't seen as labour – its seen as air, that little thing you do on the side.[23]

These miracles are still not widely appreciated. As gendered stereo-types play out in queer communities, all that is solid melts into air. Femmes enact reciprocal caring labour, often without their communities acknowledging openly the nature of this work.

In Piepzna-Samarasinha suggestions for a Fair Trade Emotional Labour Economy based in reciprocity, she emphasises the importance of consent over 'expectations of automatic caretaking'. We need to build from the knowledge of sick and disabled people when it comes to care – given the particular skills, needs, and experiences that sick and disabled people have in giving and receiving care. Piepzna-Samarasinha cautions that skills of providing emotional labour are not innate, and can be learned.[24] She hopes an equitable economy would recognise and appreciate the work that keeps queer and disabled communities alive. That equitability would require opening space for respect, time off, pleasure, and explicit acknowledgement.

The modesty of such demands for recognition may be compared to that of Time Off For Women campaign's demands to international governments and the UN to count and remunerate women's unpaid labour as part of GDP. The scale of a small, autonomous economic vision of care at the level of queer and disabled communities is enough of a demand to challenge so many bigoted assumptions that continue to inform demands of caring labour.

Bringing into view varied queer and trans people, in all our mul-tiplicities, within a theory of social reproduction requires a fresh perspective on the history and boundaries of the heterosexual family. We need to consider the institutions and policing of racial capital-ist society. We need to bring into view how structures of ableism and gender normativity are reproduced in, and through, the state.[25]

Even as it has extended liberal measures, such as same-sex marriage, the state has done so under the aegis of a new, moral conservatism, invoking a new politics of the family. Through austerity and other conservative measures – it has retrenched the family unit as a site of welfare and social support, and with it its necessary corollary – enormous demands of emotional and caring labour, naturalised as freely given gift. In the neoliberal period, the ascendant politics of 'homonormativity' was described by Lisa Duggan in *The Twilight of Equality* as 'a politics that does not contest dominant heteronorma-tive assumptions and institutions, but upholds and sustains them'.

Homonormativity emerges in the wake of neoliberal capitalist structural adjustment, and its transformation of the conditions of socially
reproductive labour.[26] It offers specifically a 'promise' of 'a demobilized
gay constituency and a *privatized*, depoliticized gay culture *anchored
in domesticity* and consumption'.[27] The neoliberal phase of capitalist
restructuring privatises the 'costs' in the labour of social reproduction
through a disinvestment in social security.

Next to the facilitation of an upward redistribution of wealth,
and government subsidy of private businesses, such disinvestment,
has taken the form of austerity measures in public expenditure as
we've witnessed in the cuts to social services and welfare provisions
around the globe since the 2008 Financial Crisis. Duggan emphasises
that this occurs alongside the political rhetoric that caring labour –
including supporting disabled persons, child care, and adult social care
– is a 'personal responsibility' of families, rather than that of the state.[28]
With this disinvestment, the costs of socially reproductive labour –
both the financial costs of providing social services and welfare, and
the portion of socially necessary labour time required to undertake it
– are left to individual families. Private households are left to pick up
the fiscal slack (or at least, are expected to). Duggan clearly intends
for us to consider this material context, describing the deal on offer
as: 'we get marriage and the military, then *we go home and cook dinner
forever*'.[29]

For queer activists, these are familiar concerns. Arguments that gay
marriage reassures a key institution of capitalist society are commonplace among revolutionary queer circles.[30] However, Marxist theory
has so far paid little attention to the material costs in socially reproductive labour that underwrite the inclusion of LGBTQ subjects into the
institution of marriage. Or to demands on queer social reproduction
intensified by neoliberal capitalism more broadly. Social divestment
and austerity measures have become defining features of the daily
lives of many LGBTQ people – precarious work (both waged and
unwaged), precarious housing, precarious benefits, precarious healthcare, precarious immigration status. This has been especially harsh on
those of us who are disabled, migrants, or people of colour.

In the UK since 2010, consecutive Conservative-led governments
have introduced austerity measures across public services (including
social housing and the National Health Services), while also restructur-

ing and cutting welfare and social security benefits. This includes cuts to disability benefits, such as ending the Disability Living Allowance (DLA), and introducing a highly-criticised, eugenic regime of private assessments.[31] The benefit sanction scheme, introduced in 2012, gave welfare officers the power to withhold benefits such as Employment and Support Allowance (ESA) and Job Seekers' Allowance (JSA) from periods between seven weeks to two years for arbitrary reasons; the closure of over 350 Sure Start Centres, responsible for childcare provisions[32] and cuts to Working Tax Credits. The policy also introduced limits to Housing Benefit Payments and a cap on total benefit payments. Cuts to Legal Aid services and the introduction of fees for Employment Tribunals restricted even the limited legal representation Britain's most vulnerable could easily procure. Financial disinvestment in the NHS, opening up NHS service provision to competition from private providers. Migrants were also targeted with the introduction of restrictions and costs to service users who don't have UK Citizenship, including passport checks at the point of access. Cuts to HIV/AIDS services and ongoing chronic underfunding of trans-specific health-care services. Cuts to domestic abuse/domestic violence services; cuts in the Voluntary Sector, resulting in the closure of LGBT support services Pace and Broken Rainbow.[33] Further targeting of queer migrants under the 'Hostile Environment' placed pressures on recent and long-term migrant people and asylum seekers by restricting access to jobs, housing, bank accounts, welfare, etc., through the introduction of mandatory passport checks.

These policies were part of a global move by states against queer life. As Holly Lewis has it: 'the reproduction of daily life and the reproduction of workers themselves are factors in keeping the value of the working class high and thereby retaining as much quality of life as possible; from the employers' perspective, the overall goal is to reduce labour's standard of living as much as possible'.[34] The UK government's divestment of capital from the welfare system, a system of social wages aiding social reproduction, are part of a neoliberal ideological divestment in the poor, one that disproportionately impacts disabled people, people of colour, women, LGBTQ people, and people with a history of migration. This should be read as a disproportionate attack on those particular groups, given that they/we are more likely to already be bearing the burden of socially reproductive labour while simultaneously finding them/ourselves in a much more precarious relationship to wage labour, or out of work, without material fallbacks or support.

Any radical theory of queer and trans social reproduction needs to thread the needle between queer particularity – recognising the specific labour of creating and reproducing queer and trans life against the social and material pressures of capitalist society – with the spectres of LGBT assimilation.

Such 'queer world-making'[35] opposes the virulent forces of homophobia, transphobia, whorephobia, ableism, and racism that have been deployed to shore up the boundaries of the nuclear family across the twentieth century and that find new articulations in the current neo-fascist period. This chapter attempts to highlight the various forms of socially reproductive labour that queer and trans people undertake under conditions of social abjection, stigma, and marginalisation, arguing that such work undergirds queer and trans community building and social support – and deserves its day of account, and full recognition.

This in turn necessitates an expansion of the concept of socially reproductive labour. To argue that our lives as LGBTQ persons span varied familial and community formations within a trans and queer socius – affected by our material, cultural, social, legal positions within capitalist society – is to give socially reproductive labour a different orientation to the reproduction of labour power for capital's consumption alone. While constituted by and working to support the needs of predominately Latinx and Black homeless transfeminine and gay youth, Street Transvestite Action Revolutionaries (STAR's) political platform demanded an end to racist, homophobic, transphobic, and whorephobic state policies and free provisions of what we might cognise as social welfare – namely 'free education, health care, clothing, food, transportation, and housing' for '[t]ransvestites and gay street people and all oppressed people'.[36]

Queer and trans social reproduction

Queer Marxism and trans studies have, at various points, made gestures towards analysing the forms of socially reproductive labour that reproduce queer and trans lives, workers, and worlds.[37] Addressing the relation of gender to certain productive practices, Miranda Joseph suggests that '[i]f child socialization or heterosexual sexual activity ... can be recognized by [materialist] feminist arguments as valuable labour, then gay sex is also certainly analyzable as a valuable, productive act: productive of relations, identities, communities and social spaces'.[38] Joseph points towards the role of anonymous gay public sex as a form of reproductive activity, enabling gay identities and defining public gay communal space – cruising grounds and parks, bathhouses, bars, and so forth. However, her otherwise excellent work on the supplementary relation of capital and communities refrains from developing this analysis further. Such activity undoubtedly enables queer social formations: yet the criminalisation of, say, public sex, attempts to stop such behaviour if deemed to have a 'negative' effect to an area by a state, thus criminalising queer social formations and public space, and criminalising queer reproductive activity. As with the case of New York City's zoning laws in the 1990s/2000s, the impact of such laws are often felt most by queer and trans of colour youth who may also be homeless. Queer social reproduction is not assured, often frustrated, and constantly finds itself under threat from police harassment, marginalisation, and socially endorsed violence.[39]

In her essay on queer value, Meg Wesling highlights the importance of the 'myriad forms of social activity that go beyond subsistence and reproduction – those activities that work towards the aims of the body's comfort, pleasure, and the satisfaction of desire – and that we would want to acknowledge as labour'.[40] Wesling's reading of the 1996 Cuban film *Mariposas en el Andamio* (*Butterflies on the Scaffold*)[41] highlights the labour of a group of *transformistas* in post-revolutionary Cuba to produce and perform their feminine gender expressions from limited materials. Wesling's reading of the film emphasises the 'social utility' of drag – and the laboured production and performance of feminine gender – as pleasurable and 'important cultural work', where the situation of gender is importantly understood in the unique context of 'post-revolutionary Cuba'.[42] She argues that the success of the *transformistas* performances – to construction workers on their lunch breaks – provide both 'a vision of gender as the self-conscious production of human work' and through this 'integrate the politics of sexual transgression to the aspirations of a utopian, anti-capitalist revolutionary project'.[43]

In considering the collective work of gender transgression between trans men and queer femmes, Jane Ward notes that only minimal attention has been paid to the intimate and caring labour that produces transgender worlds, homes, and lives by trans studies.[44] Focusing on such labour, Ward defines the term 'gender labour':

> To describe the affective and bodily efforts invested in *giving gender to others*, or actively suspending self-focus in the service of helping others achieve the varied forms of gender recognition they long for. Gender labour is the work of bolstering someone's gender authenticity, but it is also the work of co-producing someone's gender irony, transgression, or exceptionality.[45]

Ward describes such labour as constituted of both the affective labours that 'keeps genders ... in motion', alongside the 'physical and feminized labours that contribute to the production of queer (and normative) genders (e.g. cooking, sexual services, nursing care, administering gender technology/hormones, chest-binding)'.[46] Describing the gender labour that produces various expressions of masculinity and femininity, she emphasises that while 'these efforts are often "labours of love" enacted for and by people who are denied gender validation within mainstream culture (women, men of colour, queers)', such labour 'must not elide the ways in which gender is reproduced through routinized forms of care work'.[47] Ward's study, undertaking interviews on the West coast of the USA in 2004, specifically considers the intimate labour undertaken by queer femmes – the subjects of her interviews – to bolster the masculine subjectivity of their trans male (specifically FtM) sexual partners. The orientation of the study allows her to emphasise how 'some genders, principally those that are masculine and especially those that intersect with other forms of power (such as wealth and whiteness), make their demands less visible and more legitimate, or deliver them with more coercive force'.[48]

Arguing that 'all genders demand work, and *therefore all people both give and require gender labour*', she emphasises that '[g]ender labour, like other forms of caring, weighs down most heavily on feminine subjects, the people for whom labours of love are naturalised, expected or forced'.[49]

Like Piepnza-Samarasinha, Ward argues that the production of queerness falls more heavily on feminine subjects in a manner that is often not acknowledged, and which finds itself reflected in queer theory's 'embrace' of models of life that are 'made most possible or necessary for masculine subjects', leaving the patient work of 'reproductivity, caretaking, shopping, home-making, and safety-making' theoretically disavowed.[50] But Ward's analysis unfortunately effects a complete erasure of transfeminine bodies and the gender labour of trans femininity – gender labour is analysed only as work done by non-trans, feminine subjects for trans men. However, if we place this next to the analysis of queer value production by *transformistas* as formulated by Wesling, who collectively produce their feminine gender expressions from limited, re-appropriated materials due to a scarcity of cosmetics and material resources in Cuba, it could be argued that transfeminine subjects in (or from) the Global South often find themselves at the bottom of a hierarchical, international division of *gender* labour, innovating their genders out of material necessity.

In an essay on queerness *as* a situation of precarity, Joni Pitt (Cohen) and Sophie Monk plot the (in)accessibility of the heteronormative household as conceived in Marxist feminism through the familial rejection of queer and trans people. They argue that for 'estranged queers', due to the widespread rejection and abuse queer and trans people face from families, 'the responsibility for taking care of oneself and managing one's life is privatized to the individual' – living within individual bedrooms in shared houses, estranged queers often lack the conditions required for 'sharing' the costs of reproductive labour more easily managed in the heteronormative household.[51]

Facing social marginalisation and precarity for one's queerness or transness within both the workplace and within domestic households, 'the proletarian queer is required to do both productive labour – for the wage – and the reproductive work necessary for the continuation of their labour power, through self-care, and the management of their own individual micro-household'. Formulating the negative situation of Piepnza-Samarasinha's emotional labour economy discussed above, Cohen and Monk write that under such conditions, 'proletarian queers'[52] fall ill, as 'traumas of living in a cis-heteropatriarchal world have to be dealt with alone, or with the care of friends suffering the same conditions: those who are least equipped taking on the responsibilities of caring for another person'.[53] Cohen and Monk describe 'the queer household' as 'where the class of immiserated queers is sustained', such that 'we may reproduce subjectivities and bodies that can withstand the violence of capitalism and even confront it'.[54] The authors' examples of sharing medications, cleaning rooms for depressed housemates, providing each other food, a roof, affection, creating nightlife as a space of safety, and fighting off street and bathroom harassment, are common themes among queer and trans communities and communal housing projects.

Robert McRuer has provided a historical account of the development of the domestic family. The space of the home in the twentieth century was constructed and imagined as an 'able-bodied space' (intersecting with ideologies of domesticity and the family), visiting great violence upon disabled people within the hierarchies of social and domestic life.[55] McRuer argues for the importance of recognising and enacting 'crip domesticities' and their possibilities, which productively intersect with our theorisation of queered domestic relationships.[56] He reads *Why Can't Sharon Kowalski Come Home?* – a book that details the struggle (across the 1980s and into the 1990s) of co-author Karen Thompson and her partner Sharon Kowalski to live together after Kowalski suffered a debilitating accident. These included their encounters with the homophobia and ableism bound up with the provision of care from hospitals, nursing homes, and religious institutions; and their legal battle over Kowalski's guardianship with her parents. Ruer emphasises that while Kowalski's father is 'unable to imagine a queer and disabled domesticity ... confin[ing] Sharon to a nursing home', which 'keeps [Sharon] from coming in contact with all those (public) movements and identities that would make queer and disabled publicity (and domesticity) imaginable', Thompson's struggle for guardianship leads her to a public life of activism and queer, feminist and disabled people's communities.[57]

The strength of these communities to contest homophobic, sexist, and ableist institutions provides more than 'an alternative model of home and community, where individuals, couples, and "families" are dependent on each other and where "home" is always contiguous to other sustaining locations',[58] but a basis for radical and transformative political activism. And it's her experiences within these communities that leads Thompson to develop a critical, feminist conception of interdependency, based on the mutual dependency of queer and crip relationality and domesticity. McRuer argues that '[t]he feminist, queer and disabled relations of interdependency [that Thompson] encounters expose the inadequacies of the able-bodied/heterosexual family', elucidating the structural fictions between the 'private' family and the 'public' sphere, which respectively support 'heterosexual and able-bodied intimacy and security' and 'sustain relations of exploitation ... by privileging ideologies of "independence" and protecting heterosexual and able-bodied identities and homes'.[59]

Such structural fictions and ideologies are crucial for upholding the racial and gendered division of labour structuring the heteronormative, able-bodied nuclear family that devalues disabled and/or LGBTQ persons' lives.

Between these readings, we have an emphasis on the public character of queer sexuality and its role in defining queer communal spaces; a vision of the collective production of gender and feminine gender expressions; a concept of the affective work of gender as gender labour that supports gender expressions; and two conceptions of queer and trans, and queer and crip domesticity, respectively, produced through queer households, and queer feminist and disability activist communities. Each of these emphasises the interdependent, communal character of supporting the conditions and politics that make queer, trans, feminist, and disabled lives more liveable in the face of capitalism. Each reading elucidates a different communal practice of queer and transgender and sexual expression that performs caring, affective, and/or creative labour that directly services LGBTQ communities and lives – each a different vision of queer and trans social reproduction.

Domestic resistance: women of colour feminist perspectives on socially reproductive work

Orienting our analysis of domestic labour around women of colour provides a significant shift in standpoint of the role of socially reproductive labour from that advanced by Marxist feminism. Patricia Hill Collins argues that Black feminist scholarship 'suggests that Black women see their unpaid domestic work *more as a form of resistance to oppression* than as a form of exploitation by men', and that such work 'remains a fundamental location where the dialectical relationship of oppression and activism occurs'.[60] Furthermore, Hill Collins emphasises that the dichotomy of public and private spheres, equating 'male' economic provision with the workplace and 'female' affective provision with domestic space holds for neither African-Americans, whose families 'exhibit ... fluid public/private boundaries because racial oppression has impoverished disproportionate numbers of Black families', or for low-income families, who do not necessary 'equat[e] private with home and public with work'.[61] Aida Hurtado and Chandra Talpade Mohanty also emphasise that 'the economic conditions that underlie the public/private distinction' have not benefited women of colour.[62]

Hill Collins' argument may be situated historically next to the context of chattel slavery. Between her readings of masculinist and sexist conceptions of gender in work from the Black Power movement and the particular forms of violence that Black women experienced during and since slavery, LaKeyma King undertakes a reading of Hortense Spillers which emphasises the contradiction of the social reproduction of gender for Black women.

> Gender, according to Spillers, originates within the domestic sphere where the sexual division of labor first manifests itself. For the slave, the 'home' is obliterated and replaced by the slave quarters, the opposite of the domestic haven that shields its inhabitants from the evils of society. The absence of a domestic realm within chattel slavery de-genders Black women, relating them to 'femaleness' rather than 'womanhood'.[63]

King argues that Black women have inhabited a position under the system of chattel slavery where the (re)production of one's gender is theoretically impossible, while inhabiting 'the slave quarters' as a site that is the very negation of 'home'. However, as Zhivka Valiavicharska discusses in a recent essay in *LIES Journal*, articulating trajectories of social reproduction in the thought and practices of Black and migrant communities that challenge Eurocentric formulations of social reproduction, the 'home' under the conditions of slavery could also be a site of reprieve from violence and surveillance.[64] The work of Angela Davis and other Black feminist scholars, Valiavicharska argues, show that the home was a site of self-determination 'where [Black women] could define their lives on their own' and also where 'resistance was organised, rebellions planned, and fugitives harboured'.

Valiavicharska argues that for enslaved Black women, domestic work undertaken in the home 'acquired social meaning and social value because it was not directly extracted and expropriated out of them to benefit masters'. To undertake socially reproductive labour in a space not overdetermined by enslavement demonstrates an alternate schema of value in the face of the total expropriation of economic value. This labour enabled forms of resistance, and established a means to gender self-determination. Black trans history appeared in the context of distinctive efforts undertaken by Black American families to sustain Black communities.

In Audre Lorde's work, Black lesbian domestic space is framed as an interdependent site of resistance-through-nurture. In The Master's Tools Will Never Dismantle the Master's House, Lorde writes that 'for women, the need and desire to *nurture* each other is not pathological but redemptive', and that with this knowledge comes power.[65] She states that '[i]nterdependency between women is the way to a freedom which allows the *I* to *be*, not in order to be used, but in order to be creative. This is a difference between the passive *be* and the active *being*'.[66] The queer of colour domestic space, and the understanding that comes through the desire which forms it, is for Lorde – and also for STAR, as we shall see in the following section – a potent site of knowledge and praxis for resistance. Domestic spaces as fashioned by queers of colour have served both as means of survival and loving or caring more broadly. Knowledge borne through desires that exist in a relation of excess to the nuclear family under capitalism.[67]

Queer and trans of colour domestic resistance:
Street Transvestite Action Revolutionaries

While a thoroughgoing theoretical account of queer and trans social reproduction may be absent from the canon, trans activist praxis is another story. A thoroughly radical and politicised understanding of such labour, and the necessity of collectivising it, has always occupied transgender revolutionaries. This is particularly true among trans and queer people of colour.

If we turn our attention to the queer and trans communities of the 1970s, we find a readymade critique of the 'bourgeois nuclear family' as a site productive of gender conformity. This position was advanced most famously by the revolutionary groups that made up the left wing of the gay liberation movement. Third World Gay Revolution (TWGR), formed in New York, USA, in the summer of 1970, argued that the family was a central site for the perpetuation of heterosexist and homophobic 'sex roles', and sexist and cis-sexist 'sex definition'. In this view, mothers and fathers are instrumental in teaching and enforcing the gendered 'behavior necessary in a capitalist system'.[68] The idea that such socially reproductive labour should be collectivised through the formation of communes was common – one example being the work of the STAR, the radical Third World and Black Gay/ Trans Liberation group founded by Marsha P. Johnson and Sylvia Rivera in New York, 1970.[69]

STAR combined caring labour, sex work, prison solidarity, and political activism. As Reina Gossett, Eric Stanley, and Johanna Burton argue in the introduction to *Trap Door: Trans Cultural Production and the Politics of Visibility*, 'STAR engaged a particular set of issues generally overlooked by the white middle-class gay movement'.[70] Pointing toward the group's example of renting a space to create STAR House, Gossett, Stanley and Burton describe STAR's

small, personal acts of resistance and refusal [which] created space for those unruly to the demand of assimilation to come together and to support one another. At a time of heightened violence, just by hanging out with and taking care of one another, the members of STAR were doing revolutionary work.[71]

STAR's care work centred sheltering and supporting Latinx, Black and white 'street queens'[72] and other homeless gay, trans, and lesbian youth. This work was done in the face of active state and social persecution. The group's activities were situated at the intersection of gay and lesbian liberation and the Latinx and Black liberation movements of their time – struggles that marginalised *and* welcomed STAR's members' deviance from racial, class, gender and sexual norms, and may be read today as an example of queer and trans social reproduction that put into practice a transfeminism of colour. Reflecting on these campaigns remains profoundly important for trans and queer politics today and highlights the need to centre the struggles of racially and economically marginalised trans people. The group's members met each other on the street, in jail, or at gay liberation meetings, mixing a politics of transgender expression with radical civil rights struggles for poor and homeless trans and gay people.[73]

STAR's activity with the wider gay liberation movement in New York included participating in demonstrations and marches (including the Christopher Street Liberation Day Parade, where Rivera gave a now-famous speech). They protested the incarceration of LGBTQ people in prisons and psychiatric hospitals, joined occupations, interventions, and 'zaps' (confrontational and theatrical sit-ins) of politicians.[74] They played a key role in the collective running of the Gay Liberation Front (GLF) affiliated Gay Community Centre, organising gay dances to fundraise.[75] They attended demonstrations led by the Young Lords and Black Panthers, and alongside the TWGR and the GLF were 'active in the support' of Communist Party (CP) member Angela Davis, in spite of the CP's pointed dismissal of their support.[76]

Having previously helped street queens and homeless gay youth by sheltering them in hotel rooms and in the back of a trailer, in 1971 the group established STAR House. Renting a building from the Mafia and paying the $200 rent through sex work, STAR provided shelter, food, clothing, friends, and political solidarity, primarily for Latinx street queens.[77] STAR House consisted of four rooms, housing up to 25 street queens and homeless gays and lesbians at once. The labour producing STAR House as a shelter included fixing the building up for inhabitation (plumbing, etc.) and the production of a politicised space, adorned with 'Free Angela Davis' and 'Free All Political Prisoners' posters.[78] In addition, earnings from sex work supplemented by the maternal care work of Sylvia and Marsha, directly enabled the creation of the space for the survival, support, and politicisation of poor trans and gay people. Susan Stryker writes that STAR intended 'to educate and protect the younger people who were coming into the kind of life they themselves led', and that 'envisioned establishing a school for kids who'd ... had their formal education interrupted because of discrimination or bullying'.[79]

STAR House functioned with a division of labour: the older group members selling sex to shield the younger queens from the dangers of working on the street, while the younger queens 'liberated food'.[80] This labour built upon the solidarity and kinship among queens working the street – Jessi Gan highlights that on leaving home aged 10 to her new home among queens on 42nd Street Times Square, Sylvia 'was excited to find so many drag queens, some of whom adopted her and helped out'.[81] Gan emphasises the importance of Sylvia's (and by extension STAR's) 'visions of kinship, family and community' as 'both inclusive and dynamic. Like her lifelong attempts at building "home", they are unpredictable, impatient but generous, provisional yet welcoming'.[82]

Located at 213 East 2nd Street, Manhattan, STAR House was situated in the primarily Puerto Rican, working-class neighbourhood known by locals as Loisaida.[83] Sylvia Rivera recalls that STAR House had a positive relationship with the neighbourhood. She describes STAR's work as including babysitting for locals, and feeding 'half of the neighborhood because we had an abundance of food the kids liberated'. Rivera described such solidarity as 'a revolutionary thing'.[84] Noting the political, pleasurable space that such work created, Sylvia remarked that '[t]here was always food in the house and everyone had fun'.[85] Such forms of care work as activism were not uncommon in the Black Power and third world liberation movements. The Black Panther Party had instituted a programme of 'Free Breakfast for School Children' and the Young Lords undertook healthcare pro-grammes for the Puerto Rican community of East Harlem.[86] As with STAR, these programmes were often staffed by women.[87]

STAR asserted that the lives of street queens of colour who were sex workers were valuable, in need of support, and worth protecting and nourishing, serving as a lasting testament to the value of acting for one another in solidarity. They did this work when white America and the aspirational quarters of the gay rights movement did not recognise the importance of such lives.

From the early 1970s to the present day, Black feminist politics would affirm the value of the lives and work of women of colour. A significant example is the response of the Combahee River Collective to the deaths of 12 Black women in Boston in 1979. Grace Kyungwon Hong and Roderick Ferguson argue that the Collective provided an analysis linking the murders, 'insisting that race and gender are the names for the processes that ushered these women to their untimely deaths ... killed because their lives were not valued and, in this way, were outright extinguished'.[88]

Similarly, STAR's praxis challenged those murderous processes that devalue feminised people of colour – those who were poor, homeless, gender-deviant, queer, and/or sex workers – asserting that such lives were valuable and worth loving amid violently oppressive social and material conditions. STAR's work both assumed, and assured, that their lives were more than the stigmas that attached to them; that they were not just defined by the labour (from sex work, to less stigmatised proletarian labour) that dominated their daily lives.

Conclusion

To formulate a queer and trans social reproduction requires expanding the concept of social reproduction to make legible the caring labour that enables and maintains queer and trans people and lives – the loving and sexual pleasure, cooking and feeding and housing, resting and rearing, cleaning and washing and dressing, the emotional and psychological support, transition advice and specialised counselling, healthcare support, the work of creating our genders, performances or expressions, the very fabrication of *us*.

Reconceiving socially reproductive labour from the trans and queer perspective allows us to consider such labour *both* as work of resistance that enables our *being* (as in the case of STAR, and as discussed by Piepnza-Samarasinha, Cohen, and Monk) *and* as unpaid labour (as in the case of Wages Due Lesbians), work that is valuable and *necessary*. A struggle that is always challenging, and sometimes pleasurable.

We must recognise and affirm the necessary work for our survival within racial capitalist society *as work*. Work is required to flourish, when our lives are marked for destruction within racial capitalist nation-states (from imprisonment, to maiming, to deportation). Our labour, love, caring; and the forms of community, sociality, and worlds that are produced – breaking out of and pushing against the expectations of gender, race, ability, labour, and desire – are each important forms of work.

There is a merit that exists to each of these facets of queer life, despite their minimal exchange value (if any). Such work must be situated within the political economy of the racial and gendered division of labour under capitalism. The labour of feminised, radicalised, queer, trans, disabled, and/or migrant workers is material and socially devalued,[89] a division of labour under which we are often poor, often overworked or underpaid or underemployed or unemployed. The devaluation of our work and lives is a historically specific phenomenon. It relates to the world of racial capitalism that we inhabit.[90] In its rabid drive for commodification, such caring labour is being subsumed as a form of low waged work.[91]

The reproduction of queer lives and worlds often takes place within communal and subcultural spaces, or queer households. These socially reproductive centres have often remained marginal, emerging outside of the confines of the homophobic, racist nuclear family. They exist apart from and against the racialised and gendered division of labour that is reproduced by private households. This is not to say that queer and trans bodies, lives, and monogamous familial forms are not dependent on domestic spaces. As Wages Due Lesbians argued, the familial forms we have been inhabiting and creating for decades are often rendered invisible as sites of social reproduction. Often queer households have existed in unrecognised or clandestine forms, actively delegitimised by the state. Even the limited state recognition of monogamous LGBT family forms today occurs alongside a material disinvestment in social security and welfare. This process further rests the costs of social reproduction on private relationships. The state has begun to recognise homosexual households only as the meeting of social needs has become more thoroughly privatised than ever before.

So how might queer and trans social reproduction inform political strategies? This question seems especially pressing in the contemporary context of the International Women's Strike on 8 March, including forms of queer and trans feminist Gender Strikes[92] and Sex Workers' Strikes. It should be clear that such articulations emerge from positions of being surplus, if not precarious in respect to capital's demands for labour power and the state's valuations of lives. Surplus life is responded to by the state through cutting welfare, as much as through police surveillance and incarceration. The disproportionate demands of socially reproductive labour on queer and trans, femme or feminised, disabled, and/or of colour people results in the impoverishment of our communities. How might we be able to maintain and build our resources, including our valuable skills in organising caring

labour, to ensure we work for ourselves? How can we resist the appropriation of our efforts by capital?

Four decades after the hegemonic extension of the New Right, how
can our survival continue? Can we continue to substantively resist the
coercions of capital's demands that we undertake socially reproductive
labour for free, while simultaneously dismantling and ending the capitalist world[93] within which our lives are debased and devalued? For the
time being, we struggle for our lives even as this very struggle is being
turned to the ruling classes' riches.

Notes

1. Wages Due Lesbians described themselves as 'an international network
   of lesbian women who are Black/of colour and white, with and without
   disabilities, of different ages/backgrounds, and occupations' (Wages Due
   Lesbians (1991). *Policing the Bedroom and How to Refuse It.* London:
   Crossroads Books, p. 1) The group were part of the International Wages
   for Housework Campaign. The London group continues to exist today
   under the name Queer Strike.
2. The *Time Off For Women* campaign pushed 'for the implementation of
   the 1985 UN decision that governments count women's unwaged work
   in every country's gross national product' (Wages Due Lesbians, *Policing
   the Bedroom*, p. 1). Wages Due argued 'Counting lesbian women's work
   ensures that we will not be deprived of the wealth we are entitled to
   which our work has helped created' (ibid.).
3. Ibid.
4. Ibid., pp. 53–56.
5. Ibid., p. 1. The London group were not alone in this analysis – in her
   work on the Wages Due Lesbians Toronto group in the 1970s, Christina
   Rousseau's discusses how Wages Due addressed the 'material impossibility' of lesbian visibility and the problem of the low paid, precarious
   and 'feminized job ghettos'. Rousseau, C. (2015). Wages Due Lesbians:
   Visibility and Feminist Organizing in 1970s Canada. *Gender, Work and
   Organisation,* 22(4), 364–374, citing 369–370.
6. Counting Women's Unremunerated Work Act 1989. HCA/CHE2/9/40,
   Women, Hall-Carpenter Archives, London University: London School
   of Economics Library, Archives and Special Collections. Wages Due
   Lesbian's co-ordination of TOFW and support for the Bill are discussed
   address in a Letter to Bernard Crowe, 4 September 1990, Rossi, D.
   (Wages Due Lesbians), HCA/CHE2/9/40, Women, Hall-Carpenter
   Archives.
7. 'Counting Women's Unremunerated Work' Bill, *Hansard* HC Deb
   11 April 1989, Vol. 150, No. 82, cc. 747–750, accessed 4 April 2018,

https://api.parliament.uk/historic-hansard/commons/1989/apr/11/counting-womens-unremunerated-work#S6CV0150P0_19890411_HOC_198. The Bill was introduced under the House of Commons' ten-minute rule. The Bill was due to have a second reading in July 1989, which appears to have never taken place.

8. The law also banned local government from 'intentionally promot[ing] homosexuality or publish[ing] material with the intention of promoting homosexuality'. Local Government Bill 1988 – Clause 28, quoted in Wages Due Lesbians, *Policing the Bedroom*, p. 2.

9. Ibid., pp. 15–26.

10. Wages Due understood the connections between the sexual agency of queer women, compulsory heterosexuality, and government policies and state harassment of precarious women, especially of sex workers. In a 1977 statement of international solidarity to sex workers facing police crackdowns and gentrification in San Francisco, the London group stated that '[t]he attack which governments are organizing against prostitute women everywhere in the world is an attack on every woman's right to determine whether, and on what terms, she will have sexual relations with men'. 'Supporting Statement by Wages Due Lesbians', cited in Wages Due Lesbians (2012). '"All the Work We Do As Women": Feminist Manifestos on Prostitution and the State, 1977'. *LIES Journal*, 1, 217–234, 227.

11. See 'Social Reproduction' (2015). *Viewpoint Magazine*, https://www.viewpointmag.com/2015/11/02/issue-5-social-reproduction/ (accessed 10 April 2018); the reissue, new introduction by Ferguson, S. & McNally, D. (Vogel, L.) (2013). *Marxism and the Oppression of Women: Toward a Unitary Theory*. Leiden: Brill; Mojab, S. (2015). *Marxism and Feminism*. London: Zed Books.

12. Laslett, B. & Brenner, J. (1989). Gender And Social Reproduction: Historical Perspectives. *Annual Review of Sociology*, 15, 381–404, 382.

13. For the canon of this argument, see Costa, M. D. & James, S. (1975). *The Power of Women and the Subversion of the Community*. Bristol: Falling Wall Press Ltd; Federici, S. (1975). Wages Against Housework. In Federici, Silvia (2012). *Revolution at Point Zero: Housework, Reproduction, and Feminist Struggle*. Oakland, CA: PM Press, 2012, pp. 15–22; Vogel, L. (1983). *Marxism and the Oppression Of Women: Towards a Unitary Theory*. New Brunswick, NJ: Rutgers University Press; Fortunati, L. (1995). *The Arcane of Reproduction: Housework, Prostitution, Labour and Capital*. New York, NY: Autonomedia. For a detailed reading of social reproduction theory from a queer and trans-inclusive, Marxist feminist perspective, focusing primarily on Vogel, see Lewis, H. (2016). *The Politics of Everybody: Feminism, Queer Theory and Marxism at the Intersection*. London: Zed Books, Chapter 2.

14. Weeks, K. (2011). *The Problem With Work: Marxism, Feminism, Antiwork Politics and Postwork Imaginaries*. Durham and London: Duke University

Press, p. 119; Marx, K. (1990). *Capital: A Critique of Political Economy, Volume 1.* London: Penguin.

15. Federici, *Revolution at Point Zero*, p. 19.
16. Ibid.
17. Farris, S. R. (2015). Migrants' Regular Army of Labour: Gender Dimensions of the Impact of the Global Economic Crisis on Migrant Labour in Western Europe. *The Sociological Review*, 63(1), 121–143.
18. For instance, see Federici's 1975 essay Why Sexuality is Work (in *Revolution at Point Zero*, pp. 23–27).
19. See also the politics and praxis of the gay liberation movement, calling for the abolition of the nuclear family, and for gay communalism and interdependency (Jay and Young, 1992).
20. Federici, *Revolution at Point Zero*, pp. 15, 22, original emphasis.
21. Two recent essays mark new directions in queer and trans social reproduction: Jules Gleeson's 'An Aviary of Queer Social Reproduction' analyses the fertility of queer and trans feminised subjects and trans 'egg' discourse through social reproduction theory; and Harry Josephine Giles' 'Wages for Transition' manifesto makes political demands in the context of the collective, communised labour of gender transition. These essays were published after the completion of my essay. See Gleeson, J. (2019). An Aviary of Queer Social Reproduction. *Hypocrite Reader*, 94, http://hypocritereader.com/94/eggs-queer-social-reproduction; and Giles, H. J. (2019). *Wages for Transition*. Edinburgh: Easter Road Press, https://medium.com/@harrygiles/wages-for-transition-dce2b246b9b7.
22. Piepzna-Samarasinha, L. L. (2017). A Modest Proposal for a Fair Trade Emotional Labour Economy (Centered by Disabled, Femme of Color, Working Class/Poor Genius). *Bitch Magazine*. Accessed 11 April 2018, https://www.bitchmedia.org/article/modest-proposal-fair-trade-emotional-labour-economy/centered-disabled-femme-color-working.
23. Ibid.
24. Ibid.
25. Such a theory ought to also highlight how heterosexist, racist, ableist and cissexist norms play out within wider social, economic and scientific regimes – often rooted in eugenics – and how they have policed sexual reproduction. These factors have especially restricted access to social services and healthcare for poor queer, trans, disabled, and people of colour, and have thus been a key focus of the feminism articulated by these marginalised groups. This policing of sexual reproduction has led to forced sterilisation of trans people (trans women in particular), disabled people and certain groups of people of colour. It has meant the limiting or refusal of access to reproductive technologies, abortions, and medications. It has resulted in the denial of family rights of LGBTQ families, including the removal of children from parents. It has seen the withdrawal of social security and welfare, and marginalisation in broad

medical provisions. More actively, it has meant state harassment, incarceration and psychiatrisation of trans and gender non-conforming people. These are all matters which LGBTQ activists have been central in contesting directly or inventing alternatives to since the 1960s. For a Black feminist perspective on reproductive justice, see Roberts, D. (1997). *Killing the Black Body: Race, Reproduction, and the Meaning of Liberty*. New York, NY: Pantheon Books. For work addressing the incarceration and psychiatrisation of queer, trans and disabled people, see Ben-Moshe, L., Chapman, C., & Carey Allison, C. (2014). *Disability Incarcerated: Imprisonment and Disability in the United States and Canada*. New York, NY: Palgrave Macmillan.

26. Duggan, L. (2003). *The Twilight of Equality: Neoliberalism, Cultural Politics, and the Attack on Democracy*. Boston, MA: The Beacon Press, p. 50.

27. Ibid., emphasis added.

28. Ibid., p. 14.

29. Ibid., p. 62, emphasis added.

30. For canonical arguments, see Conrad, R. (Ed.) (2014). *Against Equality: Queer Revolution, Not Mere Inclusion*. Edinburgh: AK Press; Warner, M. (1999). *The Trouble With Normal: Sex, Politics and the Ethics of Queer Life*. New York, NY: Free Press.

31. Euphemistically known as the 'Personal Independent Payments' (or PIP).

32. Walker, P. (2 February 2017). More than 350 Sure Start Children's Centres Have Closed Since 2010. *The Guardian*, https://www.theguardian.com/society/2017/feb/02/sure-start-centres-300-closed-since-2010.

33. Pitt, J. (Cohen) & Monk, S. (28 August 2016). 'We Build a Wall Around Our Sanctuaries': Queerness and Precarity. *Novara Media*, http://novaramedia.com/2016/08/28/we-build-a-wall-around-our-sanctuaries-queerness-as-precarity/. Hereafter cited as Cohen and Monk.

34. Lewis, *The Politics of Everybody*, p. 147.

35. Berlant, L. & Warner, M. (1998). Sex in Public. *Critical Inquiry*, 24(2), 547–566.

36. STAR, 'Street Transvestite Action Revolutionaries' [circa 1970], reproduced in Lewis, A. J. (2017). Trans History in a Moment of Danger: Organizing Within and Beyond 'Visibility' in the 1970s. In Gossett, R., Stanley, E. A., & Burton, J. (Eds.), *Trap Door: Trans Cultural Production and the Politics of Visibility*. Cambridge, MA and London: MIT Press, pp. 57–90, 76–77.

37. See Joseph, M. (2002). *Against the Romance of Community*. Minneapolis, MN and London: University of Minnesota Press; Wesling, M. (2012). Queer Value. *GLQ: A Journal of Lesbian and Gay Studies*, 18(1), 107–126. Ward, J. (2010). Gender Labor: Transmen, Femmes, and Collective Work of Transgression. *Sexualities*, 13(2), 236–254; Sears, A. (2016). Situating Sexuality in Social Reproduction. *Historical Materialism*, 24(2), 138–163,

141; McRuer, R. (2006). *Crip theory: Cultural Signs of Queerness and Disability.* New York, NY and London: New York University Press.

38. Joseph, *Against the Romance of Community*, p. 40.

39. There are numerous considerations of the impact of zoning laws on gay male public sex, for instance, see Berlant and Warner, Sex in Public. One might go as far as suggesting that this has become a critical norm within queer theory centred around cisgender men. For various accounts of how zoning laws, particularly in New York City, have impacted on queer and trans youth of colour and homeless persons, see Shepherd, Rosado, and Stanley's essays in Sycamore, M. B. (Ed.) (2008). *That's Revolting: Queer Strategies for Resisting Assimilation.* Berkeley, CA: Soft Skull Press, pp. 123–140, 317–328, 329–336. For a consideration of female public sex, see Mbessakwini, E. (2008). Sex, Gender, and Letters to Myself. In Sycamore, *That's Revolting*, pp. 199–209.

40. Wesling, Queer Value, p. 108.

41. Dir. Luis Felipe Bernaza, 1996.

42. Wesling, Queer Value, pp. 118, 117.

43. Ibid., pp. 120, 115.

44. Ward, Gender Labor, p. 239. Ward specifically cites Stryker, S. & Whittle, A. Z. (2006). *Transgender Studies Reader.* New York, NY and London: Routledge.

45. Ward, Gender Labor, p. 237, author's emphasis.

46. Ibid., p. 239.

47. Ibid.

48. Ibid.

49. Ibid., pp. 239–240, emphasis added; the later clause cites Nakano Glenn, E. (2004). *Unequal Freedom: How Race and Gender Shaped American Citizenship and Labor.* Cambridge, MA: Harvard University Press.

50. Ward, Gender Labor, 241.

51. Cohen and Monk, 'We Build a Wall Around Our Sanctuaries'.

52. Cohen and Monk's formulation of the 'proletarian queer' deserves to be considered at length. They write: 'To be queer is not only to adopt an identity through which one is oppressed through violence and hatred, but is also materially implicated in class relations in a particular way. Even previously instantiated class privilege can be disrupted through forcible ejection from the bourgeois household' (Cohen and Monk, 'We Build a Wall Around Our Sanctuaries'). Given the direction of this essay, I refrain from discussing this conception.

53. Ibid.

54. Ibid.

55. While McRuer does not focus on questions of how race shifts the forms that domesticity and the family takes, the institutions that he outlines are shaped by Western Euro-American ideals that privilege and reproduce whiteness.

56. McRuer, *Crip theory*, pp. 99–100.

57. Ibid., pp. 99–100.
58. Ibid., pp. 100.
59. Ibid., pp. 101.
60. Hill Collins, P. (1991). *Black Feminist Thought*. New York, NY and London: Routledge, pp. 44–46, emphasis added.
61. Hill Collins, *Black Feminist Thought* , pp. 46–47, citing Stack Carol B. (1974). *All Our Kin: Strategies for Survival in a Black Community*. New York: Harper & Row; and Rapp, R. (1982). Family and Class in Contemporary America: Notes Toward an Understanding of Ideology. In Thorne, B. with Yalom, M. (Eds), *Rethinking the Family: Some Feminist Questions*. New York and London: Longman, 1982, p. 180.
62. 'There is no such thing as a private sphere for people of Color except that which they manage to create and protect in an otherwise hostile environment', Hurtado (1989, 849), cited in Talpade Mohanty, C., Russo, A., & Torres, L. (Ed.) (1991). *Third World Women and the Politics of Feminism*. Bloomington and Indianapolis, IN: Indiana University Press, p. 9.
63. LaKeyma King (2015). Inversion and Invisibility: Black Women, Black Masculinity and Anti-Blackness. *LIES Journal*, II, 31–48, 43–44.
64. Valiavicharska, Z. (2020). Repression and Struggle on the Terrain of Social Reproduction: Historical Trajectories, Contemporary Openings. *LIES Journal*, III.
65. Lorde, A. (1996). *The Audre Lorde Compendium*. London: Pandora, p. 159.
66. Ibid.
67. This insight is also hinted towards by Wesling in the discussion above, in a politicised excess of both the insertions into the systems of wage labour of the people reproduced within the nuclear family.
68. Third World Gay Revolution (1992). What We Want, What We Believe. In Jay, K. & Young, A. (Eds.), *Out of the Closets: Voices of Gay Liberation*. London: GMP Publishers Ltd, pp. 363–367, quote on 365. It's important to note that 'Third World' here referred to groups primarily representing those who'd today more typically describe themselves as western people of colour. Karla Jay argues that '*radical* lesbians and homosexuals' as 'the negation of heterosexuality and of the nuclear family structure', who have 'as such been driven from our jobs, our families, our education, and sometimes from life itself' – to exist as the negation of these structures entails feeling the brunt of their repressive values (Jay, 'Introduction to the first edition'; Jay and Young, lxi, quoting Martha Shelley).
69. While STAR emerged directly out of the gay liberation movement, the group and its members were also visible and active in Latinx and Black movements – most specifically Puerto Rican revolutionary organisation the Young Lords – and their work took forms similar to that of these movements. I discuss STAR's connection to New York's Young Lords and Third World Gay Revolution in detail in my essay (Spring 2015). 'Out of Jail and on the Streets Again': Street Transvestite Action Revolutionaries and the Praxis of Transfeminism of Color. Unpublished Manuscript. For

a brief discussion of Sylvia Rivera's connection to the Young Lords, see Wanzer-Serrano, D. (2015). *The New York Young Lords and the Struggle for Liberation*. Philadelphia, PA: Temple University Press, pp. 117–119.

70. Gossett, Stanley, & Burton, *Trap Door*, p. xvii.

71. Ibid.

72. 'Street queen' was used as a self-description by STAR's members denoting a classed position of living and/or selling sex on the street. It must be emphasised that STAR were a group of poor, primarily Latinx and black street queens – in Sylvia Rivera's words '[a] majority of the queens were Latin'. Cited in Cohen, S. L. (2008). *The Gay Liberation Youth Movement in New York: 'An Army of Lovers Cannot Fail'*. New York, NY and London: Routledge, p. 134. While Sylvia Rivera and Marsha P. Johnson occupy significant positions in transgender history and the trans political imaginary, their canonisation has often erased their positions as people of colour, street queens, and the political praxes that emerge from such positions. As Jessi Gan importantly emphasises in the case of Sylvia Rivera, Rivera's visibility and reclamation by trans activists as 'transgender Stonewall combatant' have 'concealed' her 'subjectivity as a working-class Puerto Rican/Venezuelan drag queen' Gan, J. (2013). 'Still at the Back of the Bus': Sylvia Rivera's Struggle. In Stryker, S. & Aizura, A. Z. (Eds.), *The Transgender Studies Reader 2*. New York, NY and London: Routledge, pp. 291–301, 292.

73. Martin Duberman writes 'As a Hispanic, Sylvia strongly identified with those righteous revolutionaries of the Third World, the Black Panthers and their Hispanic counterpart, the Young Lords' (Duberman, M. (1993). *Stonewall*. New York, NY: Plume, 1994 Edition, p. 251).

74. On 'zaps', see Cohen, *The Gay Liberation Youth Movement*, p. 178; Benjamin Shepherd cites Arthur Evans' recollection of the Gay Activist Alliance's petitioning of the Village Independent Democrats in 1970, when Sylvia hit a councilwoman over the head. This was described as 'climbing up the liberals' (in Sycamore, *That's Revolting*, pp. 125–126).

75. Cohen, *The Gay Liberation Youth Movement*, pp. 130–146; Teal, D. (1971). *The Gay Militants*. New York, NY: Stein & Day, p. 222. Teal emphasises STAR's role in the Gay Community Center's organising collective.

76. *Gay Flames* 7, cited in Teal, *The Gay Militants*, p. 166. Addressing the dismissal of STAR, TWGR, and GLF's support by the CP, *Gay Flames* reported that '[w]e can march beside them as long as we do not carry our own banners or camp it up too much. Three times, GLF or STAR people have been thrown of the picket lines. So far, we haven't the numbers to physically resist, be we hope to do so at the next demo, November 20 [1970]'. Angela Davis herself would come out as a lesbian in the early 1990s.

77. Cohen, *The Gay Liberation Youth Movement*, pp. 131–135.

78. Bell, A. (Thursday 15 July 1971). 'STAR trek', *The Village Voice*, 1, 46. On their eviction, STAR trashed the building so that their mafia landlord

could not benefit from the work they did on the house. Missed rent payments would lead to the eviction of STAR house after around nine months.

79. Stryker, S. (2008). *Transgender History*. Berkeley, CA: Seal Press, pp. 86–87.

80. Rivera, S. (2002). Queens in Exile: the Forgotten Ones. In Nestle, J., Howell, C., & Wilchins, R. (Eds.), *GENDERqUEER: Voices From Beyond the Sexual Binary*. Los Angeles, CA: Alyson Books, pp. 71–85, 81–82.

81. Gan, 'Still at the Back of the Bus', p. 294.

82. Ibid., p. 299.

83. Cohen, *The Gay Liberation Youth Movement*, p. 131.

84. Rivera, Queens in Exile, p. 82.

85. Feinberg, L. (1998). Portrait: Sylvia Rivera, 'I'm Glad I was in the Stonewall Riot'. In *Trans Liberation: Beyond Pink or Blue*. Boston, MA: Beacon Press, p. 108.

86. On the Black Panther Party's breakfast programmes, see 'To Feed Our Children', *The Black Panther* (26 March 1969), accessed 11 March 2016, https://www.marxists.org/history/usa/workers/black-panthers/1969/03/26.htm – which notably does not discuss the gendered character of this labour. For more on the latter, see Brown, E. (1993). *A Taste of Power: A Black Woman's Story*. Norwell: Anchor Press.

87. While this care work had a revolutionary function, it was generally conceptualised in a denigrating fashion as 'women's work' by the men of the parties.

88. Kyungwon Hong, G. & Ferguson, R. A. (Eds.) (2011). 'Introduction' to *Strange Affinities: The Gender and Sexual Politics of Comparative Racialization*. Durham and London: Duke University Press, pp. 14–16, quote on p. 15.

89. In my essay 'Transfeminine Brokenness, Radical Transfeminism', I theorise the connection of transmisogyny in particular to such devaluations. Raha, N. (2017). 'Transfeminine Brokenness, Radical Transfeminism'. *South Atlantic Quarterly*, 116(3), 632–646.

90. In her conception of a 'second skin', Rosemary Hennessy connects the cultural, normative and symbolic meanings that adhere to the bearer of labour power, emphasising the devaluation of the feminised labourer in the context of capital's social relations that devalue reproductive labour (Hennessy, R. (2013). *Fires on the Border: The Passionate Politics of Labour Organizing on the Mexican Frontera*. Minneapolis, MN: University of Minnesota Press, p. 129).

91. For discussions of how transfeminine migrant sex workers cognise the valuation of their work by capital, see Aizura, A. Z. 'Trans Feminine Value, Racialised Others and the Limits Of Necropolitics'. In Haritaworn, J., Kuntsman, A., & Posocco, S. (2014). *Queer Necropolitics*. Hoboken: Taylor & Francis, pp. 129–147. For an elaboration of transfeminine subjection

while performing low paid caring labour in a dysfunctional care undergoing privatisation and restructuring, see Spott, V. (2017). *Click Away Close Door Say*. London: Contraband Books.

92. See SomMovimentonazioAnale (2014). Social Strike: Gender Strike. Accessed 9 April 2018, https://sommovimentonazioanale.noblogs.org/post/2014/07/18/social-strike-gender-strike/.

93. van der Drift, M. (2018). Radical Romanticism, Violent Cuteness, and the Destruction of the World. *Journal of Aesthetics & Culture*, 10(2) 1–8.

6

Notes from Brazil

Virginia Guitzel

I.

At his inauguration, Jair Bolsonaro hailed Brazil's 'liberation from socialism, the inversion of values, the bloated state and political correctness', promising to 'unite the people, rescue the family, respect religions and our Judeo-Christian tradition, combat gender ideology, and [conserve] our values.'[1] Here, then, was not just a declaration of intent but a declaration of war, drawing a stark dividing line between his administration and the past, and promising a full-throated assault on the 'gender ideology' that has allegedly poisoned the minds of many young Brazilians. But Bolsonaro did not randomly fall from the sky, nor is the hatred against trans people a recent development. Brazil has the highest rate of murder of trans people in the world. The average age of the victims is 26. The life expectancy for trans people is just 35. Despite this, Brazil also has the largest LGBTQ+ Pride parade in the world, and has made attempts in recent years to brand itself as an LGBTQ+ friendly tourist destination.

For Bolsonaro's base, the 'traditional Brazilian family' has been under sustained attack from LGBTQ+ activists. The claim that 'gender ideology' was being imposed on children and youths in schools by the left circulated widely in sensationalist media and WhatsApp groups during the last presidential campaign. But it first made headway during the Dilma Rousseff administration in 2014, when Evangelical and Catholic churches presented a united opposition to her National Education Plan, demanding that any mention of the word 'gender' be removed from classrooms, stating: 'we do not want schools that confuse our children'. This campaign was successful, and gender and gender identity education was removed from curricula. Bolsonaro's supporters openly long for 'simpler times'.

The Brazilian right has long been empowered by its interlocking relationship with the Catholic Church. While credited as a religious reformer with a modern perspective, Pope Francis has in fact used his position to uphold the clergy's aggressive stance towards trans people. Francis said in a hearing on 15 April 2015: 'Gender theory is born of an expression of frustration and resignation that seeks to erase sexual difference because it is no longer known how to deal with it'. He peppered the rest of the decade with denunciations of trans-gender people, culminating in 2019s document Male and Female He Created Them, which reaffirmed the Church's anti-trans stance, and also mandated surgeries on children born with ambiguous genitals. It was in this context that Bolsonaro appointed Damares Alves to head the Ministry of Human Rights, Family, and Women, with a remit of attacking so-called 'gender ideology'.

There should be no doubt that the myth of leftists imposing 'gender ideology' is little more than a bourgeois attack on Brazil's trans pop-ulation. Bolsonaro positions himself as the primary defender of the traditional family, and the arch-enemy of sexual freedom and the free construction of gender identity. In this sense, his presidency marks the end of an era, the end of Brazilian 'progressive neoliberalism' witnessed under successive Workers' Party (PT) administrations. This period witnessed the expansion of 'Pink Money' in the gay and lesbian movement. Our current era is seeing the reversal of even this modest breakthrough.

Bolsonaro is the standard-bearer for the most hateful, reaction-ary forces in Brazil. During the elections, his rhetoric whipped up a feverish climate of hate that encouraged the murder of Mestre Moa do Katende, an important capoeira master and a tireless activist against racism. The campaign also coincided with the murder of two trans women. He is well known for controversial statements such as telling a woman member of Congress: 'I won't rape you because you're too ugly', and 'I'd rather have my son die in a car accident than dating another man'. As part of his culture war, Bolsonaro has proposed a law known as 'Escola sem partido' (school without political affiliation), which seeks to attack teachers' rights in the name of 'fighting Marxist indoctrination', while legitimising reactionary historical revisionism.

After his election victory, femicides and transfeminicides have increased exponentially. Perhaps the most brutal was the murder of

Quelly da Silva, whose heart was torn from her chest. Although the murder of trans people is nothing new in Brazil, these murders have gained an air of legitimacy under the presidency of a man who says that people are queer because they were not beaten during childhood. But we must examine: How did we get here?

Brazil has undergone intense political and economic turmoil in recent years. To borrow from Gramsci, elements of organic crisis are at play: this era has been characterised by an economic crisis, a crisis of traditional political parties, and the emergence of 'new' ways of thinking. Yet despite intense moments of national protest surrounding flashpoints such as the 2014 World Cup, this crisis has developed without ever reaching a revolutionary or even a pre-revolutionary situation. We can trace the roots of the crisis to the millions who took to the streets in June 2013 when the self-described progressive Workers' Party ordered bus fare hikes. The youth that took to the streets broke the paralysis of the masses, expressing the mounting disaffection with the PT's narrowly ameliorative administration. This street resistance highlighted the contradiction between, on the one hand, the aspirations of the working class for economic and social progress and, on the other, the limits that constrain it under capitalism in a semi-colony. It was in this context that the US began a campaign of subversion and naked interference in the political affairs of Brazil.

This imperialist offensive reached a crescendo in the Operation Car Wash (Operação Lava Jato) investigation led by federal judge Sérgio Moro, a massive political manoeuvre by the judiciary, whose transparently anti-democratic intent was all but confirmed with the later appointment of Moro as Bolsonaro's Minister of Justice and Public Security; a payment for services loyally rendered. Operation Car Wash first laid the groundwork for the parliamentary-judicial *coup d'etat* against Dilma Rousseff. It later led to the arrest of former President Luiz Inácio Lula da Silva based on the testimony of questionable characters offered shady plea bargains in exchange for their statements – in a trial devoid of incriminating evidence – making a mockery of his right to a fair trial. Lula was consequently barred from running in the presidential elections, with polls showing he was the favourite to win in the first round of voting. This was the sharper end of a broader campaign to delegitimise and destroy the PT by the media, the ruling class, and the US government.

However, throughout the process, the Workers' Party, the main opposition to Bolsonaro, continued to fuel enormous illusions in the coup-mongering judiciary. Even as he was being imprisoned, Lula said he trusted the judicial apparatus, and legitimised the blatantly manipulated electoral process. Far from launching an unflinching defence of himself, Lula argued that Operation Car Wash had served the interests of the country!

This weak response did not match the potential for worker action against the right. Just a year before Bolsonaro's rise to power, there had been a general strike and several massive mobilisations against President Temer's austerity cuts and the imprisonment of Lula. Rather than strengthening and radicalising these tendencies, the Workers' Party attempted to channel this anger towards the upcoming election, even as the democratic institutions of the capitalist state were being undermined and subordinated to the authoritarian and arbitrary judiciary, with the open support of the armed forces.

In doing so, Lula and the Workers' Party sought to paint themselves as the 'responsible alternative' to Bolsonaro, ignoring the intense culture war being waged by the right wing against oppressed people. This reactionary campaign has especially targeted LGBTQ+ people, women, and Black people. In this way, the Workers' Party reaffirmed its programme of administering neoliberal capitalism in its decline.

The Party of Socialism and Liberty (PSOL) is the primary left-wing alternative to the PT, and was hit hard by the reactionary offensive. The deepest wound was the brutal political assassination of Marielle Franco, a direct result of the institutional coup and military intervention in Rio de Janeiro. Almost a year later, two militia men were accused of her murder, both with ties to the Bolsonaro family. Afraid of becoming the 'next Marielle', Jean Wyllys, the first openly gay member of Congress, left the country after receiving numerous death threats.

The PSOL doubled its members of parliament in the last elections. However, while revolutionaries certainly can and should run in elections, the PSOL has demonstrated its own strategic limits by putting electoral victory at the centre of their political practice. Vote-winning became an end of its own, rather than a means for building class struggle. They correctly focus on the defence of the most oppressed sectors of society, through attempting to build social movements. But if the PSOL do not use their seats to demand that trade unions build up a fight against austerity and for the working class paying for the crisis, this approach ends up being mere parliamentarianism. Instead of helping to build a combative left, they have built a Democratic Front in parliament, which aims to be a 'responsible' opposition that will respect even the arbitrary rulings of the judiciary.

In summary, then, the PSOL lacks a programme for the capitalists to pay for the crisis that they themselves created, a strategy to accumulate forces to confront Bolsonaro and the financial capital that backs him, as well as a strategy to fight to win in battles for the emancipation of sexual and gender identity. It would make an enormous difference to have a revolutionary party rooted in the working class with a strategy that brings together the tactical struggles in parliament, in the unions and in the social movements to strengthen the power of the working class. Despite its potential, the PSOL does not, at least at present, represent such a party.

Now, the second year of Bolsonaro's government begins with an important revival of class struggle at the international level. In this second cycle, after the important uprisings of the Arab Spring in 2011, gigantic demonstrations from North Africa, the Middle East to Latin America, crossing from Sudan, Algeria, Iraq, Hong Kong, and Catalonia. Or the demonstrations that followed Ecuador's turn to austerity under IMF tutelage, the huge protests in Chile, the resistance to the coup in Bolivia and the enormous movement in France, one of the hearts of European imperialism, in the struggle against Pension Reform.

The first half of 2019 saw enormous instability and uncertainty about developments in Brazil, including large student mobilisations that took more than 1 million people back onto the streets against the government's attacks on education, and several media scandals that demonstrated the intent of the Lava Jato process to consolidate a dramatic, regressive transformation in Brazil's political system. This whole period was crossed by a huge dispute about the future of North American imperialism, between Republicans and Democrats which also involved other countries, in particular China, that found its expression as a division between Brazilians themselves.

If, on the one hand, the Bolsonaro/Trumpist wing concentrated on strengthening the executive to bring about a more Bonapartist regime, which begins by submitting the other institutions of government to the direct control of the executive, the influence, on the other hand, is expressed by the Democrats' attempts to weaken Bolsonaro and Lava Jato.

This latter wing could be termed 'Institutional Bonapartism', represented by the National Congress, part of the judiciary and a wing of the military, who have played a role in limiting the excesses of Bolsonarism, at a time when their own sub-existence within the Brazilian political regime was also in question. However, Bonapartism is none other than the government of financial capital. That is why, in order to achieve the central objective of the coup of forcing through fiscal retrenchment against workers in a more accelerated manner, it was necessary to discipline both wings. Through this, a bourgeois consensus on the economy has emerged. The approval of the Social Security Reform with the help of this truce, defended by the Union Centrals (mainly directed by the PT and PCdoB) justified the existence of the Bolsonaro government and guaranteed its permanence, at least in the medium term, despite the several crises that appeared.

Lula's release marked another turning point, as it instigated a new PT offensive to rediscover his place within the new dispensation, one still difficult to define. But what is already clear is that this return entails a retreat from questioning the economic plan of the coup, since the party's most institutionally powerful organisations – the trade unions – continue to avoid mounting a real counter-offensive against the attacks directed at the working class. Meanwhile, their governors in the Northeast have duly applied the Pension Reform with little resistance in states that they govern, essentially operating as agents of the right unloading the crisis on workers.

Sexual repression, moreover, remains an essential feature of this government. Damares Alves, the Minister for Women, Family and Human Rights recently launched an official campaign for 'sexual abstinence', alongside attacks on the health of people living with HIV. Strikingly, according to national polling Damares is one of Brazil's most popular politicians. This demonstrates the active conservative base on which the government's support rests, revealing one of the most worrying factors in Brazilian politics in the medium term. Whether or not left-wing movements concern themselves with questions of trans oppression, Brazil's reactionaries are fully engaged with these questions, and use agitation featuring these themes as key recruitment tools.

As I write, workers in the oil industry are in the middle of a national strike with more than 100 paralysed units, and thousands of workers mobilising. This display of worker militancy is the first confrontation of this kind against the Bolsonaro government and its oil surrender plan. I dedicate this article to these workers, to Marielle Franco, and to everyone who seeks to build a real struggle for sexual liberation and the free construction of gender identity.

II.

We cannot put forward a truly revolutionary programme or strategy without a basis in historical materialism. As Brazilian socialist feminist Diana Assunção has stated, 'Preventing the new generations from knowing the history of struggles of the old generations is also a way of dividing us'. Divide and conquer has always been a favoured strategy of the ruling class.[2] We do not have to start from scratch: history does not begin the moment we enter it. In this sense, we must go back to and critically learn from the history of our struggles for sexual liberation and the alliances built between LGBTQ+ groups, and the labour movement. Reclaiming our history is a necessary step in building the tools we need to defeat our enemies and fight for true emancipation.

We are at the end of an era: one in which the enormous growth of LGBT visibility and acceptance in recent decades clashes with the insurgent growth of the far right. We are now witnessing the end of the idea of legislative breakthroughs as progressive steps in our emancipation. There is now the risk of losing the few rights we already have. Our victories, although important, are not permanent.

Understanding oppression against the LGBTQ+ sectors is to understand a mechanism of capitalist domination based on the economics of sexual misery. It is one which encourages and points to consumption as the only viable 'solution' that reaches those who declare themselves outside the prevailing norms: non-heterosexual and non-cisgender people. This hetero- and cisnormative order imposes a binary division of gender and sexuality tied to biological reproduction. This process is the basis of the reactionary morality of the religious institutions that campaign openly against our lives. Beyond the front lines where we trans revolutionaries stand, capitalism also inflicts brutal sexual repression on the whole of the working class. This results in illnesses, unwanted pregnancies, and numerous restrictions on one's own bodies and desires. Those brought in line by the capitalist order suffer in their own fashion, fostering reservoirs of resentment and self-loathing consistently drawn on by right-wing movements.

Control over others' bodies, the imposition of binary genders pre-defined by genitalia, heteronormative sexuality, and cisgender conformity are not 'natural'. These norms are at the service of a specific economic system, which favours a specific social class that organises society (and consequently its morality) to serve its own class interests. This is how permanent sexual repression under capitalism fulfils various roles in the relation between oppression and exploitation. We should embark on a sexual revolution capable of destroying repressive sexual morality.

The sexual question is not separated from class domination. Capitalism allows us to consume not only sexual acts, but films, ideas, fetishes, and a wide range of products that seek to stimulate pleasure and imprison it at the same time. Capitalism, resting on centuries-old institutions such as the patriarchal family and religious dogma that espouse misogynistic, homophobic, and sexist prejudices, aims to transform sex into an almost pleasureless routine act with the sole purpose of reproduction. This is imposed upon billions as the only 'normal' sexual expression.

In order to understand the strong links between the control of our bodies – and the hindrance to the free construction of non-normative gender identities – it is worth considering the 1973 essay by Argentine poet and anarchist Nestor Perlongher 'Sexo y revolución':

> Genitalization is destined to remove from the body its function of reproducing pleasure to convert it into an instrument of alienated production, by only sexualising what is indispensable for reproduction. That is why the system condemns with special severity all forms of sexual activity other than the introduction of the penis into the vagina, considered 'perversions', pathological deviations, etc. In order to imprison the human being in alienated labour, it is necessary to mutilate it by reducing its sexuality to the genitals.[3]

Let us examine the historical trajectory of the debates surrounding sexual and gender emancipation.

III.

While Stonewall looms large in most contemporary accounts, the political movement against sexual repression can actually be traced as far back as 1862 in Germany. Germany had the largest and most influential socialist movement in the world until WWI, and the German Social Democratic Party fought against the persecution of so-called sodomites. The issue was raised when Jean Baptiste Von Schweitzer was arrested while walking in a park with his partner, charged with 'sodomy', jailed for two weeks, and banned from practising law. August Bebel, one of the leaders of the SPD, condemned the hypocrisy of this imprisonment: 'You have no idea how many respectable, honourable, brave men, even in the upper ranks, are driven to suicide, year after year, some out of shame, others for fear of blackmail'.[4]

Years later, in 1885, when Oscar Wilde was arrested, still in the absence of a homosexual or sexual liberation movement, it was once again the left wing of the Social Democratic Party that came to his defence. Eduard Bernstein wrote a lengthy article in defence of the writer, rejecting a naturalistic view of sexuality, stating that:

> The argument that [homosexuality] is unnatural says nothing, because it is as unnatural as the capacity for writing. What is natural and unnatural is, ultimately, related to the development of society ... Moral attitudes are historical phenomena ... Sexual relations between individuals of the same sex are so widespread that there is no stage in the history of humanity that can be said to have been free from this phenomenon.[5]

The Marxist tradition is of enormous importance in understanding the oppression of human sexuality as a social phenomenon. Friedrich Engels reflected on the power that this question has in challenging the capitalist order, saying: 'It is a curious fact that with every great revolutionary movement, the question of "free love" comes to light'.[6] It was no different in the foremost revolutionary act of the international working class – the Russian Revolution, which began to challenge the economic and political bases upon which homosexuality was criminalised and by directly combating conservative morality, thus liberating sexuality from the oppressive confines of patriarchal ideology.

But the revolution was not just a transformation of base social relations. Also challenged were ideas, mental conceptions, and ethical standpoints – critical breakthroughs in thought concerning human sexuality were produced, among them thinkers like Wilhelm Reich. Reich promoted the self-regulation of sexual life in the pursuit of pleasure and desire, and was greatly inspired by the possibilities that the Russian Revolution aroused. He sought to elaborate a programme for freeing the youth from the sources of sexual repression and the capitalist family, and to approach the struggle for sexual liberation as part of the class struggle, involving conflicting ideologies and social projects. The merits of Reich, beyond the proposals he presented, were without doubt his struggles for collective and state solutions to ostensibly private sexual concerns, aiming to create the preconditions for the realisation of true sexual freedom. One of his ideas was the creation of spaces where young people would be free to experiment, without moralism or reprisals. In this way, Reich sought ultimately to displace the patriarchal family.

American historian Dan Healey's book *Homosexual Desire in Revolutionary Russia*[7] demonstrates the immense obstacles that the struggle for sexual liberation faced, even as the revolution decriminalised 'sodomy', which comprised all non-heterosexual sexual relations for non-reproductive purposes. Still today more than 75 countries punish homosexuality, and in seven of them it carries the death penalty. By approving the penal code of 1922, the Bolsheviks had recognised the weight of medical and legal opinions that recommended decriminalising same-sex relationships and had included in the objectives of the nascent revolution the battle for the liberation of sexuality, the abolition of discrimination and limitations based on sex and gender, and the emancipation of women, with the aim of eliminating all repressive laws that were, in their view, 'contradictory with a revolutionary conscience and legality'.

However, those victories in the early years of the revolution clashed with the reality of the isolation of the Russian Revolution and the defeat of the German Revolution in 1923. These failures led to the consolidation of a Soviet bureaucracy that usurped power from the workers. In order to secure its privileges, this bureaucratic regime, known as Stalinism, implemented a counter-revolutionary policy that prevented the Socialist Revolution from expanding throughout the world, and which also had the need to repeal many of the rights won by the heroic workers who fought against 14 different armies to secure proletarian power in the Russian Civil War. In 1928 the setbacks had already begun, when Dr Nikola Pasche Oserki defined homosexuality as a 'potential danger', and in 1934 it became a crime with an eight-year prison sentence.

Sexual liberation and the freedom to determine our identities are not based simply on a more-or-less advanced awareness of our own desires and bodies. It rather emerges from the sources of power of a given society, which uphold both our standards of sexuality and identity. This can only be overturned by the conscious effort of trans people seizing the enormous potential unleashed by the advancement of humanity's productive forces, and the abolition of scarcity. Through communist measures, we will fulfil our sexualities and our identities freely.

IV.

The sexual liberation movement, which reached its peak in the 1960s and 1970s, had to contend with both capitalism and Stalinism upholding the repression of sexuality and gender identities. It was in this context, amidst anti-war protests, that students gave rise to what would come to be known as May 1968, as students and workers in France occupied universities and factories to demand a sexual, lifestyle, and social revolution. One year later the Stonewall uprising took place.

Stonewall is probably the most enduring LGBTQ+ rebellion in popular culture, spearheaded by lesbians and trans women who refused to endure the indignities of repeated, systemic brutality at the hands of the police, who invaded the underground bars attended by the LGBTQ+ community night after night – arresting and assaulting the patrons. That movement received support from the feminist movement, the Black Panther Party, and other leftists and taught us a powerful lesson: the police and the capitalist state are enemies of the oppressed and the struggle against exploitation. When the trans women of colour of Stonewall led the uprising against the police, one could not have known that their outcry for sexual liberation would echo around the world. Over the following years of struggle, activists such as Sylvia Rivera and Marsha P. Johnson questioned those who would settle for a relative degree of inclusion of non-heterosexual sexualities and non-cisgendered identities within the capitalist system. One could synthesise Rivera's critique in the following phrase: 'if they cannot defeat them, profit from them'. In this, she foresaw the rise of queer liberalism, where corporations and capitalists no longer see gender and sexual minorities as subversive threats but instead as profitable opportunities and lucrative markets. This co-optation has gained strength in recent decades, as evidenced by the role of LGBTQ+ characters in entertainment media and the commercialisation of Pride, where the poor and the angry have been displaced, only to make way for corporate sponsorships. Johnson's famous slogan 'no pride for some of us, without liberation for all of us' attests to the fact that the struggle they defended was not only for the LGBTQ+ community, but for a society free from all forms of oppression.

The French group FHAR (Homosexual Front for Revolutionary Action) sought to bring attention to the link between the struggle against sexual repression and the struggle against the capitalist system, thus developing a union between the working class and the struggle for the right to pleasure. FHAR had to confront Stalinism, which came to regard homosexuality as a 'bourgeois degeneration' and prohibited any relations between its affiliate parties and the Front. On 1 May 1971, the Front marched alongside the workers with the slogan 'Down with the dictatorship of the normals'. They wrote:

> For us, the class struggle also passes through the body. Which means that our refusal to withstand the dictatorship of the bourgeoisie is freeing the body of this prison in which it has been systematically bound for 2,000 years of sexual repression, of alienated labor, and economic oppression. Therefore there is no possibility of separating our sexual struggle and our daily struggle for the fulfillment of our desires, from our anticapitalist struggle, from our struggle for a society without classes, without master nor slave.[8]

In the 1980s, groups such as Lesbians and Gays Support the Miners (LGSM) also fought to bridge the separation between the struggle for sexual and gender liberation and the class struggle. LGSM were dedicated to building solidarity with the miners who had a common enemy in the Thatcher government and the police. Another expression of this phenomenon was the conformation of 16 groups in ten countries that made up the Revolutionary Homosexual International (IHR).

But for all the radical ferment of that generation, it could not survive the onset of the HIV/AIDS crisis. When the US Centers for Disease Control announced the appearance of cases of pneumonia associated with Kaposi's sarcoma, most patients were homosexual and died within months. This triggered terror in the LGBTQ+ community, the stigma surrounding us was vastly increased, and a true witch hunt was unleashed. It took nearly a decade to establish the origins of the virus, to discover treatments for the infection, and a more precise knowledge of the pathways of contagion. During this decade, the movement had to channel its energies almost exclusively towards prevention of the disease, the dissemination of scientific data, and sick loved ones. But it also saw the rise of NGOs financed by international agencies, private companies, and state agencies. As the institutionalisation of the international sexual liberation movement progressed, radicalism was increasingly lost while more and more focus was given to strata of higher social and economic power that advocated for civil rights, inclusion, 'tolerance', and consumer rights, meaning 'Pink Money'.

It is under this new paradigm that we must view the following challenges: to develop a real working-class force with a programme for sexual liberation to raise these demands, and mobilise to confront the capitalist class. And to engage in a ceaseless struggle within sexual liberation movements against co-option. Queer liberation means the concrete struggle for hegemony waged between the capitalist state and the working class. While the current political order of Brazil may evoke despair (as with many places elsewhere the nationalist tide has triumphed), the return of class struggle at the international level breaks any material basis for the pessimism still so present on the left. If the Arab Spring in 2011, which saw the historic overthrow of dictatorships, did not, then certainly this new cycle that crossed the whole globe, from the demonstrations in Hong Kong to Ecuador, Sudan, Bolivia, Chile, Iran, Iraq, and France, marks a significant advance that brings us much closer to our shared history of working-class struggle and revolution which the bourgeoisie has worked hard to erase since Russia's capitalist restoration.

When we examine this matter in practical terms, given the visibility that the issue of gender identity has gained over the past four years in Brazil, its profound impact upon the *imaginarium* of the population is unquestionable. However, our increasing visibility has been accompanied by the unprecedented growth of neo-charismatic protestant denominations, which control a sizeable part of Brazil's Congress. These reactionary movements have come to challenge the secular character of the Brazilian state, and are now launching an open offensive against 'gender ideology' (meaning trans people).

The Brazilian right was able to exploit this situation in part due to the failed tactics LGBTQ+ rights groups adopted during the prosperous years of successive PT administrations. They believed that they could achieve a progressive and linear increase in legal rights and public esteem through awareness campaigns, based on the mistaken premise that sexual repression is the result of immaturity or ignorance rather than a means of social control. Progress in 'visibility and representation', lacking the material conditions to uphold those gains and to advance the cause of queer liberation, slipped into reverse as the far-right insurgency grew and came to accuse the media of being communist for presenting even the possibility of not being heterosexual.

It is therefore a question of building the material, cultural, and political conditions for sexual dissidence to take place, laying the foundations for genuine sexual liberation against existing inequalities and against the objectification of bodies and desire.

We must do better than the reformist ideals that prevailed in the post-WWII period, based on advancements in the culture industry and a supposed victory for visibility. Despite these surface level breakthroughs, this was not accompanied by progress in the struggle for rights for the non-heterosexual and non-cisgender masses. We must point to the material need to create those conditions for the free exercise of our sexuality and identities. Given that the capitalist system prevents us realising our liberation, this cannot be achieved in a linear path towards social emancipation through education and a gradual struggle against ignorance and prejudice.

Emancipation is based on ongoing clashes between social classes, and the struggle between them based on the pursuit of profits through exploitation. Sexual liberation is twinned with the liberation of workers from the condition of wage slavery. It is longed for by millions of people whose free sexuality and gender identity are neutered. It is a struggle that expresses the contradictions within an economic system that demands the oppression of different groups to secure capitalist hegemony. And presages quite a different future: a rationally planned economy designed to secure the realisation of all human needs as the gateway to true fulfilment for all.

Only the working class can play a leading role in this process. The proletarian class condition is not understood simply as another form of oppression, but rather as the role in capitalist production that is strategically positioned to overturn the fundamental structures of bourgeois society. Therefore, it is the task of the working class to take up those democratic demands. Moreover, as Emilio Albamonte and Matias Maiello have it: 'On the one hand, the working class constitutes a majority, even in a large part of the periphery. On the other hand, imperialist oppression made a spectacular leap during the neo-liberal offensive that makes any fundamental and lasting democratic victory in the semi-colonies, without national emancipation from imperialism, unthinkable'.[9]

It is within a new revolutionary framework that we must examine the enormous potential in the unity between the women's movement, the Black movement, the labour movement (the majority of whom are women and Black!), youth and oppressed groups such as LGBTQ+, and indigenous peoples. We must revolutionise trade unions and student organisations, to transform them into instruments of struggle. In the most exploited and oppressed sectors of society we can find the energy to sweep the labour and political bureaucracies from the comfort of their armchairs. This is our perspective for structurally confronting capitalism, sexual repression, and the patriarchy.

Liberation for trans people requires a tireless struggle against all structures of domination – social classes, the police, and the capitalist state – as a contribution to the building of a new society. One defined by relations between freely associated workers – that is, communism.

Notes

1. Phillips, D. (2020). Bolsonaro Declares Brazil's 'Liberation From Socialism' as He is Sworn In. *The Guardian*. Accessed 20 February

2020, https://www.theguardian.com/world/2019/jan/01/jair-bolsonaro-inauguration-brazil-president.

2. D'Atri, A. & Diana A. (compilers) (2018). *Lutadoras: A história de mulheres que fizeram história*. São Paulo: Edições Iskra.

3. Perlongher, N. (1973). Manifiesto del Frente de Liberación Homosexual, 'Sexo y Revolución'. *Somos*, 1.

4. Democratic Socialist Party of Australia (1982). A Revolutionary Strategy For Gay Liberation, https://www.marxists.org/subject/lgbtq/pamphlets/A%20revolutionary%20strategy%20for%20gay%20liberation.pdf.

5. Bernstein, E. (6 May 1895). *Die Neue Zeit*, 13(2), 1894–1895, 228–233.

6. Engels, F. In Hill, C. (1975). *The World Turned Upside Down: Radical Ideas During The English Revolution*. New York, NY: Penguin, p. 306.

7. Healey, D. (15 October 2001). *Homosexual Desire in Revolutionary Russia: The Regulation of Sexual and Gender Dissent*. Chicago, IL: University of Chicago Press.

8. FHAR (1971). *Rapport contre la normalité*. Paris: Champ Libre.

9. Albamonte, Emilio & Maiello, M. (2017). *Matías in Estrategia Socialista y Arte Militar*. Argentina: Ediciones IPS, p. 558.

7

Queer Workerism Against Work: Strategising Transgender Labourers, Social Reproduction & Class Formation

Kate Doyle Griffiths

Trans communist abolition or the barbarism of reaction

It is a 'best of times, worst of times' moment for the left, and working-class politics. Recent years have seen women's strikes,[1] months-long general strikes,[2] and now mass uprisings against the state, complete with self-conscious international solidarity. These moments have revived the class struggle, even in the capitalist core-countries' highly subsumed heart. Protests, strikes and direct action, feints toward commune-like autonomous zones, gestures towards workers' control, and *ad hoc* redistribution of goods have blossomed over recent years, too rapidly to easily follow. At the same time, right-wing national-ist parties and politicians have taken power in some of the world's most populous nations. This conquest of electoral politics has been a global trend: between India, Japan, the Philippines, and Brazil (to say nothing of smaller countries like Bolivia or Israel, where the far-right and legal apartheid has continued to dominate).

At this point, it seems challenging to define the 'extremes' of the right wing. Arguably, this includes the USA under Trump, elected by technicality and not plurality. For now, at least, Trump's brand of huckster right-wing populism has not completely abandoned the pretext of formal democracy. A similar situation applies to govern-ments in the UK, Italy, and elsewhere in Europe.

So we find ourselves at a point of clear dissonance: both struggle and reaction sharing their crescendo. Unprecedented numbers have hit the streets to call for concerted collective action in the face of climate change and a planet literally on fire, while the ruling class, where it hasn't yet resorted to the most severe methods of repression and an open embrace of far-right ideology, seems utterly bereft of ideas, and of any appeal to the many. Let's recall that old saw, 'socialism or barbarism'.[3] This line was always intended not to implicate pre-capitalist modes of human survival, but instead the fascist abandonment of any moral inclination towards solidarity. Heading off socialism requires the mobilisation of the state's most brutal face in service of the horrifying end-logic of capitalist imperatives in the face of crisis.

So how should we, as Marxists, respond to this concatenation of grave circumstances? What would a practical strategy of liberation, supplemented with an appropriate theoretical framework, look like? I don't like calling for 'queer' or 'trans' or even 'feminist' Marxism. Each of these additions is simply an elaboration of Marxism made into a useful tool for struggle. They are not best understood as 'identity' issues, siloed from the centre of Marxist theory and practice. There has been real progress on making this approach a reality on a number of fronts. This is particularly evident under the abolitionist framework – so to hyphenate seems like taking a step backwards.

Transgender Marxism requires us to insist both on the particular liberation of individuals, *and* to assert that that liberation cannot reliably be embodied by individuals alone empowering their way in the world.

One of the most relevant recent debates on the US left has focused on what theoretical and political approach Marxist organisers should take towards not just so-called 'identity politics'. This broader debate has focused on queer politics and the immediate demands of transgender people, in particular. Broadly, there are often assumed to be two camps, albeit with a range of nuances within them and some significant overlaps. It's a debate that often invokes, and repeats, many of the historical oppositions around questions of left strategy that emerged throughout the twentieth century, and is best addressed in that register: often what has been called the 'anti-woke'[4] side of this debate unites an overt political commitment to cis/heterosexism, natalism, and the nuclear family,[5] with an aggressively 'colour-blind' and anti-introspective approach to racism and nationalism.[6] This vein of socialism imagines as its enemy a 'camp' of the left that doesn't exist

– one myopically concerned largely with matters of representation or calculations of privilege.

One of the questions that strikes me as particularly urgent in overcoming these misdiagnoses is how we ought to understand the significance of gender, sex, and sexuality in any renewed strategy for worker organisation. A (reluctantly defined) trans-queer-Marxist-feminist frame not only calls into question any assertion of a divide between 'identity' and 'class', but also undermines any neat divide between shopfloor organising 'inside' unions at the point of production, and strategies directed towards unorganised (non-union) sectors and outside the workplace.[7]

The stakes in this debate are high, as a renewed interest in socialist organising has spread across the US since 2016. One left group alone, the Democratic Socialists of America (DSA), has surpassed over 100,000 members. The DSA has at once attracted many prominent transgender members, and voices hostile or at least dismissive towards trans politics. So how can we begin to make sense of trans people's place in workplace struggles?

That trans and queer people often risk sustained unemployment, or when we do find work are often restricted to sectors that exploit our specific qualities and skills – those self-same qualities that mark us for stigma in the first place – is just the most obvious and extreme case, but this is true of everyone's gender and of everyone's traumatic history. For trans/queer people this is often reflected in the deployment of workers uniquely suited to the intellectual labour[8] of social reproduction, and into roles tasked with organising that work. From early childhood, trans and queer people often develop the ability to mask and manage our own affect – this code-switching is a skill picked up through sometimes brutal necessity. We learn to appear impassive or pliant in response to the immediate needs and anticipated reactions of others. We are formed by the need to make ourselves indispensable as 'extra' caregivers in families that might otherwise dispense with us out of embarrassment.

The stereotype of the effeminate gay man, unusually attached to his mother and living with her late in life, can have a basis in reality. In a queer paradox, those least palatable to heterosexual norms can be least well placed to escape those households founded around them. But rather than viewing this in the mid-twentieth-century psychoanalytic model, where homosexuality is but a symptom of excessive identification with the mother, or a pathological reaction to the withholding of maternal love – this arrangement, to the extent that it exists, might more plausibly be read as a survival strategy, based on an appeal to the only plausible ally in a heterosexist family formation.

More broadly, the skills to manage trans and queer existence on a social level lend themselves to exploitation as skilled labour in the spheres of social reproduction and hospitality. This view offers one possible explanation for the (otherwise paradoxical) fact that queer and trans people gravitate disproportionately to professions in which it is more difficult to be comfortably 'out'.

Queers are often found in posts where it is more likely to result in abuse, stigma, dismissal, and blackmail when we are discovered: education, childcare, service labour, health care, and the Church. These industries present unique and intensified dangers when trans and homophobic parents and parishioners react to the idea of queer/trans people's close proximity to children or the intimate details and embarrassments of their social life. Yet they nevertheless lend themselves to queer-coded skills of meta-social analysis – the dispassionate eye of an outsider excluded from the mico-politics of cis/heterosexuality: worldly mentors lacking a more direct role in reproductive responsibilities, with an ability to offer 'creative' solutions to the dilemmas of everyday life.

This intensified familiarity with social reproduction is specific to queer, trans, and other marginalised experiences.[9] But it's also one expression of a personal dilemma familiar to most people – alienated from the means to sustain yourself, you instead find yourself forced to submit to contortions and deformations demanded of you by employers on the labour market. Equally universal are decisions to modify your style, affect, and self-segmentation. These bargains are struck in an effort to resist some of that violence – or at least to partially mitigate and avoid its worst assaults.

This acknowledgement of expediency has specific implications with respect to left strategies for resisting the right. Further, it is a perspective that is necessary for a class politics in general, and any Marxist politics in particular. The Marxist perspective we need here is one that can go beyond the failures of liberal feminism and a queer politics which emphasises 'diversity', 'inclusion', and 'tolerance' – precisely *because* it raises the possibility of resistance to liberal cross-class co-optation, and distinguishes itself from reductionist invocations of 'class'.

Crucially, a Transgender Marxist lens highlights how reductive engagements with class necessarily mirror and replicate liberal 'identity' politics, instrumentalising class as merely a container or stand-in for other (unmarked) identities: whiteness, heterosexual cisgender masculinity, and nationalism. Here, class is imagined as rooted in demography and identification rather than in the patient, transformative work of building a class-for-itself, through organising in and beyond the workplace.

This chapter argues for the strategic necessity of organising queer and trans workers and the political possibility of a deeper, more thoroughgoing, universalist politics. Just as 'identity' and 'class' are a false dichotomy, so too are the oppositions between workplace organising, *ad hoc* affinity-group models, and so-called community struggles. No distinctions of this analytic kind appear so clearly during actual moments of class war. Struggles in many contemporary workplaces occur *through* looser gatherings of affinity and wider networks built on trust, solidarity, and social support formed through shared recognition arising from similar circumstances.

Marxist strategy and gender as the terrain of class

This conclusion is suggested by another book that's been much celebrated among both critics and proponents of 'anti-woke' workerism, Kim Moody's *On New Terrain*.[10] Moody is probably the most well-known Marxist analyst of class composition and strategic power in the Anglophone world. His research has been a central touchstone for many socialist organisers attempting to implement rank-and-file and shopfloor strategies for worker self-organisation. Despite this popularity among many of the most vocal class reductionists who propose themselves as strategists of the US socialist movement, Moody's latest book-length intervention challenges notions that are widespread on the left and in academia. Especially the idea that deindustrialisation and precarity are a universal tendency in class composition. Moody complicates this picture by emphasising the dialectically simultaneous tendency for workplace power to be concentrated in only a few job categories, and then in specific sectors.

In the stark absence of strategy-focused Marxist analysis that looks beyond or primarily outside electoral efforts, or that which reverts entirely to a celebration of spontaneity, Moody's decades of writing emphasise the changing structure of the working-class-in-itself. His work adopts a dogged focus on the potential role of Marxists in organising the working class *beyond* efforts to rebuild either a labour or working-class party. Specifically his approach to rank-and-file organising has lately been popularised within both the right and left wings of the DSA, and well beyond.

For this reason, I think it is both fruitful and illustrative to reread Moody through a transgender – which is to say, a fully Marxist – lens. Both as a counter-position to the most stagnant and apolitical forms of class-reductionist workerism that is still gaining traction on the socialist left, but also as a method of conceptualising a new Marxist strategy for class organisation. One that not only affirms 'trans rights' as a moral or even tactical position – but transgender liberation. A struggle through which trans workers deploy Marxism in service of a practical strategy to bring communism about though working-class self-activity.

This mashup – of Moody's rank-and-file strategy, and Transgender Marxism made explicit – isn't exactly obvious. But considering them together provides a means to go beyond simply countering transphobia on the left, or in broader social discourse. And towards one that specifies and elaborates concrete and detailed efforts to outline how Marxists can best apprehend the changing structure of class society – and then most effectively intervene.

On New Terrain builds upon Moody's previous work outlining the rank-and-file strategy.[11] Here, he expands the breadth of its initial focus on the power of logistics workers and union democracy. This orientation provides for a strategy combating conservative union leadership, in favour of a labour movement built on an active 'militant minority'. Militants are defined by their focus on class politics proper, rather than narrow sectionalism. In this earlier iteration – and even more so in its practical translation into socialist strategy – the rank-and-file strategy heavily emphasises the importance of 'chokepoints' in logistics. Bringing clearly into view the work of dockers, warehouseman, truckers, and the like, these forms of labour appear as critical points of intervention for Marxists. A strike or slowdown at these points can wield significant gains through their power to disrupt profit-making. This opportunity appears both at the point of production, and in sectors further downstream. Actions by even a small number of logistics workers can offer remarkable leverage during broader class struggles, and therefore these are the sectors that should be a high priority for Marxist and socialist organisers.

On New Terrain introduces the necessity of analysing a second category of 'chokepoint', adding to Moody's focus on the strategic power of workers in logistics. In the book, Moody recognises waged social reproductive labour in education and healthcare as strategically critical. This is a significant development in Moody's rank-and-file strategy, which has seen revived interest over the past five years. Though written in 1990, this book was canonical for DSA activists and others looking to build socialist politics 'from below' within the labour movement. This follows its longstanding interest among many others who are simply interested in 'thinking through' the most pertinent strategies on the US left, for building socialist and working-class politics.

This revision, following in the wake of significant interventions by social reproduction theorists over the last several years, is extremely welcome. But I argue that trans and queer experiences can be seen as offering us additional access to an often neglected aspect of the fragility of capitalist relations. Namely, chokepoints of social reproduction.

The teacher strike wave demonstrates that social reproduction chokepoints are now central to a new wave of struggle; workers who are paid to do the work of the daily remaking of the working-class-in-itself play a central role in expanding and politicising workplace struggles. These moments allow for raising universal class-wide demands, precisely because workers in feminised reproductive sectors like education are in daily contact with the deepening crisis of care that impacts the entire class. Moody himself has taken up much of this argument in an essay for the 'workerist' socialist magazine *Jacobin*.[12] This suggests a different emphasis than earlier discussions of the 'chokepoint'. These actions usher onto centre stage previously underappreciated aspects of the debates about what 'particularism', class politics, and the 'rank-and-file strategy' looks like in practice.

The periodisation of the recent history of class struggle and the model of its development that Moody maps is one that he presents as complementary to an Arrighian frame, which analyses the development of historical capitalism over the *longue durée*, tracing its ascent and expansion through the rise and fall of successive hegemonic centres of capital accumulation.[13] This precisely lends itself to incorporating and validating Beverly Silver's globe-spanning, and comparative analysis of the role of social reproduction struggles and public sector strikes at the early stages of periods of class struggle over the last century.[14] Silver's book provides a quantitative overview of strikes over the last 150 years. With remarkable continuity, she demonstrates that time and again social reproductive strikes and public sector strikes are often predominant or concurrent in early waves of struggle. Rather than a sideshow, these are the crucial foundations for those more explosive moments in working-class history. Struggles around crises of care are interwoven with those broader movements in the history of working-class resistance.

Transitional organisations and trans strategy

Classically workerist formulations often counterpose workplace struggle with other forms of working-class organising. This opposition is at the crux of class-reductionist conceptions of a counter-position between 'identity' and 'class' politics. Moody's formulation of transitional organisations can help us break down these dichotomies, which are never so rigid or apparent in practice. In *The Rank and File Strategy*, Moody proposes that cross-sectoral 'transitional' organisations and multi-union campaigns, like Labor Notes or Our Walmart, can play the role of connecting shop floor organising to larger class-wide and movement politics. Alongside movement coalitions, these organisations can connect labour struggles to other forms of pro-immigrant, feminist, anti-racist, and ecosocialist organising. Through considering queer and trans communities, we can address arguments Moody raised concerning the undeveloped aspects of the rank-and-file strategy; most urgently, how it relates to socialist politics and organisation.[15]

Rather than lay out the further details of that argument here,[16] I'm going to supplement it by explaining the role I think trans and queer workers play in this strategic elaboration.[17] If the workplace and community distinction is collapsing (such as it ever held), what do struggles by queer and trans workers today tell us about chokepoints more generally?

It's not enough to say that logistical and productive, and social reproductive, chokepoints are each necessary, but not sufficient, to express the power and breadth of any potential class-for-itself politics. A third element of strategy is, I think, crucial to its full development. Rather than stretch the chokepoint image too far, let's take a simpler view. Socialists and communists must recognise and engage the uneven development of class consciousness. We have to recognise that this unevenness is rooted in experiences that are particular – but ones which foreshadow and make possible the development of a class consciousness. The implications of this goes beyond the politics of 'bread and butter', to one of bread and roses.

Roses here signify a humane and insurgent response to and recognition of the deeper and universal depredations and alienations of working-class exploitation:[18] from the length of the workweek as a perpetual site of struggle, to the experience of direct violent repression by the state and the family, to the embodied humiliations and alienations of working-class subjectivity that are particularly crystallised in the experiences of trans and queer workers. Through the figure and the social reality of the transgender worker, I want to arrive at a new 'workerism'. A politics that can effectively confront work as the defining experience of life under capitalism. This transgender workerism will allow us to think through a left strategy with a practical shot of achieving utopia.

This proposed relation between trans and queer workers and class formation is not distinct from what we've seen developing concretely in terms of the connection between feminist activity and workplace organising. Rather it is an intensification of this dynamic. Gender and workplace struggles are already merging: from strikes of thousands of workers at hotels and in the fast-food industry sparked by the #MeToo movement against sexual harassment as a modality of labour control, to walkouts of tech workers at Google and Amazon against sexism and racism at work and in favour of climate and immigration justice,[19] to the developing and generative interaction between teacher-wildcatters in West Virginia with anti-Kavanaugh organising and the grassroots struggle in the state against an abortion

ban.[20] A wave of rail and port blockades in Canada, by and in solidarity with the Wet'suwet'en people (and echoing the Dakota Access
Pipeline struggle) have demonstrated potential for white and indigenous workers as effective comrades. These breakthroughs have shown
a new possibility for a politically effective interplay between 'particular'
struggles, and an overarching strategy leveraging the profit-disrupting
power of targeting chokepoints of circulation.

Trans/queer workers have the potential to intensify this connection between workplace organisation, targeted strategy with respect to
logistics, and class consciousness. And also between shopfloor struggles and social movements – united around class demands. The first
task is to locate trans and queer people in the labour market, and then
move through a concerted effort of worker inquiry.[21] An investigation
that will no doubt uncover unexpected and surprising connections.

But even before that work is complete, I want to *hypothesise* that
queer and trans workers represent a dynamic and specific sliver of
the class. A sliver that is vastly over-represented in the work of paid
social reproduction, and particularly in the material organisation of its
expression as intellectual labour.

In the present and historically, trans/queer people have also tended
to find themselves grouped into key nodes of distribution and logistics
networks[22] – in warehouses, in air travel and air cargo, and shipping
and trucking of various kinds. This holds even as these are not the most
common occupations of trans people taken as a whole (as they aren't
for cis people as a category, either). This holds so widely for reasons
that may not be immediately obvious. Several accounts detail the lives
and experiences of trans/queer workers in production and logistics, but
few offer any systematic quantitative accounting of our presence. In
Semi Queer, Ann Balay illuminates the lives of 'trans, queer, and Black'
long-haul truckers. Balay uses personal accounts that demonstrate
how these workers are often the most marginalised in an industry hard
hit by deregulation and increasingly exploitative labour conditions. In
Steel Closets, Balay similarly uses an ethnographic approach to draw
attention to the lives and oral history of trans and queer people in that
quintessential 'working-class' industry, steelworkers. Through this, she
criticises the dominant, bourgeois LGBTQ politics disseminated by
major NGOs and other liberal institutions. However, her account does

not shy away from the often horrific homophobic and transphobic treatment these workers encounter on the job.

Trans and queer people have at various times drawn on the social worlds of queer life. These scenes serve to bridge the kinds of social division segregation and isolation that are reproduced in the organisation of work, labour, and housing markets. We have been drawn to radical organisation in disproportionate numbers – even where these organisations have been formally and practically hostile to queer and trans people. For the purposes of tracing the contribution and potential of a living, political, and strategic 'Transgender Marxism', the reasons why this is the case should be concretely investigated and understood. Through exploring the connections between these points of practical interest we can provide more detailed accounts than the usual offhand gestures toward queer/trans people. Concrete investigations of how queers navigate the everyday demands of exploitation must come to replace us serving as quaint representatives of the expansive tolerance, or emblems of social radicalism, of the left (contra wider society). The left is not only unusually 'tolerant' of queers and trans people: it also consists of us.

Double freedom from the family: queer proletarianization

I want to link these specificities of queer/trans labour relations to the (often negative) dynamism of the precarious and flexible family as a capitalist institution.[23] Through this I'll come to suggest that – as a group – we present a politicised network that bridges each of the three nodes of strategic catalysation. Here maybe queers can demonstrate the role that 'affinity groups' can actually play in a broader left strategy. Or perhaps be considered as a kind of vanguard-in-itself. One of several vanguards, but representing that potential as an actually existing social force, a basis of militant minority organising across and between workplace and community. This potential is both produced by and arrayed against sexual violence, reproductive authoritarianism, and the coercions of the family and workplace. The positioning of queer/trans proletarians as inevitably 'against' these, also place us to challenge the forces through which they limit and damage working-class people, and which present barriers to the actualisation of class politics. Queer/trans workforces are the revenge of the margins.

Queers have historically played an important role in politicising health care access as a question of class politics. Securing relevant treatment has required us to make political and organisational linkages between patients, providers, and researchers. Queer and trans people have rarely been able to expect humane and expert treatment as a given. Instead, we have secured it only through organising to advance research agendas, and test protocols. These are often formulated by working-class people through our lived experience, and autodidactic expertise.

The particular role of queer people in making healthcare access a matter of class politics over the last 40 years is especially important to highlight. The first example is of course the struggle through the gay liberation movement to depathologise 'homosexuality' itself, when it was classified as a psychological disorder. Then more recently, the related struggle to do the same for 'transsexuality'. The most often cited organisation in LGBTQ healthcare access efforts is of course ACT-UP, who deployed direct action to demand care for HIV positive and AIDS affected people. Today, trans healthcare can be seen as playing a similar equally politicised role.

Healthcare is often precisely raised as the archetypal Erfurt-style 'universal' demand for the class-reductionist left. From that perspective, illustrated by its advocates in the figure of tragically closeted civil rights leader Bayard Rustin,[24] queer and trans people represent an obstacle to the imagined negotiation with the ruling class for the adoption of this reform. (The same well may be true of disabled people or immigrants and other overlapping categories of people whose needs can be seen as particular or identity-based.) From this view, we appear as an extra expense, or a distracting 'culture wars' set piece that disrupts and divides simpler struggles.

But from an organising and class struggle perspective, queers represent a reservoir of movement history, strategy, and experienced cadre for healthcare struggles. And at the level of consciousness, the demand by trans people for care raises the possibility that healthcare battles may become a politics that refuses to separate self-fashioning from survival. Our struggle to secure social reproduction leads us to refuse to surrender ourselves to a one-size-fits-all profit-driven standard of what constitutes the bare minimum necessity for human survival.

Here, the lived experience of a small group of people recalls and exemplifies that original demand central to the socialist or communist vision – that 'to each according to [her] need' entails a *recognition* of different individual and particular needs. And that the distinction between need and desire is as much an artificial product of capitalist logic as the division between politics and economy, or between public and private. While we are obliged to meet the same demand as any other part of the capitalist workforce, through the unique demands of queer life, we find ourselves spilling over those divides readily, and shamelessly.

Further, queer/trans existence and class formation plays a crucial role in the development of the ongoing global feminist wave as a working-class project. While any given category of 'identity' has its quislings or avatars of bourgeois representation, the lived reality of trans/queer people brings to the fore gender as a relational and political process – rather than a seemingly transparent and natural one. We make plain the absurdity of, for example, Jordan Petersen's lobster-based naturalistic fallacy. But also the feminist version of this sort of thing – i.e. perspectives that insist on a biologically reductive 'sex class', contra a Marxist politics of social class, and class as war. Queer and trans communities are defined exactly by how the pressures of reproducing ourselves plays out in ways that are unexpected, or even unimaginable, from perspectives that boil down intergenerational exchanges into these familiar heterosexual terms.

Our lives and experiences insert indeterminacy and uncertainty, both in the sense of compelling feminism to reckon with the possibility of actually existing non-binary forms of gender, made liveable through a combination of self-assertion and community recognition. But also by revealing that even binary genders are changeable across time, and an individual lifespan. Trans/queer people make visible in the world that crucial Marxian analytic move – that what 'appears' is often enough the opposite of what 'is'.

Reading this indeterminacy through the labour theorisation of Moody highlights the material reason for this similarity. Analogous to the foreshortened ambitions of liberal feminism or the staid LGBT politics of NGOs, in Moody's work the attachment of bureaucratic layers of the labour movement to class-reductionist and conservative politics is made plain. The most significant revision to Moody's conception then has to be a rethinking of his understanding of the role and root of transitional organisations – and implicitly, socialist or communist ones. The particulars of queer proletarianisation are relevant to this rethinking. While there is not one single experience – and many individuals may experience some, none, or all of these features – queers collectively represent a concentrated group that tend to be alienated. Which is to say we are dispossessed not only as all proletarians are by definition,[25] but also from the social means of reproduction and redistribution, which is to say from the family.

These reproductive pressures are not unique to all self-identified queer people, but it is specific to us collectively. It's common that in response to this, queers and other similarly displaced people form alternative arrangements, today most commonly referred to as 'chosen family'. These are social relations which are simultaneously more free and open to creative adaptations, among more relatively equal individuals. But they are also more precarious, pressed, and less stable for precisely those same reasons. These circumstances shape the past and potential role of trans/queer people in organising, and organisation.

In historical accounts, like Chauncey's *Gay New York*,[26] or Feinberg's historical novel *Stone Butch Blues*,[27] we see how the rise of industrial urban environments attracted queer people to large cities. These migrating queers often found work in ports and warehouses, and as sex workers serving both working-class and wealthy urban clients. This work was taken up in part because these roles accommodated those whose presentations violated the gender norms of polite society. And because this work assumed or tolerated a certain laxity with respect to legal niceties.

Through the twentieth century, these clandestine communities tended to be exceedingly diverse, in all respects. These were the elements of the working class least capable or predisposed to 'aspiration', or earnest imitation of bourgeois values and customs. In urban watering holes one might find workers from across the globe. Patterns of migration not only leaves racialised minorities open to direct confrontation with the dual 'freedom' of market forces, but often far from the support of families (and their disciplinary strictures). Of course, this milieu also provided a part-time playground for the wealthy and the middling. This double minority of wealthy queens pursued living 'double' lives, straight and bent, or who simply wanted to let their hair down here and there.

Gentrification and the financialisation of real-estate in most urban centres worldwide has now dispersed communities of dock and warehouse workers, remodelling what were once accommodations for transient sailors, and 'cleaned up' red light and gay districts. Yet, still today, shipping and distribution draws queer and trans workers together through their proximity to urban centres, and relative amenability to those with 'unprofessional' presentations. Given this dispersal and the ascent of elite gays to the status of respectability, it's still true that queer social and sexual relations bring together individuals and groups among whom intimacy is prohibited or taboo in wider society[28] – across hetero norms of sex and romance, but also across race, class, religion, educational experience, language, profession, and national origin.

Friendship as a mode of struggle: queer comradeship

This provides fertile ground for making unlikely connections. Queer sociality throws up opportunities for comradely relations that may otherwise seem unlikely, extending across the division of labour and social prohibition. The historical record includes many examples where this proves true, such as one wealthy industrialist, a trans man living in New York City, Reed Erikson.[29] Styling himself as something of a twentieth-century Engels, Erikson was of such means that his family yacht *Granma*, came to be owned by Fidel Castro.

Less serendipitous perhaps but more typical was the role of queer people in the mass struggle against apartheid. In conditions where cross-racial sociality outside formalised conditions of servitude was all but outlawed, those willing to break legal restrictions on queer relations were more often to be willing to break both apartheid bans, and informal norms against race-mixing. Relationships across the juridical racial divide were outlawed along with homosexual relations, and 'cross-dressing'. So it's not surprising then that many of the 'underground' organisers of the movement to overthrow this system were LGBTQ. A kind of outlaw solidarity appeared in the face of state racism. This formed a shared basis for significant political action, even if they largely remained closeted in the context of the struggle-era

African National Congress, and then in its attendant union and social movement formations.

Simon Nkoli, writing to his covert lover from prison, where he had been detained for banned political activity with the United Democratic Front, wrote: 'I have another idea about launching a new gay association when I get out of prison – maybe a progressive association'.[30] Before Nkoli's death he achieved this dream, playing an important role in winning the liberation movement over to active defence and affirmation of LGBTQ rights. Remarkably, these efforts were formally enshrined in the nation's post-apartheid constitution. Zachie Achmat's life history similarly demonstrates this tendency to organise across social divides, with him founding and joining a series of organisations. As a student organiser and member of the Marxist Workers Tendency, Achmat was imprisoned for anti-apartheid agitation. Later, in free South Africa, he launched the Treatment Action Campaign (TAC) – pushing back against the AIDS-denialist and medically austere policies of President Thabo Mbeki.

In the USA, Leslie Feinberg among others was similarly drawn to radical organisation. This held true even as most left groups during this period directly opposed gay and trans rights. Whereas now American transgender communists are ubiquitous, New Left groups were usually sceptical to hostile, only later coming to advocate directly for the rights of working trans people.

Part of the explicit purpose of transitional organisations for Moody is to develop and cohere a minority of unionists. Such workers operate as actors who are not only militant, but political. Transitional organisations build concrete solidarity across unions and sectors. But they also necessarily operate across the divides of race, nation, gender, sexuality, and other divisions within the working class. These schisms are expressed as occupational and sectoral divides, and reinforced by chauvinist policies, attitudes, and harassment at the hands of the boss. The assumption here, critics have grumbled, is that there is a stagist logic to radicalising the working class. And particularly because it's often the case that workers in its most organised – and often most militant – sectors can also be among the more conservative sections of the class.

We can do better than viewing the working class as always-already radicalised and for-itself, and merely held back or restrained by conservative leadership. The rank-and-file strategy assumes that development of consciousness – from trade union to class, and perhaps from class consciousness to a socialist one – is the project of socialists through the process of building concrete solidarity, within overlapping layers of organisation.

With this horizon in mind, *The Rank and File Strategy* lays out why the small and shrinking sectors of unionised workers are a crucial arena for socialist intervention. This holds true both on practical and political grounds, and in ways that remain quite salient for anyone intending to commit themselves to a life of organising. We can sustain ourselves as militants without working on the basis of charitable grants or government funding. We can organise from and toward our own deeply held beliefs, rather than working primarily as a paid staffer beholden to the agenda of our employer – whether union, NGO, or government service provider. The piece is particularly sharp on the question of the necessity of workplace action in achieving even basic reforms, let alone the advancement toward or achievement of socialism. In the context of the community-heavy and particularistic 1990s that inspired it, it was a little-made and crucial point.

It must especially be pointed out these days that *The Rank and File Strategy* does not assert that the workplace is the only or the most important source of workers consciousness – in fact it explicitly denies this. It is exactly this recognition that drives its vision of 'social movement unionism'. A lengthy section of the piece roots the weakness of the USA workers movement precisely in the history of African slavery and indigenous genocide in building a working class. In this context of racialising colonial subjugation, the American working class was historically divided against itself. They were often more mobilised in an explicitly political way around its own internal divisions than against capital.

Moody's *Rank and File Strategy* saves space for a special interlude on the role and history of the union bureaucracy as both a repository of some of the most backward historical forms of worker consciousness and as a brake on militancy in moments of upsurge or even simply of militant fightback. Due to this bureaucratic tier's specific role as an engine of anti-communism, what followed was a purging of all leftists and radicals from the labour movement. The book attempts to synthesise both a non-sectarian assertion of the crucial role of socialists in potentiating rank-and-file rebellion when the conditions become ripe, and elucidates a compelling set of historical examples that underlie both the urgency of this, as well as some of the recurring obstacles to the full development of a conscious and active class-for-itself. Not only rear-guard action by the bureaucracy, anti-communism, racism, and other chauvinisms, but also sectarianism among socialists broadly committed to the strategy.

The brief sketch above shows historical organisers moving within broad class struggle formations that were initially hostile or unreceptive to queer politics, to advancing queer interests, where they worked with the aim of securing rights and material support for queer people specifically. It is only under conditions of greater organisation and working-class power that queer rights and gains could be proposed, let alone won, where they have been. But from the perspective of a much greater degree of visibility for queer people, it is worth thinking about our current moment and what stage in history we have arrived at. Following the legal affirmation of some specific rights, where now for queer struggle?

Does the need to build worker and social movement formations once again require queer and trans militants to save self-assertion and defence for another future date, as implied by anti-identitarian social democrats? Or might defence of gains in LGBT rights, and further pursuit of them, lend themselves to the kind of broad class organising that the anti-apartheid movement against legal race segregation once did?

What barriers did the closet and the danger of blackmail place on the kind of subterranean queer connectivity of the past, even as it played a crucial role in cohering a militant minority in and beyond workplace struggle? What role did the devastation of HIV/AIDS play in late twentieth-century lulls in class struggle organising? This history is harder to trace, but should concretely put to rest appeals to cheap cultural populism in the name of working-class politics. Even absent this full accounting, it's clear that queer and trans workers today provide one concrete way of reframing an analysis of the militant minority model.

Trans politics provides transitional organisations with a route away from a coalitional politics based either on identity or nominally against it. This investigation has not supported an emancipatory drive organised through bureaucratic alliances and stitch-ups. Instead, it suggests transitional forms that organise the transition to a communist horizon along class lines, rather than around them.

What can we expect from Transgender Marxism in the 2020s? There are three distinct moments we can anticipate: firstly, identification of the role of trans and queer workers in workplace struggles. Secondly, clarification and analysis of our role in existing social movement organisation and movement. And thirdly, elucidation of the potential trans and queer people may play in the development of radical organisations that connect these. Through this organisation, trans people can involve ourselves in pushing transitional forms to transformational ends.

In workplaces we have already seen organising around wages and benefits. But also resisting workplace discrimination and harassment, specifically against trans people. These struggles can be a unifying point of class action, from retail workers in megastores,[31] to teacher–student solidarity in action.[32] These workplace struggles simultaneously take up working conditions and questions of union democracy and reform.[33] In street marches and social movements, at times culminating in mass strikes, we've seen the question of transgender peoples' rights become a focus of radicalising demands. These struggles have paved the way for renewed militancy within the long-captured and staid mainstream feminist and LGBT movements, long-dominated by NGOs.[34] Trans liberation has not existed at odds with 'bread and butter' concerns, but has been mobilising as a concern for workplace organising – along with the defence of sex workers, the liberation of Palestine, and opposition to racist police repression. These concerns have never been at odds with workplace organisation.

Instead, queer and trans workers are at the forefront of workplace and social struggle. They will provide crucial social linkages between different levels of organisation: workplace, social movement and 'transitional', and socialist organisations – as we do already, and have historically. Where socialists have long imagined themselves – as the linkage between strategic locations in the working class, in broader social struggle and between differing levels of organisation with the potential to radicalise and leverage working-class power for liberation – queers have long lived. As queers radicalise in response to this urgent moment, we can draw on our history and specific positionality. We draw on our history in order that we may transcend the most aspirational or hypothetical aspects of that socialist vision. Far from being an obstacle to be overcome in the class war, trans and queer workers are and can be organised as its leading edge.

Notes

1. Pashkoff, S. (27 August 2019). There is a New Wave Of Feminism! Organising for our Future and the Planet! *International Viewpoint*, http://www.internationalviewpoint.org/spip.php?article6197.
2. 2019 saw the beginning of a month-long general strike in France, against cuts to government pensions as well as massive general strikes in Chile, India, and elsewhere.
3. Rosa Luxemburg most famously put forward this construction in her Junius Pamphlet of 1915, saying 'Bourgeois society stands at the crossroads, either transition to Socialism or regression into Barbarism', paraphrasing Engels – it is her characterisation of the dangers to humanity presented by capitalism in crisis and the duelling possibility either of descent into fascism or transcendence beyond capitalism that informs my quoting of this concept; it is well worth revisiting her analysis for some of the historical antecedents to any 'Transgender Marxism', not because she herself might have anticipated this development but because her theoretical and political approach to a living and lived in Marxist class politics is one that takes up seriously the counterintuitive revolutionary potential in the defence of besieged minorities as part of, definitional to, and necessary for a mass, working class and revolutionary movement that might practically answer the questions raised by global capitalist crisis. See Luxemburg, R. (2010). The Crisis of German Social Democracy (Junius Pamphlet). In *Socialism or Barbarism: Selected Writings*. London: Pluto Press.
4. Often this 'side' of the debate is attributed to popular 'socialist' media platforms like the *Chapo Trap House* podcast, *Red Scare* (described in *Spiked*'s interview Meet the Anti-woke Left, by Fraser Meyers) and attendant internet discussion fora, to writers in and around *Jacobin* magazine or alternately to the post-2016 Democratic Socialists of America, a once staid and fairly moribund organisation infused with tens of thousands of new members following Bernie Sanders first run at the Presidency (of the United States of America) and the election to that office of Donald Trump. I think that characterisation is too broad a sweep. *Jacobin* has published many articles including some that take up important elements of a more thoroughgoing class politics and even specific defences of trans rights. Meanwhile, as a multi-tendency organisation lacking any mechanism of line discipline, includes a range of thought on these matters that more or less reflects the range that exists on the left as a whole.
   That said, for a minority viewpoint in terms of socialist or even progressive opinion, a kind of class-first or class-reductionist politics that

is aggressively anti-trans and anti-black, pro-natalist and which enter-
tains even positions (such as the pro-life socialism of columnist Elizabeth
Bruenig) that would seem well beyond the pale of even the most milque-
toast leftism has maintained a surprising resilience despite its general
unpopularity, bolstered by the exigencies of electoral coalition-building
and majoritarianism in the context of a second Bernie Sanders campaign.
Initially represented in an editorial, *The New Communists* by Connor Kilpatrick and Adaner Usmani that kicked off *Jacobin's* 100th anniversary
issue on the Russian Revolution, an aggressive stance towards 'identity
politics' is a theme that has been repeatedly revisited. Melissa Naschek's
review of Haider, *The Identity Mistake*, was another such broadside, and
with respect to trans issues most clearly addressed in *Its Good that Joe
Rogan Endorsed Bernie. Now We have to Organize* by Michael Brooks and
Ben Burgis.

The piece, while *formally* and unequivocally defending trans rights as
a point of principle for socialists, nevertheless presents Joe Rogan's views
(namely that trans women are men) as representing in an uncomplicated way the general opinion of everyday Americans, presented as a kind
of homogenous mass, rather than as what they in fact are; a chauvinist
political position strongly held and actively advanced by an exceedingly
popular and right-populist media figure, pushed repeatedly and purposefully to millions of listeners, conflating addressing Rogan with the object
of socialist responsibility to 'meet the people where they are', engage in
debate, solidarity and ultimately transformation. In so doing, it undermines that very project, whether from cynical expediency or lack of clear
strategic thinking and Marxist analysis, it is impossible to say.

5. Socialist magazine *Jacobin's* Childhood issue (Summer 2018) included
a range of articles discussing the politics of reproduction and social
reproduction, with the notable exclusion of any taking up the classic
but notorious communist call for family abolition as part and parcel
of the revolutionary horizon beyond a capitalist political economy; all
of the contributions neatly avoided any explicitly natalist calls to positively bolster the family as such, rather they highlighted the devastating
impact of neoliberal externalization of the costs of social reproduction
on to existing families. Kilpatrick's essay *Its Okay to Have Kids* posits
this approach against a purportedly liberal tendency to succumb to
and valorise that pressure as overt anti-natalism, and even Malthusian
moralism against reproduction. In *Catalyst*, Nivedita Majumdar is much
more explicit with pro-natalist and politically heterosexual social democratic politics in a broadside review of Sophie Lewis's *Full Surrogacy
Now*, in which she incorrectly conflates Lewis's elaboration of a communist anti-work horizon that envisions biological reproduction as fully
detached from gendered labour with advocating capitalist surrogacy as a
form of prefiguration. In it, she argues that any form of 'collective' child
rearing would cause 'considerable harm', contra the family, which, she

seems to imagine, against a great deal of evidence, does not cause harm. This I think is the most considered elaboration of the most current social democratic natalism, and quite revealing in this respect.

6. With respect to race and racism, the most prominent proponents of 'anti-woke' social democracy, specifically in its anti-anti-racist vein are Adolph Reed, his student, Cedric Johnson and Walter Benn Michaels. Across several articles in *Jacobin*, *Catalyst*, and Reed's online project Nonsite.org, these authors rail against past efforts to confront racism as such, beyond the confrontation with de jure segregation represented and won by the Civil Rights Movement. Any efforts to characterise or resist *de facto* racism as such are presented as liberal deformations of a unifying class politics at best and at worst as cynical vehicles for the career advancement and collective empowerment of a slice of self-appointed black '(mis) leaders', directly counterposed to any meaningful project of class politics. For this school of thought, the slogan 'Black Lives Matter' is identical to the right-wing NGOised instantiation of that movement and one that inflames and divides the working class by trolling the (seemingly natural) racism of the white worker who still make up a slim majority of the USA working class demographically. Similarly, debates concerning reparations are seen as a misdirection counterposed to any path toward cross-racial solidarity and shared struggle.

7. The reclamation of 'workerism', usually invoked as a smear for varieties of class-reductionist politics is here, somewhat tongue in cheek, used in that same spirit of reclamation through which 'queer' and other terms of cis/heterosexist abuse have themselves been reclaimed. It is also taken up in full recognition that the 'rank and file strategy' itself, at least as elaborated by Kim Moody and discussed in this piece is already an idea that has been reduced positively and negatively to 'workerism' in its most class reductionist iterations, but not correctly or fairly so, by my account.

8. This conception of 'intellectual labour' draws on Braverman's use of the phrase in *Labor and Monopoly Capital*, as applied specifically to social reproductive labour.

9. Put another way, the idea might well be rendered through DuBois 'double consciousness', which describes Black social and psychological accommodation to whiteness as both an effect of oppression and a source of skill and insight.

10. Moody, K. (2018). *On New Terrain: How Capital Is Reshaping the Battleground of Class War*. Chicago, IL: Haymarket Books.

11. Moody, K. (2000). *The Rank and File Strategy: Building a Socialist Movement in the U.S.* London: Solidarity.

12. Moody, K. (20 April 2019). We Just Remembered How to Strike, *Jacobin*, https://www.jacobinmag.com/2019/04/strike-wave-teachers-nurses-labor-unions-kim-moody.

13. Arrighi, G. (2010). *The Long Twentieth Century: Money, Power, and the Origins of Our Times*. London and New York, NY: Verso.

14. Silver, B. J. (2013). *Forces of Labor: Workers Movements and Globalization Since 1870*. Cambridge: Cambridge University Press.
15. Moody, K. (2018). Reflections on the Rank and File Strategy. *Jacobin*, https://jacobinmag.com/2018/08/rank-and-file-strategy-update-moody.
16. For a full attempt at this, see my three-part series at Doyle Griffiths, K. (5 August 2000). The Rank and File Strategy on New Terrain, Parts 1–3, *Spectre Journal*.
17. For the general case I am using queer/trans as a broad category to describe working class LGBT people. These populations have self-described in shifting and changeable ways, but consistently have included, incorporated and often celebrated gender nonconformity, overt sexuality, and either rejected or been substantially excluded from the dominant tendencies of bourgeois LGBT politics, largely oriented toward inclusion and assimilation into existing class society, including conventional governing norms of the family and their gendered, classed, and racialised exclusions. These tendencies are by no means neatly separable, but the aim of my formulation is to resist the impulse to read back any purely 'trans' or indefinitely 'queer' identification onto individual figures, past or present, who do not neatly fit into present and fast-changing categories of identification. Inspired by Mieli's use of 'gay', my aim is to indicate open and processual resistance, rather than fixed relations of identity. And specifically to emphasise the long-standing but long overlooked significance of trans-genders to this universalising conception of gay or queer social worlds and politics. At the same time, I wish to resist the hardening of 'transgender' identities, lives and political possibility as wholly distinct from queer sexualities, rather than constituted through and by queer or gay sexuality, desire and human relationality. This goal however conflicts with the task I set for myself, because debate on the left today largely revolves around the 'trans question' marked as a culture wars hotspot within and beyond the left.
18. Haider, A. (19 November 2018). Insurgent Universality. *New Frame*, https://www.newframe.com/insurgent-universality/.
19. Newcomb, A. (16 September 2019). Google Workers to Join Amazon and Microsoft Employees on Sept. 20's Walkout for the Environment. *Fortune*. Accessed 8 September 2020, https://fortune.com/2019/09/16/global-climate-strike-protest-google-amazon-microsoft-walkout/.
20. Doyle Griffiths, K. (7 March 2018). When Women Organize, We Win: Lessons From the West Virginia Teachers' Strike. *Truthout*. Accessed 8 September 2020, https://truthout.org/articles/when-women-organize-we-win-lessons-from-the-west-virginia-teachers-strike/.
21. Haider, A. & Salar M. (27 September 2013). Workers' Inquiry: A Genealogy. *Viewpoint Magazine*, https://www.viewpointmag.com/2013/09/27/workers-inquiry-a-genealogy/.
22. Personal interview with Dave Stringer-Hughes of Out Leadership on employment sector research and LGBTQ employment, September 2016.

23. Doyle Griffiths, K. and Gleeson, J. (30 June 2015). Kinderkommunismus. *Subversion Press*, https://subversionpress.wordpress.com/2015/06/30/kinderkommunismus/.

24. Trasher, S. (27 August 2013). Bayard Rustin: the Man Homophobia Erased from History. *Buzzfeed*, https://www.buzzfeed.com/steventhrasher/walter-naegle-partner-of-the-late-bayard-rustin-talks-about.

25. From the land and other means of production.

26. Chauncey, G. (1994). *Gay New York: Gender, Urban Culture, and the Making of the Gay Male World, 1890–1940*. New York, NY: Basic Books.

27. Feinberg, L. (2014). *Stone Butch Blues: a Novel*. Syracuse, NY: Leslie Feinberg.

28. Drucker, P. (2016). *Warped: Gay Normality and Queer Anti-Capitalism*. Chicago, IL: Haymarket Books.

29. Swanson, P. (23 February 2018). The Amazing True Story of Fidel Castro's Mystery Motoryacht. *Passagemaker*, https://www.passagemaker.com/trawler-news/granma-yacht-changed-history.

30. Ndlovu, A. (10 November 2017). Gay Heroes' Fight for Freedom Was Not In Vain But The Struggle Continues. *Times Live*, https://www.timeslive.co.za/ideas/2017-10-11-gay-heroes-fight-for-freedom-was-not-in-vain-but-the-struggle-continues/.

31. Target Workers Unite!, https://targetworkersunite.com/.

32. Geanous, J. (19 February 2020). Children Stage Mass-Walkout after Teachers Were Forced to Quit for Being Gay. *Metro*, https://metro.co.uk/2020/02/19/students-walk-class-catholic-school-forced-gay-teachers-quit-12269247/.

33. Featherstone, L. (2019). How Flight Attendants Grounded Trump's Shutdown. *Jacobin*, accessed 17 September 2020, https://jacobinmag.com/2019/02/flight-attendants-union-sara-nelson-shutdown.

34. Merelli, A. (27 June 2019). There is a Radical New Alternative to the NYC Pride March That Rejects Corporate Influence. *Quartz*. Accessed 17 September 2020, https://qz.com/1651608/nyc-pride-rivaled-by-the-anti-corporate-reclaim-pride-march/.

8

The Bridge Between Gender and Organising

Farah Thompson

Being out as a Black trans woman takes a lot of wondering, thinking, and fighting. You can be well-versed in the street life of Los Angeles, know a lot about US Imperialism in the Middle East, or have studied in meticulous detail the history of the rise and fall of white feminist thought in America. But what gets through to people is a willingness to look into someone else's eyes, and face them. And that hasn't been easy for me. I can't always get people to care or to see me, no matter how nice, smart, or hardworking I am. You'd think I'd just retreat inward, and live only for myself. But I can't. Not while I'm still gendered. Not while I'm still deemed a body made for extraction and consumption. And not while even those who rhapsodise in public about how critical they are about exploitation, privately still see me as an adversary, a traitor, and perhaps a resource.

My own gender journey was harsh. I was outed by my abuser when I moved out of my old home eight years ago. I left behind my journal, which she then exposed to my immediate family and others. It contained all of my private feelings about my identity, my hopes, my dreams. And a drawing of a woman with a penis. After I left, my abuser sent me a text message saying that my 'aberrant' behaviour is the result of me being possessed by a demon that leapt out of my grandmother's VHS copy of *The Crying Game*. Then she pledged to never speak to me again. She reached out to me again almost two years later. Out of familial guilt, I told her that I have a normal girlfriend now, feeding her a lie that I am conforming to the heterosexual, patriarchal, and upwardly mobile dream she and most of my immediate family forced upon me since I was six. But on 4 July, when I finally came out to her and asked for her to call me by my name and pronouns, that was the last straw. She berated me, told me that my name is 'a fetish', and tried to get me into a hotel room using the last dollars I had. I just walked away. Afterwards she told me, 'I ain't fucking with you any more'. I haven't spoken to her since.

I will probably be dealing with people who are like my mother, in varying degrees, for the rest of my life. People asked me lots of questions about my identity throughout middle school and high school, often in mocking tones. Because of this, I found myself spending a lot of time at home, in online communities, learning about queer history through anime, furry, and gaming fandoms. I resented being assigned male and the social impositions that came with it. I approached things like *Xena: Warrior Princess*, *Sailor Moon*, fashion, and other sources of momentary release out of pure love. But I couldn't embrace these things openly, not without a heavy dose of corrective violence.

Over time my embrace of 'feminine' things and behaviour came out of spite. I treated my increasingly obvious bisexuality with the same contempt. The only people who could offer comfort were my school teachers and my late grandmother, who encouraged me to try to love myself even when I was at my worst. But self-love only goes so far in a racist society that hates you for failing to be that 'strong, handsome young man' expected of you.

In a Jehovah's Witness household, that would eventually turn to other religions and beliefs, I was expected to embody all the usual aspirations my parents had for their first-born child. I was told to take my hands off my hips, and to walk on the outside of the sidewalk when a woman is around. I was told only the most rudimentary and idealised things about love, duty, and sex. I was given no advice on how to reconcile this with vivid memories of domestic violence and divorce. I was scolded for crying after a fight. I was told that I would be a great husband with a beautiful wife and kids. Sex at a young age with an older girl was supposed to be a source of pride according to friends, and my abuser joked about me finally becoming a man because of it. This was me eating the Fruit of Knowledge early, both in regards to the 'gay shit' I was told I wasn't supposed to be interested in, and learning how women (too) can subjugate and dominate. Same with friends later in life as I shared with them my shady encounters with porn directors in my home city, a mix of mocking admiration and victim-blaming. I have been punished and mocked for my sexual experiences, some good and some bad, while being told to live up to nebulous standards of manhood.

Before I knew I was trans, I would spend a lot of time on the internet and in libraries. And, at first, I found more comfort and power in the writings of women than men. I looked through the writings of Mary Daly, bell hooks, Andrea Dworkin, Alice Walker, and others. Women whose words were meant to break down the world and provide avenues for freedom, but did so by reducing masculinity to a pathology. Or by embracing my manly self-stylisation for womanhood's empowerment. I took this example to mean that my own small way of doing good would be by trying to understand why I was miserable, and then dealing with it through forms of harsh self-discipline directed towards some possible transcendence. I would refuse to pick fights or fix my lisp, but in another way I would struggle against myself. Sometimes this feminist self-education would give me something to fill the void from years of abuse, a framework to understand why I suffered. Through it I found some solidarity with others (especially those who had read this same literature). But other times I've witnessed that knowledge be deployed as a way to make oneself out to be better than the people they're supposed to be liberating, with everyone outside the group treated like diseased, dangerous people. Victims of patriarchy, who either have to be saved or eliminated.

And as far as I understood it, a failed man like myself is still a man. I was still a probable threat. 'Self-discipline' could be demanded of me in ways that could never be reasonably imposed on those readily accepted as women. If I was nothing but a failed man with a fucked up voice, a desire for true love and ambitions to boot, then the least I could do was reduce my collateral damage. That was how I understood myself, in relation to my abuser, to my sister, and to any other woman who stood next to me – even in admiration. Maybe I would never be an outright good person, but at least I could try not to repeat the echo of male domination. I could resist the regulatory violence that has defined my past, and still serves as the focus for my neuroses.

The thing is though, that only gave me temporary comfort. I still felt chained. I still hated my body, and would spend nights interrogating myself in front of the bathroom mirror. All of my self-monitoring for signs of evil maleness did nothing to combat the misery. They offered me no new communion with the (other) women around me.

And while I was able to do some good and make friends, I still felt broken. My neurosis spilt out the longer people knew me. Simple words sent me over the edge. Over the years I've learned that I am just an echo of someone else's expectations, and that my humanity is contingent on responding to that. From being someone's ghetto fucktoy, to being considered a possible school shooter for being too introverted, to being a bigots' token they can lean on while speaking broadly about heavy concepts to whoever listened. None of that displaced the alienation I felt. Sure, I wasn't the spitting image of a domestic abuser from a TV crime drama. But I still wasn't given room to be a whole person. To be whole meant being 'dangerous' and barred out of the few 'safe spaces' I was permitted to be in.

So it is with femininity – whether innate or compulsory, a matter of what you call yourself, or the judging gaze of someone else. As I try to be free from heterosexual, masculine expectations, I want to be seen. People had seen me as a strange, awkward boy for over 20 years. And perhaps still do, given their furtive stares and fumbling of my name and pronouns when I'm in the room.

In 'boy mode' I had friends and relationships, but I was still expected to live up to the same toxic norms even with people who claimed to be against them as marginalised people themselves. Other times I did wrong and apologised to a neurotic degree, wishing that the disease I apparently had by being assigned male at birth would just melt away. A few people even questioned me on my gender, noticing how much time I spent around trans women online, and reading their literature. But I did not allow myself to be forgiven for living through all of this. After all, if I am really a girl or am really a worthwhile, innocent person, I should not have lived like this. I should not have made mistakes like a man, overshared to a friend and had them tell me how irritating I am to talk to, wore the wrong clothes, said the wrong things, used the wrong tone of voice.

Poor and Black, I had a difficult time feeling like a person, much less a woman.

To their credit, bell hooks and Alice Walker at least laid out capitalism's role in racialisation and gendered exploitation. Working through their writing and speeches, I've found portions of their struggle to be a lot more nourishing for my contemporary fight. I struggle alongside those who quote them often. Even so, I'm not sure if they would like me. bell hooks in particular has condemned the trans women subjects of *Paris is Burning*, as if people like us are problematic reifications of gendered oppression. Alice Walker's anti-Semitism seems to suggest the same reflex of hostility towards minorities, scapegoating us for society's ills. That these are the attitudes of supposed radical theorists hasn't helped my sense of isolation.

As much as people talk about the virtue of marginalised people, to this day I'm caught in waves of shame and fear. There are days where I feel that none of my marginality or struggle justifies me even waking up in the morning, just because of guilt. Sometimes I hate myself for not adhering to the performance of what a woman is supposed to be. I find myself falling short of matching an ever-shifting ideal, whether that's docile or hypercritical, because of a battle between my survival and what wider society allows.

I'm only seen as myself half of the time, the ugly and beautiful alike. One night, two older gay men kissed me all over in a favourite dive bar of mine. I'd arrived wearing makeup and told them that I am trans. One of them said to the other, 'I think she might make me switch'. A lesbian bar welcomes a friend and me, wearing makeup and a dress, but I've heard stories from other trans women who have been harassed here.

A night out is no longer the only place to find oneself. My body is plastered all over parts of the internet, because I put it there on occasion. I sometimes talk about my sex life with joy while fielding messages from guys with dicks for avatars in my inbox. A popular Tumblr blog I used to follow to learn about radical feminism equates sex with trans women to corrective rape. I interact with all of these things, only showing parts of who I am, worrying if I am overstepping my line, doing the wrong things, and being the wrong person at that moment, as if it is all a moral imperative I should've answered in advance. One guy with a miniDV camera back in Pasadena may still have a video of me accidentally saying my deadname when I was supposed to be using a pseudonym.

Working while trans aggravates the indignities of work in general. I was often misgendered while talking on the phone at my last tech job, with occasional correct guesses because of my chosen name and what my voice sounds like over a fuzzy VOIP call.

I can't decide which of these parts of me are acceptable. I can only dissect them, share them, act from them, and hope that somehow my efforts are deemed acceptable, productive, and materialist by the people I work with. Some of the things I share are 'too abstract' in some circumstances, triggering in others, and only a small part of what I provide survives the deliberate filtering of others. There's a line I have to be conscious of at all times when I speak, so I can be considered rational, civil, and materialist. Materialism is a kilogram, with social consensus as the treaty, and the force of that consensus represented in the NIST's shiny platinum-iridium cylinders. But like all measurements, it can change.

I still wrestle with all this, as I collaborate with organisers and community members today. I got here out of a broad anti-war stance. Like millions around the world, I saw the war on Iraq as an injustice, pushed to action by images of protests across the globe on the cover of the *Los Angeles Times*.

During Occupy and in my newer social circles, I saw in real time how socialist organising gave people frameworks to care for others and advance their interests in a common struggle, from people striking against student debt and crowdfunding for basic/debt payoff, to online communities where sex workers detailed encounters with police who preyed on them in the name of 'public good'. Even with their differences, by the time Black Lives Matter worked in Ferguson, multiple people gave historical and contemporary perspectives on what led up to that point. Suddenly a lot of things clicked.

The conversations with my late grandmother about the gutting of mental health care under the Reagan Administration, which affected her and a cousin who struggled with schizophrenia. My experiences with the police in Compton under Three Strikes Law, passed by the Clinton Administration. The aftermath of the 1992 LA Riots. Katrina. As marginalised as I am, without people bringing together the totalising nature of class struggle into the streets and through media, I would have been even more isolated. Without class consciousness, my work would be much more limited.

But it's still hard. Black folk have been siloed into advocating for themselves while also expected to sacrifice ourselves for others for years. These expectations have then been further divided by gender and class. I see my position as not unlike that of Sylvia Rivera and

Marsha P. Johnson, queers who have been placed in lines between labour, advocacy (for oneself and others), and marginalisation. While cis people like to parade around us, get some fashion tips and illicit pleasure from us, show support for us in the abstract, we are still treated like either dirty secrets or used to buttress their own egos. If we dare go any further than the image of clean, palatable gayness that is projected onto us, we get tossed to the kerb, and even killed.

But Blackness is often coerced, in and out of gender, in service of 'the greater good'. So separatism on trans lines serves as no more a solution for me than organising in mass parties. My Black skin is considered a threat almost everywhere I go. If I came to separatism, by what basis could I trust that other separatists have my back? Angela Davis in Reflections on the Black Women's Role in the Community of Slaves spoke of Black women being both gendered and depersonified to fulfil particular roles as 'women', but in a manner much different to white women. Their affirmation as 'women' was in service of extracting labour from them, for capital and white supremacy.

I think of how my affirmation as a Black trans woman could serve similar ends. Trans women are often placed front and centre. In the media we're represented as objects of prurient fascination, illicit transgression, or more often, vilification, and sometimes we're even invited to do the work. But that is not the same as being seen as human. We serve some purpose which is not our own, proving a point about the experiences of those who do *not* share our experiences (the more reliably human). And then, we're gone. Assuming we're even the same 'we', by that point.

Our gender divergence can't be divorced from how race has been used to divide, conquer, and harvest entire peoples in association with gender. Expressions that were once tolerated, even cherished, in some pre-colonial societies are now subject to debates about them being 'Western influences' by reactionaries in post-colonial Nigeria and elsewhere. And if we are quick, and correct, to point out the racist class contradictions in the first and second waves of Western Feminist organising and theory, how separate are we as trans women from those contradictions when we wish to organise for ourselves because of the failures and misunderstandings of people in the broader left? From where I see it, we can't be separate. As gendered subjects we carry the burdens of others, fairly or not, simply because of the nature of identity and its use for justifications of exploitation in the West and beyond. Systems that uphold some and depress others to reproduce themselves implicate all of us to varying degrees, because the very mode of reproduction we take for granted is so pervasive that even good deeds may be steeped in blood.

The only way trans women can answer all these pressures is by force, force alongside other marginalised peoples, because force is all we are allowed to be defined by. Force from dominant actors sets the limits of our subjugated life. If every step we make forms craters anyway, why retreat? If we displace space and time, and a presumed peace, just by standing around, where can we really hide? In this shifting context, poverty and pathologisation become the only stable things, and from that ethereal ground, we blossom. Through my work, I had to be more assertive and tough than I've ever been. These are things that were desired by my abuser, but are uncouth and read as predatory by the wider public. Leaning into being scary, even during moments of vulnerability, just to get a word in.

As much as some may be repulsed by me using the canvas of force to help enact positive change, there are limits to eloquent words and gentle pleas. Not all our battles can be won through deflating conflicts, clearly worded reasoning, and reconciliation. Fascists respond to power more than they do other people being right. It is the power of protesters, armed with organisational knowledge and taking collective action, which pushed Milo Yiannopoulos into bankruptcy. The gun control laws and the minimal amount of welfare US citizens get today are responses to the power of the Black Panther Party organising alongside drug users, children, mothers, and perpetually unemployed people in Watts and beyond, who mobilised people that orthodox communist parties in the US dismissed. Power is the core reason why the right is waging campaigns in Latin America, India, Australia, Canada, and elsewhere, with the coup in Bolivia and another coup in Brazil, the force of which ousted Lula and assassinated Marielle Franco in Brazil before bringing Bolsonaro to power.

Simply showing up for others is the only thing that gives even the possibility of victory. It's how I navigate my life as an artist, sex worker, and occasional employee. I fill everything in-between with self-reflection, and however much energy I have to wade through awful opinions and astroturfed popularity campaigns on social media.

In this case the very concept of Che's love for humanity is a verb, one I've had to carry with me into spaces much different to ones he probably had in mind. But largely on the same grounds of resistance to imperialism and colonialism. For Black trans women, there is always a tension between force and grace, between taking up too much space and being civil. Organising is confronting these interpersonal problems on a much wider scale. I don't know how long my comrades will stick with me, or how much of me is acceptable or good, yet I feel duty-bound to see it to the end.

I've seen the good that can be done when one steps out of oneself, carrying difference and pain with them, and working with others. I've seen people talk all of those things out almost as much as I've seen people fracture over them, seen them used as assets as much as they get derided as a waste of space. In these spaces, sometimes it falls on me to bring up the uncomfortable just to make sure everyone is on the same page, and I'm not always able to do that. I await the reprisal for speaking up like I await my abuser's words and fists. But a good group makes the discussion of the uncomfortable possible and for one to come forward, battered by alienation, yet still be able to learn and contribute. I'm happy to say that I have found that space. But it's still up to me to catch myself, in or out.

9

Encounters in Lancaster

JN Hoad

1.1: Compare the experience of walking alone down the Lancaster high street on a busy evening to a similar trip in Manchester.

1.2: One stretch of Manchester's Oxford Road is packed with bars. Usually groups of straight people, from drunken students, to hen and stag parties, take up most of the space. The crowd can feel isolating and imposing – but it's a visibly diverse city too. Many of the bars hire drag queens as DJs and hosts. This need not make the bars themselves attractive to queers. But it does make passing as a woman in this crowd more comfortable. Women with dry, deep voices, broad shoulders, heavy makeup and wigs aren't so remarkable here. The men might not be friendly, but they're not likely to look twice at a young femme among the queens.

1.3: A femme can feel lonely in Lancaster. Walking up Penny Street, you'll find groups of students, stags, hens, office workers, rugby players, in dribs and drabs amongst the cruising police cars and rough sleepers. The bars are largely on the periphery of town – Penny Street and Market Square at night are simply tiled crossroads to be hurried through, and you're less likely to be in a crowd moving together. It might be empty enough for your clicking heels to be heard down the street, but you're never quite alone. Men stop you to mumble come-ons just because you're in a dress. People will start a conversation by asking if you're getting a sex change. Once, I was walking home with a friend commonly taken to be South Asian, and a white guy approached us, his opening line: 'You're exotic'. This marks a characteristic approach to strangers. The crowds are smaller, more predictable, and it's harder to get lost. But the camouflage of the Manchester high street is absent.

It makes a difference to be just another face in the crowd, and it makes a difference who those other faces are.

1.4: What I am describing here is the way in which encounters with strangers affect a sense of being (un)gendered. A crowd can leave you feeling scrutinised and isolated, or casually adrift. It has occurred to me that there might be a queer logic of encounters which could help us understand the particular ways in which trans people, femmes, various freaks, and marginals get about in the world. Our conditions are hardly of our own choosing. Navigating social worlds of alienation, enforced heterosexuality, and class division requires laborious care.

2.1: Samuel R. Delany's *Times Square Red, Times Square Blue* considers the ways queers pass through New York City, and the spaces in which they congregate, often through brief exchanges of affection and sex. Delany uses the term *contact* to describe this mingling across classes and cultural contexts, which characterises city living. These encounters, for Delany, exist in contrast to the more hierarchical and orderly process of 'networking'.[1] Contact brings those from divergent forms of life into close quarters, for better or worse. Contact encounters, as Delany outlines them, find their scene in the porn theatres, cruising grounds, and side streets where hustlers, science fiction authors, dock workers, priests, and scholars are likely to cross paths. These encounters are likely to disturb, lead to the forging of unlikely alliances, or even liberate. A regular hustler introduces Delany to a 'lapsed Jesuit priest', who provides the young writer with a brief publishing job.[2] Visiting sex cinemas primarily frequented by gay men, he meets practising Hasidic Jews for the first time in his lifelong New York City residence. During one visit, Delany brings along a young Latina friend, a rare female visitor, and she is surprised by the unspoken norms of establishing consent which Delaney had tacitly absorbed – an underground etiquette developed through decades of semi-public, semi-anonymous sexual encounters.

2.2: Lancaster is not New York, but it has been my city of encounters. The winding, packed streets of cracked cobblestones criss-crossing the awkwardly shaped car-jammed one-way system might make this town look discordantly modernised – a less trendy Edinburgh – not the kind of place we would expect queers, anarchists, anti-fascists, or Friends of Palestine to set to work in. Still, the university brings a constant tide of young people to the rim of Morecambe Bay. Here, our curiosity about politics and our disaffection with straight campus life have led to moments that have defined my life, and my gendered relations.

3.1: Being trans requires you to develop a knack for encounters. You learn to slip away from the scowling guy approaching you from across the street; you unconsciously soften when saying 'these are my pronouns' brings a response in kind; you let strangers at the bar buy you drinks in exchange for impromptu agony aunting; you learn to be seduced while quietly demanding a respect which is more often violated. Even in a close-knit queer scene, moments of recognition in the street feel rare. You have to learn to carefully embrace them. Transition has required me, without even much thought, to develop an ethics of the encounter.

3.2: Louis Althusser gives the most widely cited Marxist account of an archetypal urban encounter: a cop shouts 'Hey you!' at a young man in the street, and at this hailing he turns his head, suddenly guilty.[3] This is the moment of *interpellation*, in which a subject is hailed only to become the name he is called, to be caught in the guilt which nabs him in the middle of the road.

3.3: Althusser returned to the scene of the encounter, expanding his concern with this chance collision into a hastily sketched metaphysics, in works written near the end of his life.[4] He begins to describe an *aleatory materialism*, derived in fragments snatched from an 'underground current' in Western philosophy. 'Aleatory' here derives from the Latin '*alea*', 'dice'. So, Althusser proposes Marxism as a theory of rolling dice.

3.4: According to Classical Greek philosopher Epicurus, in the beginning 'an infinity of atoms were falling parallel to each other in the void'.[5] At some undefinable point, one atom swerved and collided with another; the two got caught up, an entanglement of matter which clumped and congealed into the substantial, variegated world in which history can take place. For Althusser, this is the beginning of a conceptual history of the encounter that runs right through to the work of Marx and Engels.

3.5: Althusser commits to this strange and metaphysically radical thesis. He is impressed by the idea that 'the Swerve was originary, not derived'. That is to say, a break with a straight path had to occur before any measurable change, order, or reason came about in the world.[6] The atoms themselves, mere corpuscles traversing nothing, could have no worldly reality before the Swerve: *'the atoms' very existence is due to nothing but the Swerve and the encounter prior to which they led only a phantom existence'*.[7] There is nothing to distinguish between these fragments except for their direction of travel, and its random disruption. This is a certain kind of Spinozism, according to which the world is 'composed of individual bodies which are distinguished from each other merely by motion or rest, rapidity or slowness'.[8] Neither intrinsic attributes nor difference of substance makes the atoms what they are. Difference arises when they bounce off each other, like blank billiard balls. The universe, from its very origins, is but a series of encounters.

3.6: I, too, want to explore a historical materialist account of encounters, swerves, and gambles. If the world is a series of bodies in motion, how can we learn to infer their tides? If this radical Spinozist approach sees bodies and matter defined by motion, then I want to consider how bodies in labour create movement, mutually. A thick aleatory materialism would consider the lived history, felt weight, and active work each body assumes. The grind of a workday; the minutiae of makeup; sweat on the brow; each affects the flesh of bodies, in turn transforming the matrix of relations between them.

4: Transition is a roll of the dice. How a single word like 'genderqueer', a drunken confession to a friend, a friendly workshop on pronouns, can set off a chain of consequences – radicalisation, hormones, drag – cannot be accounted for in advance. But transition, like cruising, does not happen in a void. As we will see, there is a matrix of social relations which transition moves in. There is also a history to the flesh of each of our bodies that we bring with us to any social scene. A materialist approach to encounters should situate them in the fullness of the flesh and complexity of the matrix in which these interactions occur.

5.1: After a night shift, the late train back from Morecambe is packed with football fans, mostly drunk and friendly. I strike up a conversation with a twinky guy from Bradford. I'm nodding along to his enthusiasm for a 2–1 victory for the away team. I lean across the rickety luggage rack as the train passes over the Lune Bridge. Lancaster at night appears as two hills dotted with orange street lights, topped by the indigo-spotlit beacon of the Ashton Memorial, the city spilling gently over the wide dark river which flows both ways. 'View never gets old', I tell my companion, who smiles. As the train approaches my station, a friend of his comes over, stumbling. He leans close to me: 'Alright mate' (and I can take from this that he's taken me as a man, though I'm not self-conscious about that, yet). I nod and shift uncomfortably on the luggage rack, where he spots my chipped pink nail varnish. His affect changes immediately. He leans in close and winks, makes to paw at my work jacket, starts mumbling 'Hey love have I seen you around'. I seize up and quietly cross the carriage. His friend is less drunk, looks apologetically at me, and holds back his leering comrade.

5.2: To be objectified by a detail as small as chipped pink nail varnish is a fairly typical example of the unwelcome gendering that femmes often experience. This small piece of my body snagged the whole encounter, opening something casually friendly to the prospect of harassment and intimidation, colouring the moment with an unspoken history of bullying, entitlement, and vulnerability. In the worst sense, this encounter could be called 'gender affirmative' – after all, he treated me like a woman. (Put another way: I was interpellated as a trans woman, and with it cast under the inherent suspicion of the straight gaze which attends that.) But therein lies the contradiction: between safely slipping past attention and being recognised for what one is.

6.1: Transphobia, effemophobia, and other sundry sexisms are not just experiences that began since I decided to live openly as a queer trans-sexual. School bullies would pull my hair, demanding I be a boy or a girl, from the moment I began growing it out. Throughout my teen years they teased the sway in my walk, mocked my voice, threatened to castrate me. Between these formative experiences of violence and the creeps who stalk me at night in Lancaster, there is more continuity than rupture. I was queer unconsciously before I had any words to express it, and before I knew myself the more defensive straight boys at school were somehow already wise.

6.2: Transition has been a process of slowly working on myself, with and amongst others. It finds its expression in countless encounters in which I feel (un)gendered – through glances, remarks, kisses, gropes, whispers. There is more here than the motion of two particles bouncing off each other, since the bodies we are concerned with are always accruing distinct markings, habits, soft spots. Transition is that swerve away from cis-straightness, based on a gamble about what your full potential can be.[9] Embodiment philosopher Gayle Salamon calls this process *assuming a body:* both the audacious leap of faith which initiates transition, and the refashioning of one's body into something liveable and beautiful.[10]

7.1: The videogame *Pac-Man* is organised entirely around a series of encounters. In its darkened labyrinth, Pac-Man floats without limbs along the corridors, gnashing his mouth constantly. As he encounters the white pills which dot the halls, he engulfs them, and they disappear instantly. If he encounters one of the bright-eyed, colourful ghosts which criss-cross their ways towards him, he dies immediately, spinning away into nothing. Only the power-ups in each corner of the maze change this situation; these strike fear into the pursuing ghosts, turning them bright blue, so that they in turn can be chased down and eaten by the player character.

7.2: Pac-Man's relationship to the world is entirely extrinsic: he is a smooth yellow orb, with only a flapping wedge indicating a maw that faces the world. All he does is eat what is before him. He is provided with no motivation or character other than chasing or being chased, eating or being eaten. Pac-Man has no intestines: he digests nothing, nothing he consumes can satiate or change him – a phantom existence without a lively body. His sole function is to slide about the maze, turning it into an empty void, only for the entire stage to reset, beginning the cycle of encounters all over again.

7.3: I briefly take up work as an assistant for the catering service on the Lancaster University campus. It's tiring, messy, aggravating work, full of the typical grievances of temp service jobs. The managers are pedantic and bossy, fussing over our uniforms and mannerisms, and always taking care to chide us when we handle trays clumsily. Shifts last 13 hours. Legal breaks between and during these are not guaranteed. All the catering assistants share the same tired annoyance, eagerness to bitch about managers behind their back, steal food and rest where we can, and hide from being given further duties. The pay is reasonable, and I'm determined to stick at it, but after a short period I'm dropped from the rotas without a word.

7.4: One of my first shifts is at an architectural conference for potential investors in the university. During the breakfast and lunch shift in the marquee, one of the delegates showcasing a campus design service has set up a game of *Pac-Man* for attendees to play with on a large screen. As I dash about the maze of stalls, gathering plates and napkins, refilling buffet trays, and serving coffees, I can't help but think how my labour mirrors Pac-Man running endlessly about his own maze. Here I am, also trying to constantly clear away space for these hungry bourgeois speculators to network without friction.

7.5: Of course, the rules of *Pac-Man* are determined by computer programming: there's an austere limit to what the flickering inhabitants of his world can and cannot do. In dealing with begrudged temp workers, the managers could never hope to create such a strictly controlled situation. You feel the sweat on your face, your make up dripping and clotting, the smell of coffee stains which inevitably dye your shirt, the small of your back stiffening from ten hours standing up. We steal pastries from the buffet trays, learn to perch on empty coffee trolleys where there are no chairs, and linger in empty side rooms to catch a ten-minute break from our managers' attention. Our bodies have their own appetites, tiredness, and messiness, and so we adapt to the space in small inventive ways. Such acts are not necessarily liberating, joyous, or consciously political, but they express a general antagonism towards our working conditions, venting our frustration and tiredness by whatever minor, unregulated means we can.[11]

7.6: At work and on the street, in service jobs and reckless parties, the labour of holding the flesh together, making myself ready for contact, is ongoing. Transitioning is one such long project of new encounters, where pitilessly paid service work is more cumbersome and punctual. Still, an aleatory materialism which can address each scene of labour must see the body in the full flesh. Pac-Man must only consume, speeding through the void; we, human, tire, grow, and unfold along the way.

8.1: Social discipline treats othered, unremitting bodies as raw material, mere substance to be moulded, and so denies our agency and social life. Whatever your appetites, they can only be fed to you through the recognition of the state, managers, and forces of sexual control. From this view, the bodies which inhabit and make the world are featureless, except in as much as they must be disciplined, arranged, and put to useful work.

8.2: A 'materialist' analysis which sees only particles falling through the void regards individuals exactly as modern capital regards precarious workers. Deliveroo drivers darting across the city are seen by the corporation solely in terms of their trajectory, speed, and a checklist of encounters with picks-ups and deliveries. Precarious workers must be smooth and speedy – able to slip past any difficulty towards their defined goals. Bodies which are tired, clumsy, messy, grouchy, poorly dressed, queer, sticky, unionised, or which otherwise gum up the smooth functioning of the system are to be chewed up and spat out. These appetites, affects, impairments, and resistances are exactly what an atomistic account of the encounter fails to see – as they concern the distinct flesh, markings, desires, and motives of individuals and crowds.

9.1: And what of the scene?

9.2: I first stumble onto the club night drunk, but quickly turn back, too closeted yet, but pick up a badge featuring a grinning bi-gender crimethinc character.

9.3: 'Are you a fan of Queer Boots?' asks a local anarchist freedom fighter, who spots the badge pinned to my new Breton cap months later. 'Sure' – why not?

9.4: I find myself at a meeting with what I take to be mostly older lesbians. It's long and slow and pragmatic, but there's also food and jokes and brief naps; I am quiet with anticipation – how easy it is for these people to talk about being gay. How obvious it feels, here.

9.5: This begins a five-year stint as an organiser, DJ, and queen at a licentious dance night. Queer Boots feels like an ongoing party experienced in bursts, tucked ever away, impossibly large for the top room of the grotty anarchist pub which is its home. Bodily transcendence, on a budget.

9.6: 'But what *this* experience said was that there was a population – not of individual homosexuals, some of whom now and then encountered, or that those encounters could be human and fulfilling in the way – not of hundreds, not of thousands, but rather of millions of gay men, and history had, actively and already, created for us whole galleries of institutions, good and bad, to accommodate our sex'.[12]

9.7: We found this, in Lancaster: an encounter, not with one fellow queer, human and fulfilling, but with the fulfilment of being queer. An older punter whispers in my ear: 'I have always considered myself to be a transsexual' – and I am proud, yet feel no need to be astounded. We deliver Valentine's cards during the night. More than a few that I have passed on read, 'congrats on coming out'. Men who identify as 'straight' reveal themselves as restless bisexuals on the dancefloor. The one-night drag queens spend hours before arrival, sharing touch-ups in toilet mirrors with workaday femmes. Even stark naked, we can make no presumptions here about people's inclinations. These are encounters with difference which let us know that we are not alone. The straight world wants the femme drifting the streets at night to be nothing but an isolated tranny. But we are not mere isolated perverts in this glittering crucible. Rather each of us is a fractal fragment encountering countless other fragments of our myriad sexual diversity.[13]

9.8: 'From dance we learn that matter is not stupid, it is not blind, it is not mechanical, but has its rhythms, has its language, and it is self-activated and self-organising. Our bodies have reasons that we need to learn, rediscover, reinvent. We need to listen to their language as the path to our health and healing, as we need to listen to the language and rhythms of the natural world as the path to the health and healing of the earth. Since the power to be affected and to affect, to be moved and move, a capacity which is indestructible, exhausted only with death, is constitutive of the body, there is an immanent politics residing in it: the capacity to transform itself, others, and change the world'.[14]

9.9: 'Another point that people lose track of: Public sex situations are not Dionysian and uncontrolled but are rather some of the most highly socialised and conventionalised behaviour human beings can take part in'.[15]

9.10: The night itself is woven together from a half dozen bags of DIY materials which slumber most of the year in my basement. A dusty old banner, piles of zines, lacy tablecloths, tatty wigs, a hanger of 'instant drag', too many fairy lights, duct tape, a Princess Diana tea tray, a hefty though unreliable sound mixer: with these humble decorations we make the tape-chipped, black-painted venue unrecognisable. Out of them, we weave a matrix of encounters, transformative and enlightening, which make the night possible. There's a carefully drafted safer spaces policy, too – I remember the night we had to start calling ourselves a 'safe space for nudity'.

9.11: A single photo captures this ecstatic matrix of encounters. From the stage, we look down upon the dancing crowd, packing the room front to back, the shadows and awkward angle making the venue seem cavernous and labyrinthine compared to its stumpy reality under the houselights. Limbs and faces form a warm, collective blur. The long digital exposure fills the air with coils and scratches of green, red, and white laser light, bouncing and spiralling among the performers. Charged particles of glitter falling in a void, orchestrated and expressive.

9.12: It feels like a rehearsal for utopia. This frenzy of bouncing bodies may seem chaotic. But in fact it has required years of craft, coordination, and oversight. Both social bonds and ephemeral products make this scene possible – posters, friendships, recognisable faces, safer spaces policies, lighting, gestures. Someone can start grinding on me on the dancefloor, and I am into it, but without a word I can communicate 'stop, I'm not interested' – nowhere else in the world.

9.13: 'They were encounters whose most important aspect was that mutual pleasure was enhanced – an aspect that, yes, coloured all their other aspects, but that did not involve any sort of life commitment. Most were affable but brief... Beyond pleasure, these were people you had little in common with. Yet what greater field and force than pleasure can human beings share?'[16]

9.14: You can see that shared field of pleasure in the dregs left over when the house lights go up. Typically, on a busy night out, six hours of heat and exertion have coated the walls in condensed sweat, rolling down like ectoplasm as the room cools – an airborne sea of sticky intimacy.

9.15: 'This potentiality is always in the horizon and, like performance, never completely disappears, but, instead, lingers and serves as a conduit for knowing and feeling other people'.

9.16: The same freedom fighter eventually takes me along to Antifa queer self-defence classes in Manchester. I learn to punch their gloved hands in full force hundreds of times. Those repeated exertions transform my body, its capacities and habits. As much as sex, dancing, or even hormones have. Over weeks of playfighting, I come to assume my body with confidence. Time was when leering straight men on an enclosed train, or handsy strangers on the dancefloor, would reliably cause a panic attack. Now I move confidently in the dark.

9.17: The same friend asks me to accompany them to take sociological notes on a similar DIY night in Manchester. During the opening meal, another femme moves past us to sit alone in the corner of the room. 'It looks like someone needs a friend', I suggest to my companion. We move across the room, and strike up a conversation. She turns out to be an editor of this book.

10.1: Who or what draws queers together in this way? Invention and deliberation, raw luck, a controlled orbit ...?

10.2: We need a fuller account of how an encounter can constitute – or disrupt and shatter – bodies: how whole scenes, movements, cadres, riots, can have their origin and substance in the sudden, transformative appearance of strangers. In short, we need to be able to account for encounters like Mary Burns and Friedrich Engels, Marsha P. Johnson and Sylvia Rivera.

Coda – who is the aleatrix?

Who does the work of staging encounters? Contact of the kind I relish requires a careful sense of queer ecology – the diffuse agency embodied in individuals, institutions, political movements: the local geography which makes certain forms of life possible. We resist the insistence that our drives and their trajectory are strictly programmed in advance. Fear and anger, hunger and tiredness, dysphoria and effeminacy are among the bodily attributes which lead us to swerve away from the expected trajectory for our desires.

Judith Butler sketched the 'heterosexual matrix' which violently aligns assigned sex, gender identity, and sexual orientation. They remark that the word 'matrix' itself derives from the Latin for 'womb' – that 'originating and formative principle which inaugurates and informs a development of some organism or object'.[17] This matrix is not simply natural, however, state sanctions and casual brutality are always operating to make straight subjects seem coherent, assumed. The world has never been quietly empty, merely there for us to inhabit and desire. Those individuals that conform to the straight path are, then, not falling in a void, but living in a world whose substance has already been historically and violently moulded to give way to their drives, swimming with the tide. We others indeed inhabit an underground current.

Misunderstood, unproductive, roving, and promiscuous appetites tug at the matrix in which we desire. To turn down the advances of straight men at a bar, or to begin an orgy in one, creates tears big and small in this world of control. We learn to work at encounters, at every level, from paths taken in the street, to the details of our clothing and gait, dance moves, flirtations, Valentine's cards, sweat.

To intervene in these scenes of encounters, violent and liberatory, is to work as an *aleatrix* – one who rolls the dice.[18] Becoming an aleatrix means to have an ethical concern with encounters. And to practice the ethics of expecting, and savouring. To feel the heat of other bodies, the chill of rejection, to allow ourselves to be enticed towards hostile prospects. To guide bodies towards a moment of transformation. This care in rolling the dice is what empowers us to swerve away from straightforward, to merge with 'the aleatory constitution of a world'.[19]

Notes

1. Delany, S. R. (1999). *Times Square Red, Times Square Blue*. New York, NY: New York University Press, p. 125.
2. Ibid., p. 124.
3. Althusser, L. (2014). *On The Reproduction of Capitalism: Ideology and Ideological State Apparatuses*. Balibar, E. (Trans.). London: Verso.
4. Althusser, L. (2006). The Underground Current of the Materialism of the Encounter. In Matheron, F. & Corpet, O. (Eds.), Goshargian, G. M. (Trans.), *Philosophy of the Encounter: Later Writings, 1978–87*. London: Verso, pp. 163–207.
5. Ibid., p. 168.
6. Ibid., p. 169.
7. Ibid.
8. Spinoza, B. de (1969). *Ethics*. Boyle, A. (Trans.). London: Heron Books, p. 51. Spinoza's monism leads him to conclude that bodies are distinguished by relative motion, rather than difference in substance. See Axiom II of Part 2 in the *Ethics*.
9. Sara Ahmed sees queerness, migration and other deviant ways of being as swerving away from the straightening effects of heteronormativity and whiteness. See Ahmed, S. (2006). *Queer Phenomenology*. Durham: Duke University Press.
10. Gayle Salamon offers a phenomenological account of transgender experiences which declines to assume that the body is a unitary whole. Rather, Salamon draws attention to the felt sense of our flesh and bodily contours, and how dysphoria requires us to renegotiate our relation to our bodies over time. See Salamon, G. (2010). *Assuming a Body: Transgender and Rhetorics of Materiality*. New York, NY and Chichester: Columbia University Press.
11. Stefano Harney and Fred Moten point to a general antagonism in workplaces, universities, cities, plantations: this indicates how conflict and

struggle are latent in the everyday of capitalist life, in ways not perceptible to official politics. See Harney, S. & Moten, F. (2013). Politics Surrounded. In *The Undercommons: Fugitive Planning and Black Study*. Wivenhoe: Minor Compositions.

12. Delany, S. R. (1990). *The Motion of Light on Water: East Village Sex and Science Fiction Writing: 1960–1965*. London: Paladin, §34.1 (p. 267).

13. Ibid., §34.1 (p. 266).

14. Federici, S. (2016). In Praise of the Dancing Body. *Gods & Radicals*, https://godsandradicals.org/2016/08/22/in-praise-of-the-dancing-body/.

15. Delany, *Times Square*, p. 158.

16. Ibid., p. 56.

17. Butler, J. (1993). *Bodies That Matter*. New York, NY: Routledge, p. 7.

18. This designation, aleatrix, also evokes the dominatrix who guides willing subjects through kinky sexual encounters. Compare also the Dungeon Master of tabletop role-play: the lead storyteller who infers a world through a series of dice rolls. Equally, we might think of Lucy Mercer's procuratrix, 'one who manages another's affairs', as the sculptor of social reproduction. See Mercer, L. (2017). The Procuratrix Self, Simone Weil & Lonely Motherhood in Mega-City One. *New Socialist*, https://newsocialist.org.uk/the-procuratrix-self-simone-weil-lonely-motherhood-in-mega-city-one.

19. Althusser. The Underground Current, p. 169.

10

Transgender and Disabled Bodies: Between Pain and the Imaginary

Zoe Belinsky

The Phenomenology of Perception's missing chapter on labour

Work and its 'work' (or work and its object, its artefact) are the names that are given to the phenomena of pain and the imagination as they begin to move from being a self-contained loop within the body to becoming the equivalent loop now projected into the external world. It is through this movement out into the world that the extreme privacy of the occurrence (both pain and imagining are invisible to anyone outside the boundaries of the person's body) begins to be shareable, that sentience becomes social and thus acquires its distinctly human form.[1]

This chapter deals with labour as a category for phenomenology. Phenomenology is a subdiscipline of philosophy that brings experience into focus. The bounty of this style of thinking for trans communists is often not fully realised. These insights escape both those who are unfamiliar with professional philosophical writing, or jobbing philosophers who are rarely forced to consider the implications of their work for gender transgression. This is a disaster. To correct things, we must come to see trans and disabled embodiment in a new light – by considering how we put our bodies to work.

The phenomenologist Maurice Merleau-Ponty was a Marxist for much of his career, yet fails to deal with labour adequately in his published work. To correct Merleau-Ponty's limitations, I argue that what he cites as *the* foundational phenomenological experience – the 'I can' – is actually derivative of a non-foundational experience, the 'I cannot'.[2]

The 'I cannot' is the jarring, all-too-human awareness of our bodies and their limitations that we all encounter. We must come to terms with the 'I cannot', in various forms and degrees, throughout our lives. *Pain* and the *imaginary* are the central loci of the transition from the 'I cannot' to the 'I can'. It's our experience of pain – hunger, thirst, misery – that occasions the body to work, which is a function of the imaginary. We realise plans conceived in the mind in concrete form through physical labour. We imagine a future state of affairs – and by labouring, we make it so. By working, the person experiencing pain overcomes that pain. They create the means to alleviate pain in the future through the products of their labour, whatever they may be.

Which is to say that the transition to 'I can' is actually the product of conscious human labour – it is not a bare fact of life but must be created through physical toil. This labour – creating human beings in a fit condition to enter the market and exchange their labours for money wages – cannot be assumed in advance, but is the work of social reproduction. Clothing, feeding, cleaning, resting. In short, the whole ensemble of relations and actions that go into reproducing ourselves. This is the unwaged labour by which labourers arrive as readymade products on the labour market – with the 'I can' in tow. In other words, workers are expected to appear at their workplaces with *their capacities* fully intact. I contend that a process of capacitation is required before the 'I can' is achieved, that this is fundamentally a product of socially reproductive labour. *Trans* and *disabled* people, in particular, struggle with this aspect of social reproduction. While no workforce can be treated as a given, trans and disabled proletarians cope with a unique burden, an 'I cannot' which takes specialised skills to shrug away.

By honing in on the *labour* involved, and its correlates *pain* and the *imaginary*, we can gain new insights into trans and disabled labour. This will provide us with the reasons for our pronounced difficulties with both labour generally, and social reproduction in particular. In other words, we'll gain a broader and deeper picture of transgender identity and disablement as categories of capitalist exploitation. Through this, we come to understand that as trans and disabled people, our debilitating conditions of proletarian existence derive not from us alone. Instead, they arise from the economic structures that constrain us, coerce us, and in many cases kill us.

Gender transitions and disablement are not only 'facts of life', or the result of grinding social structures. They are also *experienced* processes – events in our lives we encounter directly, and cope with personally. Phenomenology is an approach to thinking which addresses this play of grander forces across our bodies. The point at which our capacities are realised, as our wills are made flesh.

To bring this into focus, let's consider several ways that labour has been considered within phenomenological literature. We can then consider some extensions that are more attuned to the distinctive difficulties of transgender and disabled lives.

(1) The phenomenological grounds of labour: organism as system

Between the musical essence of the piece such as it is indicated in the score and the music that actually resonates around the organ, such a direct relationship is established that the body of the organist and the instrument are nothing other than the place of passage of this relation ... In fact, his rehearsal gestures are gestures of consecration: they put forth affective vectors, they discover emotional sources, and they create an expressive space ...[3]

In *The Phenomenology of Perception*, Merleau-Ponty asks us to conceive of the organism as a dialectical system.[4] He draws an analogy between the human body and *performance* (for example, a musical performance). In this account, our labours are an attempt to construct a 'higher' organism out of more basic orders of causes and elements. Labour moves in this way from particular sensory elements and disconnected actions to a general labour plan, which transforms those particulars into a totality of relations springing beyond the organism itself.

It follows from the primacy of the archetype or 'plan' (*Bauplan*) that the organism evolves from the inside out, within an environment to which it is perfectly attuned. The wind is not the 'cause' of the dandelion's parachutes or the corkscrew motions of the maple key. After all, the wind has worked upon the clouds for millions of years without calling forth any organs within them: (B 115; The meaningful form that lasts is always the product of a subject and never – no matter for how long – of a planlessly worked-on object, M 151).[5]

The organism is its own efficient cause; it is not caused by its environment (*Umwelt*). Organs conform to the plan of organisms in relation to one another. As early twentieth-century biologist Jacob Johann Uexküll has it:

> The spider's web is certainly formed in a 'fly-like' manner, because the spider itself is 'fly-like' … the spider's 'fly-likeness' comes about when its body structure has adopted certain themes from the fly's melody.[6]

Importantly, the internal and systemic character of the organism accounts for the consonance of parts. Thus the fly and the spider, resembling each other, are themselves organs of a higher organism of fly-spider, which characterises their relation. Organismic conceptions of biology thus allow for a movement from the particularity of individual organs to higher levels of organisation. These levels then themselves function much like organisms, with their own particularities (organs), that they endow with special properties and rules of functioning.

Like the books in Merleau-Ponty's *Prose of the World*, labour is a 'strange expressive organism' that 'can even allow itself to be transformed and endowed with new organs'.[7] Again following Uexküll, the organism and its environments are in dialectical relationship with each other: an environment is known by being created, and it is created by being acted within.[8] As one reader has it: 'The organism as a whole works as a symphonic production of the different organ-melodies and cellular-rhythms that make it up. By adding the different chimes, rhythms, and melodies together, you get the symphony of an individual organism'.[9] The process of division of labour, similarly to this progressive differentiation of organs, constitutes labouring particulars as parts of a general whole.

This understanding is reflected in Merleau-Ponty's argument that 'the body not only flows over into a world whose schema it bears in itself but possesses this world at a distance rather than be possessed by it'.[10] A world and body are mutually constituted as a schematic dialectical system, in which the body is the particular of the general world. This system is an organism, subordinating and directing its constitutive organs subordinated and directed by the larger organism. For Merleau-Ponty: 'The significative intention gives itself a body'.[11]

This insight does not only belong to twentieth-century phenomenology, but appears in earlier theorisations of labour. As Marx puts it in *Capital: Vol. 1*:

> All combined labour on a large scale requires, more-or-less, a directing authority, in order to secure the harmonious working of the individual activities, and to perform the general functions that have their origin in the action of the combined organism, as distinguished from the action of its separate organs. A single violin player is his own conductor; an orchestra requires a separate one.[12]

This form of labour requires immersed participation. The individual human organisms and their instruments cease to be individuals, and instead become 'the place of passage of this relation' – between and among particular organs in relation to the generality of the organism.

(2) Making and its creative potential

> Once the child uses the hand as a unitary grasping tool, it also becomes a unitary touching tool. Not only do I use my fingers and my entire body as a single organ, but also, thanks to this unity of the body, the tactile perceptions obtained by one organ are immediately translated into the language of other organs.[13]

The body 'annexes natural objects' in the world, Merleau-Ponty tells us 'by diverting them from their immediate sense, constructs tools and instruments, and projects itself into the cultural objects of its milieu'.[14] It transforms those instruments into proper *organs* – which it uses to instrumentalise and transform the world. This transformation is immediately social in its form: I work alongside other human organisms; I work in coordination with the output of their labour, which I assimilate as tools of my own; I exchange the products of my labour with other products of other labour processes.

As Merleau-Ponty puts it, this exchange bridges the conceptual distinction between those around us, via analogy: 'I see other men around me putting the tools that surround me to a certain use and ... I interpret their behaviour through analogy with my own behaviour and my own inner experience, which teaches me the sense and the intention of the perceived gestures'.[15] These gestures are the material substratum of the process by which I learn to transform my world and my phenomenological horizon. After this interpretative labour, 'this created thing contains within itself the process of its own creation, the system of production and reproduction by which it comes into being, sustains and perpetuates itself'.[16]

The made-thing incorporates the human body itself. All that the body subsumes and incorporates to itself is in the service of the made-thing's imaginative gambit.

This overlap of Marxist and phenomenological insights was previously explored by Scarry:

> [Marx] throughout his writings assumes that the made world is the human being's body and that, having projected that body into the made world, men and women are themselves disembodied, spiritualized ... For Marx, material culture incorporates into itself the frailties of sentience, is the substitute recipient of the blows that would otherwise fall on that sentience ...[17]

Spiritualising herself, the human being materialises culture, fashioning it for herself as an exoskeleton, a second body that contours to her form. No human being labours in her body directly and alone, shorn of a particular time and space. It is only in the context of a political, social, cultural community that the human being labours at all.

For Marx, making is the human imaginary's function:

> A spider conducts operations that resemble those of a weaver, and a bee puts to shame many an architect in the construction of her cells. But what distinguishes the worst architect from the best of bees is this, that the architect raises his structure in imagination before he erects it in reality. At the end of every labour process, we get a result that already existed in the imagination of the labourer at its commencement.[18]

From Marx's view, capital constitutes the field of human beings' imaginative possibilities; labour, by constituting the milieu into which the human being projects her body, coordinates the terms in which making and unmaking are possible. The world becomes a function of the same making process that first instituted the world. As he puts it: 'Nature becomes one of the organs of his activity, one that he annexes to his own bodily organs, adding stature to himself in spite of the Bible'.[19] This added stature is one way for the 'inorganic body' of capital to serve as part of the organic body of living labour.

Making as a kind of 'labour, life-activity, productive life itself, appears to man merely as a means of satisfying a need – the need to maintain physical existence. Yet the productive life is the life of the species. It is life-engendering life. The whole character of a species is contained in the character of its life-activity. And free, conscious activity is man's species-character. Life itself appears only as a means to life'.[20]

Making is the reproduction of the human organism's external body: it is life-engendering life within a generative horizon.

(3) Pain and labour

[T]here is one piece of language used – in many different languages – at once as a near synonym for pain, *and* as a near synonym for created object; and that is the word 'work'. The deep ambivalence of 'work' in western civilization has often been commented upon, for it has tended to be perceived at once as pain's twin and as its opposite...it has been repeatedly placed by the side of physical suffering yet has, at the same time and almost as often, been placed in the company of pleasure, art, imagination, civilization – phenomena that in varying degrees express man's expansive possibility, the movement out into the world that is the opposite of pain's contractive potential...The more [work] realizes and transforms itself in its object, the closer it is to the imagination, to art, to culture; the more it is unable to bring forth an object or, bringing it forth, is then cut off from its object, the more it approaches the condition of pain.[21]

Pain is a central aspect of labour's creative potential: 'pain and imagining are the "framing events" within whose boundaries all other perceptual, somatic, and emotional events occur; thus, between the two extremes can be mapped the whole terrain of the human psyche'.[22] Perception is existential freedom, holding the transformative possibilities of the human organism's creative powers: '[o]rdinary perception is self-modifying because, at the very least, it alters and nullifies its own content, continually exchanging one object for another, exercising control over the direction and content of touch, hearing, seeing, smell, and taste'.[23] The imaginary is the means to *imagine the world otherwise*. A phenomenological pole extends from the sensory experience of pain to the imaginary and its transformative potentials. Pain, sitting at the base of this pole, is the organism's incapacity to transform the world through the imaginary alone. Pain is the quintessential phenomenological event. Perception 'begins to move from a self-contained loop within the body to becoming the equivalent loop now projected into the external world'.[24] Work becomes the fundamental means of extending the organism into the made-environment. The organism knows its environment by behaving within it – by constructing it. It is pain which sets this process of work in motion.

Scarry writes:

> It hurts to work. Thus, the wholly passive and acute suffering of physical pain becomes the self-regulated and modest suffering of work. Work is, then, a diminution of pain: the *aversive intensity* of pain becomes in work a *controlled discomfort*.[25]

Work begins with the incapacity of the organism to transform a situation from which she suffers; she transforms the source of pain into a source of liberation from pain by unleashing the creative potential of the human imaginary, both social and individual. The imaginary alone is impotent with respect to the things in the world. When one suffers in one's body, one's language and creative possibilities shatter – a situation one remedies through a controlled processual projection of certain relations that support the labour process and alleviation from pain. Labour is a continual passage from pain through the imagined liberation from pain into the actual liberation from pain, which is the *object of work*: food, resources, shelter, music, language, art. This reveals a central modification of the structure of perception introduced by a phenomenological consideration of labour – namely, the originary structure of consciousness itself.

'[H]unger pains, for example, are not merely interior, bodily sensations but the very substance of reality'.[26] An original moment of pain forms the prior structure of consciousness. The organism only comes to the 'I can' after transforming the world in the terms of her imaginary. So Merleau-Ponty is wrong to say that: 'Consciousness is originarily not an "I think that", but rather an "I can"'.[27] He wants to centre the *active* character of the organism in the constitution of its world. But this 'I can' with respect to the world is an *acquired capacity* that projects the organism's internal relations into the objective world in order to constitute the organism's milieu.

To *suffer* is to experience the incapacity to remove the object, which causes sensuous pain. To *work* is to remove this source of pain (hunger, thirst, cold, wound, etc.).

The organism creates her own foundation: she continually creates the being of her own species – the condition for creating the 'I can'.[28] She continually creates her capacity to create that species-being and the 'I can'. She does this through the collective labour of organisms labouring in common, in order to coordinate themselves as sensory parts in a higher organism. The labourers must move from particularity to generality in order to establish the general horizon of transformative possibilities: the inorganic body – institutions, tools of culture – that support the creative capacity of the human body.

(4) Trans and disabled bodies and the social reproduction of capitalism

The dialectic of the 'I can' and the 'I cannot' is the phenomenological horizon of the social reproduction of capitalist societies. It is the medium through which the labouring classes individually and collectively *experience* the reproduction of their existence. Here we shift from considering labour in its *positive* characteristics in the phenomenology of *making* to the question of labour in its *negative* sense: alienated labour, cut off from the object in which it invests its creative and expansive possibilities, which *contracts* human potential instead of *expanding* that potential as it ought to.

Phenomenological analysis shows us that labour has a positive, transcendental phenomenological sense, which the political economy of capitalism both obscures and systematically undermines. The labourer moving from the primordial '*I cannot*' to the epiphenomenological '*I can*' prepares herself to undertake the work of the day; the reproduction of capitalist societies is at stake in this movement. The 'I cannot'–'I can' movement thus illuminates a central precept of Marxist feminist social reproduction theory – the problem of how labour power leaps across the abyss of the labourer's suffering, her shattered phenomenological horizon, to arrive *on the market* as a readymade commodity, now prepared to be sold to the employing classes.

The labouring process brings about the 'I can', which allows the transformative making to continue. This labouring in its positive sense is everything that expands the phenomenological horizons of the human organism to be able to include newer and increasingly complex forms of mediation by the material world. This includes the reproductive labour analysed by Marxist feminists. The labourer in capitalism sells her labour power as a market commodity in exchange for a wage, but that wage doesn't directly reproduce the labourer's existence. Fundamentally *unwaged* labour outside of the sphere of production is required for the labourer to be able to return to work the next day, and for past labourers (retirees) and future labourers (children) to continue existing and receive the care they need. The worker must transform her phenomenological experience of the 'I cannot' into its opposite in order to arrive at the 'I can' through which she continues to labour for the capitalist class. The contradiction between 'I can' and 'I cannot' is the fundamental dialectic of the reproduction of the labouring class. The 'I cannot' is the primordial phenomenological experience without foundation. The hostile society in which we live constantly threatens to reduce us to this experience. Society constantly forces us to rescue ourselves from falling into the 'I cannot' which shatters our expansive capacities and renders us incapable; it constantly forces us to reinvent the 'I can' which makes this rescue possible.

The friction here is that Merleau-Ponty's 'I can' assumes an *already capacitated, able-bodied, and adult male* subject who can impose his will on the world with confidence. He does not reckon with a subject whose *in*capacities haunt the perceptual horizon through which they appraise their sense of their own bodily possibilities. This subject's incapacities need not be *merely* 'perceived', 'self-imposed', or 'internal-ised' to be real; they can also be derived from the objective material conditions in which we are situated.

In *The Right to Maim: Debility, Capacity, Disability*, Jasbir Puar introduces *debilitation* as a material force. Through debilitation, phenomenological capacities are made into incapacities, reducing the lived body to a state of 'slow death'; disability and capacity may or may not involve the 'I cannot', but in debility the 'I cannot' is primary:

> I mobilize the term 'debility' as a needed disruption (but also expose it as a collaborator) of the category of disability and as a triangulation of the ability/disability binary, noting that while some bodies may not be recognized as or identify as disabled, they may well be debil-itated ... I am arguing that the three vectors, capacity, debility, and disability, exist in a mutually reinforcing constellation, are often over-lapping or coexistent, and that debilitation is a necessary component that both exposes and sutures the non-disabled/disabled binary.[29]

In Puar's terms, *debility* is the material force undergirding represen-tations of disability and capacity. It is the *actual* phenomenological and physical reduction of certain bodies to slow death, whether they appear as 'disabled' or not.

By understanding disability's undergirding by debility, we are able to better understand disability itself. Disability is a relation of *material force* to the means of reproduction/production. Through this relation, disabled people are excluded from the circuits through which the labour force is maintained and reproduced.

The *social appearance* of disability and the state recognition that can come with it can indeed be capacitating. It might allow access to social welfare ('disability allowance') and other benefits. Those who are *not* recognised as disabled, who have no official diagnosis, or do not qualify for benefits (from the viewpoint of the state), but who still live under *debilitating* or *incapacitating* conditions are included under this rubric. As Puar puts it:

> Debilitation as a normal consequence of labouring, as an 'expected impairment', is not a flattening of disability; rather, this framing exposes the violence of what constitutes 'a normal consequence'.[30]

Such normalised violence constitutes the field of possibilities, the *milieu*, in which certain bodies find themselves located. 'Certain bodies' would include not only disabled bodies but proletarian bodies, women's bodies, transgender and queer bodies, and racialised bodies.

To conflate the 'I cannot' with disability as such would be to commit an ableist and naturalising error.[31] From this view 'disabled' bodies are assumed to be simply bodies with fewer 'natural' capacities than abled bodies. The social model of disability corrects this error by under-standing disabled people to be fully capacitated *on their own terms* – in the specificity of their own health and wellbeing. The social model holds that we are dis-abled only by the disabling conditions of society. A building without an accessibility ramp is a disabling condition: the wheelchair user is disabled not by her body, but by the material con-ditions in which she finds herself. Through having had her physical form and its capacities neglected, by all those who previously took the entrance to be fit for purpose. I depart from this 'social model' of dis-ability only insofar as I show that it is primarily *economic relations* and not ideological 'ableism' as a subjective criterion for determining the locus of disabled people's oppression.

It is our place in an exploitative world that reduces disabled people to the condition of the 'I cannot': debility/incapacity. This 'economic model' of disability is related to but not coextensive with *debility*, lets us take another view. We can speak of transgender and disabled people's debilitating conditions in the same breath, without collapsing the two groups or implying that transness is a kind of disability.

The debilitating conditions faced by both disabled and transgender people brings the 'I cannot' to continually invade our phenomenolog-ical capacities in otherwise capacitating circumstances. We struggle with reproducing ourselves as labourers in a society that deprives us of the primary means of doing so, and that is continually stripping away its own apparatus for the maintenance of proletarian survival.

Trans and disabled people, along with people of colour, the elderly, and women, bear the brunt of debilitation as states strip and undermine the social welfare programmes, economic aid agencies, healthcare, public schooling, childcare, public housing, and the like, which we depend on to survive and to reproduce our own labouring capacity. This stripping process constitutes part of a *generalised crisis of care* as capital appropriates more and more of workers' waking hours for surplus-value extraction and incorporates more and more women into the workforce, making them less available to carry out the unwaged labour of social reproduction. This crisis of care makes the reproduction of the proletariat one of contemporary capitalism's central contradictions.[32] On the one hand, the bourgeoisie needs the proletariat to continue to exist in order for the process of capital accumulation to continue; on the other hand, the bourgeoisie and its representatives in the form of the *state* are increasingly unconcerned with the reproduction of the working class, the proletariat, to the extent that they undermine the capacities of the proletariat to reproduce itself. Hence, these two exigencies, the requirement of new labour to enter the market and the parallel and opposite tendency to undermine the process of renewal of labour power, are in contradiction to one another. We simply do not have the time or resources to care for ourselves, care for our families and those around us, and then return to work with our phenomenological capacities fully intact. This is among the conditions of *debilitation* which Puar describes.

Disabled and transgender people in particular bear the force of this storm more heavily than most. In navigating ourselves through this, we must often find a differing relation to the quality and rhythms of socially reproductive labour, new ways of responding to the unique challenges that society throws up against us.

Capitalists in the formal economy cannot value disabled proletarians' labour equally to that of abled proletarians, and so cannot fully integrate disabled proletarians' labour into the labour force. Capital accumulation assumes the efficiency and productivity of a labouring subject made abstract by the form of exchange embodied in the wage. This abstract subject cannot accommodate disabled people's embodiment.

Capital demands that its workers leave their bodily needs at the door. It expects workers to grin and bear their bodily pains and needs as they clock into work. Disabled proletarians are frequently unable to do this: we bring into the workplace relationships with our bodies which we cannot set aside. And so, our labour is less valuable to capital than that of workers who can abstract their needs away. Disability is the *mode of labour relations* in which we are unable to transform ourselves into the abstract labourer that capital requires. Disabled workers' embodiment is a cost on production, just as any cisgender woman's menstruation and child-bearing capacity is. This cost is why disabled proletarians are paid less, and are fired more often. And why we struggle to find work in the first place.

Outside the sphere of production, disabled proletarians struggle with *re*production. Our relations to reproductive labour differ from those of our able-bodied peers and family in requiring more care, effort, and time in order to be able to return to work with the phenomenological 'I can' intact. Disabled people's profound need for sustained care networks in order to have the energy to care for ourselves is fundamentally a part of our relationship to the labour of reproduction. Anyone familiar with 'spoon theory'[33] will know this process of converting the 'I cannot' of being out of 'spoons' for labour into the 'I can'. This conversion *must* take place on a *daily basis* for us to be integrated into the labour force. Disability is inextricably tied to the caring labour that reproduces disabled people as labourers and enables us phenomenologically to hold onto the labouring 'I can', or the epiphenomenological *result* of prior labour in the non-formal sector, as social reproduction theory implies. Capital accumulation compels employers to create debilitating working conditions. Typical capitalist workplaces demand the impossible of disabled workers: to abstract themselves from their particular embodied condition and needs. This results in disabling conditions, and the further proliferation of debility and disability.

This understanding of disability is highly politicised: we have given a political-economic charge to disability by understanding it as fundamentally tied to labour and social reproduction. This is the economic model of disability: disability results from debilitating and disabling conditions of labour, both in and outside the workplace. This means of course that a 'disabled' landlord and a dis-abled worker cannot be understood to be 'disabled' in the same sense, without equivocation. I am more concerned with the proliferation of disablement among the proletariat due to debilitating labour conditions than with the *representation* of disability – with the material conditions undergirding disability. Disability from this view is a process, rather than an identity rubric. My terminology bears the influence of Puar's notion of 'debility' more so than her deployment of disability *qua* the representation and acknowledgement of disability in the political sphere – i.e. by the state. Disability is not an identity, nor is disabled people's oppression exclusively or even primarily 'ideological' in its source. Our abilities are shaped by those self-same capitalist relations which dominate every other aspect of our societies. To be disabled is not one identity-oppression slotted alongside our economic conditions. Disability *results directly* from our being proletarians.

Transgender proletarians' relation to social reproduction differs in originating in the home as such, rather than in the greater need for care and reproductive labour. Transgender people are frequently expelled from our homes, or subjected to the 'slow death' of lukewarm acceptance, and partial estrangement. Trans people's exclusion from the heterosexual family unit is central to our economic disempowerment and our difficulties with social reproduction. The heterosexual family is one of the central circuits of social reproduction within capitalist society. It is a place for the distribution of resources, care, and labour that daily reproduce the working class. Trans people's families, by taking these things from us, participate in alienating us from the central structures of reproductive labour – the only existing structures that can sustain us and capacitate us labourers and political subjects.

Trans people are faced daily with an atmosphere that bars us from a confident, capacitated relationship to labour. At work we may be misgendered, mistreated, or even fired for being trans. Outside of work we are faced with harassment, assault, constant misgendering, and failures of social recognition that take a strong toll on our phenomenological capacities. Reproduction of the proletariat includes the social validation from others' recognition of one's socially articulated gender. Transgender people receive even less social recognition and validation of our genders than cisgender women, whose genders are in turn validated less often than cisgender men's are due to the imposition of misogyny and patriarchy. The value attached to having a socially recognisable identity cannot be overstated – transgender people's oppression, like disability, is not merely 'ideological', but is a material force.

Both trans and disabled people thus face a series of debilitating conditions arising from the sphere of social reproduction and other economic relations. 'Debility' allows us to speak of the intersecting concerns of trans people, disabled people, women, people of colour, the elderly, children, etc., and the debilitating conditions of social reproduction that we all face. Healthcare discrimination and adequate healthcare access, for example, are concerns faced by trans and disabled people in common. Affordable healthcare institutions are one of the sites of social reproduction that are increasingly under attack by neoliberal policies and the insurance institutions and private accumulation that drive medical bills up.

This point highlights the fact not only of the economic expropriation of the working classes through their medical bills – for example, the price of insulin, a medicine that is necessary to treat diabetes, which affects one tenth of the population in the US, has tripled in price between 2002 and 2013.[34] It also indicates the alienation at the very heart of the relation to healthcare access insofar as the latter is mediated by the *wage*, or in essence *money*.

We exchange money earned through alienated labour, often performed under debilitating circumstances, for services that are intended to rehabilitate us, make us capacitated labourers again, so that we can go back to work to earn more wages to exchange for the health care that will continue to keep us alive. This requirement is doubled for disabled people, who need heightened ongoing medical attention and care. This means expenses – perhaps covered by our own waged work, perhaps by the state or its auxiliary NGOs, but increasingly often by those we have private relationships with – and upon whom we are left dependents. This is no stable basis for the development of our capacities, for us to reach the 'I can'. To have the services that keep you alive and well be mediated by the abstract medium of money, embodied in the form of the wage, is to have one's capacity to remain alive and well mediated by the *other*.

We can understand this point through Marx's *The Power of Money*, from the *Manuscripts of 1844*. Marx says of the mediating power of money: 'Money is the *procurer* between man's need and the object, between his life and his means of life. But *that which* mediates *my* life for me, also *mediates* the existence of other people for me. For me it is the *other* person'. My power to reproduce myself, whether through healthcare or simply eating the dinner I cooked with the food I bought with my wages, is mediated by the other's power to command my labour embodied in this very wage. Money has the astounding power of transforming conditions into their opposites: 'I, according to my individual characteristics, am *lame*, but money furnishes me with twenty-four feet. Therefore I am not lame'.

Here, Marx actually confirms the 'economic model of disability', insofar as he distinguishes between 'individual characteristics' and the political condition of 'lameness'. Marx plainly argues that the possessor of enough money to command the labour of others (the 'twenty-four feet') is precisely *not* lame – or disabled, in today's parlance. Personal impairment is not the limit of our relationships, indeed as Marx conceives things it does not even disqualify one from membership of an exploitative bourgeoisie.

He continues: 'Do not I, who thanks to money am capable of *all* that the human heart longs for, possess all human capacities? Does not my money, therefore, transform all my incapacities into their contrary?' This observation clearly still holds true. Money is precisely the medium of transforming the 'I cannot' into the 'I can' in capitalist society. It is the primary means by which the primordial experience of incapacity is displaced, and opened onto expansive possibilities.

> Money is the alienated *ability of mankind.* That which I am unable to do as a *man*, and of which therefore all my individual essential powers are incapable, I am able to do by means of *money*. Money thus turns each of these powers into something which in itself it is not – turns it, that is, into its *contrary*.[35]

The dialectical contradiction of the 'I can' and 'I cannot' is mediated and effected via the properties of money, namely its 'chemical' power to bind and dissolve contradictions. Marx confirms the creative thesis of the power of *making* via the medium of money in capitalist society: '[Money] converts my wishes from something in the realm of imagination, translates them from their meditated, imagined, or desired existence into their *sensuous, actual* existence – from imagination to life, from imagined being into real being. In effecting this mediation, [money] is the *truly creative* power'. So, the imaginary is now no longer an organic expression of our relation to pain. Expanding that self-contained loop into the world in an expression of pain's opposite – the imagined liberation from pain that sets the labour process in motion. Recall that the imaginary is the *productive capacity* insofar as it mediates the process of production from its inception. Now, *money* is the *'truly creative'* power'. It mediates my imagination and *'sensuous, actual* existence'. It 'converts … translates … from imagination to life, from imagined being into real being'.³⁶

I will return in closing to the phenomenological considerations that have formed the main thesis of this essay. The phenomenological 'I cannot' is a primordial structure of consciousness to which we are reduced by external constraints. Through the 'I cannot', we are surrounded by increasingly hostile environments and social, political, and economic forces that undermine our expansive capacities. Our constant struggle to reproduce ourselves in the form of the 'I can' despite these incapacitating circumstances brings debilitation, a slow death. A trans person who *cannot* be this or that kind of woman, man, or non-binary person in the world is incapacitated – just as a disabled person who *cannot* do this or that job due to lack of accommodations for their particular embodiment. Recognising this, we can work in solidarity with all those who face debilitating circumstances to (re)claim the 'I can' through which we are able to transform the world. We might expand the phenomenological horizon of the 'I can', from a mode of individual phenomenological consciousness, into a new social horizon of expansive possibilities. From this view, the phenomenological commons of positive capacities within labour appears. Latent in the pressure on us to reproduce our capacities is the prospect of reforging them in our own terms. This seizure of capacities is our means to confront and dismantle the debilitation, which undermines and constrains human potential.

Conclusion: labour and the phenomenological commons

The more deeply we go back into history, the more does the individual, and hence also the producing individual, appear as dependent, as belonging to a greater whole…Only in the eighteenth century, in 'civil society', do the various forms of social connectedness confront the individual as a mere means towards his private purposes, as external necessity … The human being is in the most literal sense a ζῷον πολιτικόν, not merely a gregarious animal, but *an animal which can individuate itself only in the midst of society.*³⁷

The civilization in which I participate exists for me with an evidentness in the tools that it adopts. When it comes to an unknown or foreign civilization, several ways of being or living can fit over the ruins or the broken instruments that I find, or the landscape that I travel across.[38]

Throughout this chapter, I have emphasised labour as a phenomenological category – in other words, as a key line of experience. Encountering the pain of labour refashions the framework from which our capacities derive. Labour expands our capacities insofar as it provides the means for transforming our incapacities into their contraries. We are coerced into work, and into otherwise unlikely forms of endurance. This is true whether we appropriate the product of our labour for ourselves – and thereby directly expand our capacities – or whether we appropriate such capacities *indirectly*, through the medium of the wage. This emphasis has in turn revealed how trans and disabled bodies bear the full weight of the force towards the incapacitating 'I cannot'. Through bearing this weight, our struggle over social reproduction is etched into the bones of trans and disabled life. Our politics begins with this struggle.

Labour is the process of fashioning tools, habits, institutions, and resources of culture. This work of fashioning will in turn support the labourer in her capacity to transform pain into its opposite, or liberation from pain. Labour is immediately social and shared. The tools and institutions of culture become the means of mapping a transforming world. They provide a self-modifying process of absorbing and transforming culture in order to support the alleviation of pain that lies at the foundation of perception. The whole of human experience is contained in the pole from the foundationless experience of pain and incapacity, through to the capacity to transform the world. We struggle restlessly to give ourselves the foundation that pain shatters. Pain and labour are our *phenomenological commons*. As suffering organisms, we attempt to transform the world while ever constrained. The dissolution of such commons under the capitalist labour relation is what Marx consistently describes as 'alienation' or 'self-estrangement'. It is through claiming these phenomenological commons that we will open revolutionary possibilities.

Notes

1. Scarry, E. (1985). *The Body in Pain: The Making and Unmaking of the World*. Oxford: Oxford University Press.

2. For Merleau-Ponty, 'I can' was opposed to Descartes' best known maxim 'I think'. Certainly, both a breakthrough and an improvement. My own opposition hopes to reveal still more, in turn.
3. Merleau-Ponty, M. (2012). *The Phenomenology of Perception.* Landes, D. A. (Trans.). New York, NY: Routledge Press.
4. Merleau-Ponty's account of the organism is rooted in prior biological theories of his time, particularly those of Jacob Johann von Uexküll. Amrine explores this heritage in The Music of Organism: Uexküll, Merleau-Ponty, Zuckerkandl, and Deleuze As Goethean Ecologists in Search of a New Paradigm, characterising the shift in register that takes place in Merleau-Ponty's thought as a special kind of causality: 'a "third way", as it were, between mechanism and vitalism, one that argued for a new kind of causality in which "consequents" are fundamentally and qualitatively different from their antecedents' (Amrine, F. (2015). The Music of Organism: Uexküll, Merleau-Ponty, Zuckerkandl, and Deleuze As Goethean Ecologists in Search of a New Paradigm. *Goethe Yearbook: Publications of the Goethe Society of North America*, 22, 48).
5. Ibid., pp. 45–72.
6. Uexküll, J. J. von (1982). Theory of Meaning. *Semiotica*, 42–41, 25–82.
7. Merleau-Ponty, M. (1973). *The Prose of the World.* Lefort, C. (Ed.), O'Neill, J. (Trans.). Evanston: Northwestern University Press.
8. Amrine, The Music of Organism, pp. 45–72.
9. Buchanan, B. (2008). *Onto-ethologies: The Animal Environments of Uexküll, Heidegger, Merleau-Ponty, and Deleuze.* Albany, NY: SUNY Press.
10. Merleau-Ponty, *The Prose of the World*, p. 67.
11. Merleau-Ponty, M. (1964). *Signs.* McCleary, R. C. (Trans.). Evanston: Northwestern University Press.
12. Marx, K. (1992). *Capital: a Critique of Political Economy.* London: Penguin.
13. Merleau-Ponty, *The Phenomenology of Perception.*
14. Ibid., p. 370.
15. Ibid., p. 364.
16. Scarry, *The Body in Pain.*
17. Ibid.
18. Marx, *Capital.*
19. Ibid., p. 189.
20. Marx, K. & Engels, F. (1987). *Economic and Philosophic Manuscripts of 1844.* Buffalo, NY: Prometheus Books, p. 76.
21. Scarry, E. (1985). *The Body in Pain.*
22. Ibid., p. 165.
23. Ibid., p. 168.
24. Ibid., p. 170.
25. Ibid., p. 171.
26. McMahon, L. (April 2015). *Vulnerability and Security: Merleau-Ponty on Personal and Political Life.* Dissertation, Villanova University, http://gradworks.umi.com/36/89/3689347.html.

27. Merleau-Ponty, *The Phenomenology of Perception*, p. 139.

28. The *Gattungswesen* or species- or *genre*-being that is characteristic of humanity.

29. Puar, J. K. (2017). *The Right to Maim: Debility, Capacity, Disability.* Durham, NC: Duke University Press, Kindle ed., p. 169.

30. Ibid., p. 186.

31. By 'naturalising' I mean reducing disablement to a 'fact of life', a simple biological reality rather than a social or economic phenomenon.

32. Fraser, N. (2017). Crisis of Care? On the Social-Reproductive Contradictions of Contemporary Capitalism. In Bhattacharya, T. (Ed.), *Social Reproduction Theory: Remapping Class, Recentering Oppression.* London: Pluto Press, pp. 21–36.

33. A model of understanding chronic illness and disability as relating to 'spoons', or units of energy for the accomplishment of tasks. Spoons are understood to be fundamentally limited in nature for 'spoonies' (people living with chronic illness and/or disability) while being relatively unlimited for people who are able-bodied, provided their needs for food and rest are sufficiently met. The point is to emphasise both the capacitating nature of spoons to accomplish tasks and their fundamentally limited nature, which can be de-capacitating when they 'run out'.

34. Hua, X., Carvalho, N., Tew, M., Huang, E. S., Herman, W. H., & Clarke P. (2016). Expenditures and Prices of Antihyperglycemic Medications in the United States: 2002–2013. *JAMA*, 315(13), 1400–1402, doi:10.1001/jama.2016.0126.

35. Marx & Engels, *Economic and Philosophic Manuscripts of 1844*.

36. Ibid.

37. Marx, K. (1957–1961 [1973]). *Grundrisse: Foundations of the Critique of Political Economy.* Nicolaus, Martin (Trans.). London: Penguin, p. 84, emphasis added.

38. Merleau-Ponty, *The Phenomenology of Perception*, p. 363.

11

A Dialogue on Deleuze
and Gender Difference

The Conspiratorial Association for the
Advancement of Cultural Degeneracy

This text is the result of a casual and spontaneous conversation between two friends. The participants in this conversation aimed to do nothing else but increase their capacity to experience life. We posited questions regarding the aporias that concern the notion of selfhood, gender dysphoria, queer identity, the body, and its many discursive prisons – and the potential for revolt. Rather than reach a final conclusion we hope to shake up all unitary regimes of truth around gender discourse. We have no wish to subsume every trans experience under a new regime of truth, but to open up the possibility for a new articulation of transhood that respects both singularity and multiplicity.

> Whatsoever increases or diminishes, helps or hinders the power of activity in our body, the idea thereof increases or diminishes, helps or hinders the power of thought in our mind.[1]

CB: I was slowly working on a Deleuzian articulation of transness that takes it beyond mere liberal identity.

An: That's a brilliant idea

CB: There is this very interesting thing, how Deleuze says true thinking only begins with the scream. That philosophy is not mere passive reflection. At the root of thought that has started to really think underlies a kind of violence.

CB: In other words, true thinking only begins in a certain affective state.

An: How so?

CB: Yes, so, my argument would be along these lines – that becoming-woman in trans always has this potential to render all these previously invisible forces visible.

CB: In the sense that this becoming is not only at the level of cognition but also viscerally felt.

CB: It affects the entire body.

CB: So there's a possible 'line of flight', a chance for deterritorialisation.

CB: What liberal identitarian rhetoric does is to reterritorialise this line of flight.

CB: Because a line of flight is always perilous and merely grabbing onto it is no guarantee of success.

CB: But the line itself nevertheless does open up.

CB: There's this moment when all of what we've been taught, the way we viewed things changes.

CB: But like there's obviously these very visceral moments that come with the realisation, right?

CB: Like the need to cry?

CB: Or even the euphoria we feel?

An: Yes, I completely agree.

CB: And it's within those moments that the grip of the present slips on us.

CB: And that's where I'm trying to locate the line of flight.

An: Outside the grip of the present?

CB: Yes, by the present I'm referring to our social reality.

CB: Since the way Empire functions is by maintaining an environment that's like a perpetual present.

An: I see.

An: In my opinion this scream is also built into how we experience dysphoria.

CB: YES, YES.

An: In the sense that

An: I consider this slightly strange, because I don't fully understand it.

CB: Or how suddenly the world feels intolerable.

An: Exactly what I meant.

An: There is a very literal alienation between the self and the skin.

An: 'The skin' is a wider thing I feel.

CB: I think the body in general is, to be honest, like Deleuze sees Spinoza's 'we do not even know what a body is capable of' to be a war cry, but to me, it seems like a very *queer* war cry.

An: In that most screams that occur through how trans women experience the world, the violence enacted upon us, the way love for us is treated, the way our self-hate is trained in, they all become important to the scream.

An: If I'm understanding what you mean by the scream correctly …

An: There is a horror in the sudden realisation that a fundamental unboundedness of the 'body', as you put it here, has been broken and bound.

CB: Absolutely.

CB: Yes, that's exactly what I mean.

CB: Affirmation preceded by destruction.

CB: That is affirmation in a Nietzschean sense.

An: I feel the cry is partly set in the language of being trapped that the liberals love, but mostly it is about said skin.

CB: That is the destruction of all established values.

An: The skin isn't just a sign of incongruity but the actual breaking and binding of the body.

CB: True. Also sexuation itself. Dysphoria is not just individual – it's experienced at an individual level, sure. But dysphoria is *produced* socially and politically by massacring the body as soon as it's born. And of course, as we know, this *massacre* is vital for the production of a productive labour force or the productive body. Vital for capitalism.

CB: By placing the body under discursive constraints that we then go on to reproduce.

An: Those constraints are like tenets of a reasoning. The entire reasoning I feel is geared towards arriving at determinism.

CB: Absolutely.

CB: Dysphoria is this radical break – a sad affect, sure. But an important one that leads to an un-becoming and simultaneously a becoming.

An: I feel a constant connect between how such constraints are created and the notion of safety. I think I told you about it once?

CB: I think you did. I think Foucault also touches on this through 'biopower', 'the medical gaze', 'pastoral power', and 'security'.

An: The liberal language is, I feel, also built from it. The discourse repeatedly seeks to declare transness 'innate' in the same way that has already been done with sexuality.

An: The goal is always the creation of the argument: 'it cannot be helped'.

CB: Absolutely. Also the sovereign individual and their 'rights' guaranteed by the state. The very idea is built into Hobbes' *Leviathan*.

An: Oh, actually I started that once.

CB: I only keep reading secondary books about it.

An: Couldn't finish.

CB: Yes, I imagine it being a painful read, lol.

An: No lol I think I may just have a reading problem.

An: It is a form of establishing safety, both of the argument, and so the state can feel safe upon hearing the argument.

CB : Right. So in the seventeenth- and eighteenth-century notions of the police state, 'health' or 'public hygiene' also fell under the purview of the 'police'.

CB: Which meant removing vagrants, sex workers, beggars, madmen from the street.

CB: Because it was believed they would 'contaminate' the air, lol.

CB: And also because population – a healthy population – was so essential to states.

An: Precisely.

CB: Because it was believed that the greater the population, the more powerful a state is.

An: I've come to realise this was also the case with doctors attempting to study trans people (even the 'good' ones who vouched for access to medical care).

An: The language is always based on 'they mean no harm'.

An: And that it is 'not something they can help'.

CB: Yes. I mean, to be honest, there is a long history of the relationship between doctors, that is to say, the modern medical establishment and the police.

An: The goal was, I believe, to convince the state to consider more people as part of the 'healthy population'.

Note

1. Spinoza, B. de (1996). *Ethics*. Curley, E. M. (Ed.). London: Penguin, p. 76.

12

Seizing the Means:
Towards a Trans Epistemology

Nathaniel Dickson

A commodity is ... a mysterious thing, simply because in it the social character of men's labour appears to them as an objective character stamped upon the product of that labour; because the relation of the producers to the sum total of their own labour is presented to them as a social relation, existing not between themselves, but between the products of their labor.[1]

Commodities are imbued with a mythical relationship to one another that bears no trace of the labour of human beings. In just the same way, gender is imagined as having an explanation that bears no trace of human effort. Our efforts, it seems, can only verify a truth that stands outside of history. Tools are not used to make gender, but to reflect it. The ultrasound and the DNA test discover what we already knew was there.

As trans people, we threaten this apparent effortlessness. If gender is *not* easily revealed by the apparition on an ultrasound screen, or the spit in a tube, but instead laboriously produced, then the certainty of the whole narrative comes into question. The work that goes into the production of gender becomes embarrassingly visible. And this labour becomes re-applied to creating the tools and interpretations necessary to describe, deny, or otherwise contain transness. What mysterious object hides within transgender people that might explain away our difference without creating too many plot holes? Revelation becomes excavation, not holy but an exhausting gymnastics of selective attention.

Since gender does clearly require work, transgender people need access to the means to produce ours. But the tools available are often both inadequate and out of reach. To use them, we must first submit our reality for inspection and garner the approval of a number of friends, partners, parents, judges, psychiatrists, clerks, nations, doctors, and more. We receive epistemological licences, with restrictions. Break the rules, lose the licence and the access that it affords.

This is nothing new. Scientific and legal discourses and practices have long been used to both justify and perpetuate oppression on the basis of race, gender, disability, and class. The construction of those discourses and their impact on how we think and relate to one another is the subject of much criticism, particularly criticism formed in response to racism and other medicalised forms of oppression.[2] As trans people, we are often required to replicate the formal conventions of a bloody medical discourse in order to access medical resources. If you want access to hormones, you must submit to diagnosis; if you want access to surgical care of any kind, you must produce a resume for your gender as a pathology necessitating intervention. Because the integrity of gender is vital to maintaining and reproducing the conditions that capitalism requires to operate, any attempt to intervene in the process of producing gender must be articulated in a way that leaves that integrity intact, or else be denied entrance.

This means sticking with an existing framework for understanding gender. There are three frameworks commonly used to describe the allegedly 'objective' reality of gender:

1. In its biological determinist form, as a characteristic of a biologically fixed feature that is defined by genitals – a binary, predetermined, and genetically verifiable fixed gender.
2. In its dualist form, as a purely social construct that is to be juxtaposed with the biologically fixed feature of sex – a social relationship between objects where the valuation is changeable but separate from its underlying, fixed biological basis.
3. In its medicalist form, as a trait that is itself biologically determined but variable from genitals – the quest for neurological evidence of difference that justifies the existence of a transgender person by identifying some fixed observable trait that simultaneously makes sense of the trans person while protecting the integrity of gender itself.

Since the biological determinist approach is the most reactionary form and by definition excludes the possibility of our existence as trans people, that one's a nonstarter. The facile version of constructivism in the second option robs my gender of its reality, and the third option reinforces a form of scientism that has been used to justify slavery, misogyny, and eugenics. In none of these will you encounter the idea that a constructed thing can itself be material, that its value might reside in the people doing the making, or that it can be transformed by the process of making itself.

And yet from the moment we begin to emerge from the closet, transness calls first for attention to the labour involved in producing 'obvious' things. Transition is estrangement. By estranging, I mean that it bears that same character that the Russian formalist Victor Shklovsky claimed as the most vital capacity of art; to add difficulty to the seeming naturalness of things, and in doing so prolong and make strange our perception of the everyday so that we might see it anew.[3] Estrangement, in other words, is a critical and contextualised attention to the experience of alienation. Transition's estrangement affects everyone involved, from cisgender people who are asked to consciously consider pronouns (and what they signify) for the first time. To trans people who are constantly negotiating how we are seen, what exactly is being seen, what connects, and what separates us from any particular category of gender.

What does it mean to want to be inside of a word, both seeking and resisting the power of other people to validate your realness? This grappling with our connection to gender does not occur in isolation, because transness is not a category that stands separate from the exigencies of race and class.[4] To move towards a trans epistemology[5] does not therefore mean to assert a special and exclusive claim to any activity or history; experiences and practices intersect, and the liberatory political potential of a trans politics that ignores those intersections is negligible. What I am suggesting is that transness draws attention to, and estranges, the social relations that produce shared oppression – while simultaneously providing an opportunity for resocialisation, and thus a potentially better model for relating to others. I am also suggesting that attention to that process of resocialisation and its implications can help make us better Marxists.

Most trans people are familiar with the difficulties of choosing a name. A trans epistemology doesn't demand fidelity to a given name, but rather to the process of naming itself. A given name should be a gift and not a catechism; kept if it's useful, and given away if it's not. To name yourself is to assert your active participation in shaping our shared reality. To claim a new name is to resist the call to submit to language as a vehicle for carrying (someone else's) objective meaning, and instead insist on meaning as a relationship, in this case made real by imagining and labouring towards a future self.

This way of thinking can also help us to conceptualise the world of difference between engaging with materialism as a science and assuming the reality of objective meaning. Take, for example, the way that a name floats through various bureaucracies, utterly detached from the process that produced it. A birth certificate speaks directly to a licence, a social security number to the ID verification systems used to secure credit reports, and an insurance card to the computer in a doctor's office. The nurse that chooses to use the incorrect name can absolve themself of any responsibility on the grounds that they are only reading out some *a priori* meaning. The objective or factual presence of a name in a computer does not describe the physical properties of anything. It implies an idealistic and ahistoric understanding of meaning as something inherent to an object, neither shaped nor changed in any way by human observation or participation. This is the cognitive foundation for many forms of oppressive social relations that masquerade as scientific practices.

Transition[6] requires intense attention to the regulations that surround the production of meaning, and their many contradictions. Through transition I make myself, in painful awareness that this is not a thing that I am supposed to do. I participate in a collective effort to fashion a language and outsmart institutions. Trans people are productive in an unruly way; social reproductive labour is spent on teaching ourselves a new gendered relationship to the world,[7] to the idea of a self and the mapping of a body. It puts the lie to so many necessary fictions, renders us deeply dangerous just for walking out the front door.

For many in the early days of transition, passing becomes an obsession. Whether passing is desirable or contemptible makes no difference – as atheism inherits theism, the measure of 'passing' is unavoidable in conversation and in thought. People will compliment, disparage, solicit, or threaten you on the basis of your ability to become nothing remarkable at all. Sometimes you yearn for it – to dissolve into the great mass of people that are arbitrarily exempted from the effort to pass, or to refuse to pass.

And yet, to think about passing is to be acutely aware of the cognitive dissonance required to simultaneously do an incredible amount of work to make a self while also submitting the enduring authenticity of that self for verification. A psychiatrist's letter in support of changing a legal document or obtaining hormones will usually specify the number of years that you have known that you are a transgender person, but it will make no mention of the number of hours you've spent researching how to convince a psychiatrist that you should get that letter. As transgender people, we must work to prove that our genders pre-exist the work we do to produce them and make them legible to others.

Transition does not vanquish that pressure to be legible and to fit within normative, profitable models of social reproduction. There is always a very tangible and sometimes life-threatening pressure to fit in, to be acknowledged as 'real' people, even if it means giving over definitional authority to those that oppress and exploit us. To be trans is in many ways to struggle at the border between liberal inclusion politics and something more defiant and promising. It is validating when the bank clerk uses the right pronouns. Participating in a nuclear family that reproduces the dominant values and beliefs of your community can serve as another justification of your realness: *we're just like you. We want the same things.*

But not all of us are willing or able to seek inclusion. There is also a potential in transition and transness more broadly to reimagine our relationships. Asserting gender anew, in our own terms, gestures to a collective political horizon beyond assimilation. Jules Gleeson calls it reassociation: 'an undoing of the aftermath of the closet that yet clings to us. This move is one of reunification: of easing us out of the over-individuation required for us to weather harsher periods'.[8] Reunification pushes back against the allure of being accepted by those that hurt us. Instead, we have a chance to see the process of socialisation anew, and often to support and be supported by others who are doing the same. As we shake off the closet, we re-parent ourselves and in the process interrogate what alienates us from ourselves and from one another.

Transition or transness does not smoothly produce Marxists. It is very common, particularly for bourgeois white trans people, to embrace the medicalist narrative – this is the most reliable way to be seen and see yourself as not rocking the boat, not disrupting the order of things, but merely as a necessary adjustment to the definition of reality. Transition in this view is a sort of pressure relief valve, allowing gender to be adjusted and then promptly ignored. This is inclusion in its most dangerous, liberal sense; submission in exchange for an exemption that betrays and abandons those who are also on the outside, but fighting for the liberation of all. As cultural contexts allowing for gender nonconformity bloom, trans people whose only point of structural awareness is their gender expression are much less likely to seek out spaces of queer social reproduction and politicisation.

For those who are otherwise vulnerable, for whom the bribes offered for collaborating with our own oppression are minimal or inaccessible, the blistering awareness of estrangement that comes with being a transgender person can encourage the same structure of thought that happens when Marx asks us to hold up a book, and consider what we are holding.

Learning, of course, is not the book that we are holding; it is what happens in the shape of that interaction, in the new maps we build of our relationships each time an experience or a new bit of knowledge overwhelms our existing mechanisms of explanation and understanding. The book itself is never enough, and the development of our human potential is limited when learning takes the shape of an endless series of multiple-choice questions. A person must believe that they are capable of knowledge production, and that belief is fostered in the experience of producing knowledge with others. There are no revelations waiting in the comments section. The shape of my life has taken place mostly in basements and spare rooms – I credit this as the scaffolding for much of my politics. At each step I have been reminded of the violent injunction that we avoid disrupting the order of things in their sacred appearance. There is a high price for making what is widely believed to be obvious look absurd.

And yet, a truly liberatory trans epistemology must do just that. It has to include reworking our relationship not only to our individual histories, but to our collective ones. I didn't write this chapter alone. It is also written by the questions that readers have asked me, by the work done to answer my anxious 3am emails, by the conversations I hear and the ones I do not. To say something productive that acknowledges the reality of other people means rewriting and reworking my relationship not only to an individual narrative, but to the narratives of others in all their intersecting complexity, and to the process of speaking and listening itself.

Alienation interferes with learning, draws our attention away from these relationships, and pins them instead on the mechanics of decontextualised things. The reduction of the world to objects animated by some intrinsic value, where we can only observe and interpret the ways that people peck at the buffet of options their lives afford, pervades everything. I find it in my composition classes, where I struggle to teach many of my students to move beyond viewing race as a biological difference over which we apply social values. Race is widely seen as 'real', while racism is 'constructed'. The problems with racism are clear, but beneath that artifice they believe there exists a pure and neutral world of biological fact.[9]

There is a mountain of cognitive dissonance between most Americans and the reality of constructed things. I don't know how to contend with people who are always questing after a proof that can be washed clean of human interference, despite a historical record fraught with the disastrous results of ignoring the relationship between the observer and what they see. Nor have I had or seen much success in convincing class reductionists that difference is not an additive ingredient that should be swept aside in service of a purely class-based approach to organising and analysing, that class is instantiated on the grounds of those very differences, which make up its living reality. And I cannot, after two years of trying, convince my father to say my name.

Often I think these conversations fail when there is no place for the shape that our thoughts take to intersect. To make meaning, people rely on cognitive processes to integrate the various aspects of our sensations, emotions, values, and beliefs. And yet children are tested alone, graded alone, asked to write alone, given a format to follow and expected to create a passable pastiche of critical engagement. We are somehow then surprised when many young adults find the idea of research very difficult. If every interaction is a sanitised and removed act of evaluating and choosing between predetermined objective meanings, then they are not interactions at all, because they leave no

SEIZING THE MEANS: TOWARDS A TRANS EPISTEMOLOGY

room for us to find one another, to be moved by other people. And we need each other now more than ever, even as we stand at a moment in history where our days, thoughts, and labours must endure the ever-looming presence of apocalyptic questions: fascism or communism? Capitalism or life on earth? We must decide between eulogising the world or transforming it.

We must reintegrate learning with the activity of our daily lives if we are to have a future. Scientific research is chained to whoever pays the bills and hopes to turn a profit. Most academic writing is doubly inaccessible – the language difficult, the work itself buried behind paywalls. We must ask permission to use medicine, and it is assumed that we will make bad choices without paternalistic management. The tools we use to learn and the tools we use to act are not separate categories. Our dispossession in both regards is everywhere visible, in the death of diabetics who cannot obtain insulin,[10] the black market in hormones for gender transition,[11] the use of fish antibiotics for the treatment of human infections,[12] the price of state-sanctioned medications, the racist devaluation of language systems, the gap in preventative and diagnostic care access by race, income, and gender, and the general attitude of suspicion and resentment levelled at scholars, researchers, teachers, and medical providers who are by virtue of this divide positioned as gatekeepers between those inside and outside of their respective institutions. Disintegrated knowledge production prevents solidarity and collaborative understanding and response. Reintegrating learning and activity is essential to nurturing our capacity for collective learning, thinking, and political action. The reorganisation of a life and a self in the process of gender transition is one model for this work.

The process of transition also involves a reintegration – remapping the body, language, the way I occupy a space, and what it might signify. My own life currently forms a triangle centred on three severed places[13] – each about 20 miles apart and each with its own material demands – a university campus and two houses. The first two have been mostly closets, in the sense that they require a degree of compartmentalisation and self-division that is harmful or counterproductive to growth. The campus is a series of looming concrete buildings strung together around walkways that become wind tunnels whenever October rolls around. There is little greenery and no large gathering spaces at all. I teach there for a little over minimum wage, and have amassed over

$300,000 in student loan debt, because I am poor and because it seems the more integrated and meaningful my individual and social relationships grow, the more my wages and employability shrink.

The first house is, like the university campus, suburban – a small brick cape cod with a creek behind it. A few miles behind the creek lies a high school where transgender children still have to pee in the nurse's office, despite New York State legislation. For the past four years I have rented this house from a former fiancée and his parents, sometimes for money, sometimes for work. Often I cannot pay at all. This is where I send my also transgender teenager to school. It is a space governed by the exigencies and violence of custody agreements and school districts, and the demand by one heterosexual conservative man that his ex and his estranged child live in a world of heterosexual conservatives for so long as his parental mandate holds.

The second house is a project I helped to found nearly two years ago, around the same time that I began my gender transition – the Queer Communist Community Center, or Q3C. It's a large warm building in a state of bad repair, brimming with transgender communists, all of us some combination of poor, disabled, or mentally ill. Much of our time is spent attempting to build a language and way of relating to one another. These efforts enable us to survive and to think and build things together, while recovering from the traumas transgender people accumulate over a lifetime. In these ways we can begin to reverse the patterns this trauma produces in social behaviour. This is the space where I intend to more fully integrate my life and the life of my child at the end of the next school year.

When I leave the little cape cod I will be freer, but I will not be free; inhabiting this third and final space will not obliterate my closet, because it will not in itself obliterate capitalism and with it the mandate to submit to various institutions and pass as a person who shares the values and beliefs at the base of those institutions. I will still need to describe myself to doctors.[14] I will still need to engage in wage labour as best as I am able. I will still need to code-switch into various forms of more legible masculinity to minimise violence as I move through the world. I will still have to balance the precarities of mental health against the necessities gained by these engagements. But there will be fewer presentations to manage, they will overlap more closely, and my overall reproductive labour demands will be reduced in ways that are presently difficult to imagine.

People are made like life and language and planets, in the interactions and intimacies of difference and in the creativity and desire that difference produces.[15] I am shaped by the specificity of my experiences and the ways I have learned to interpret and describe them. I might not think these thoughts at all were it not for the parts of me that are indigestible and create social friction in the spaces of normative social reproduction. This last point is important, because there is a tendency on the left towards erasing difference or finding identity divisive or extraneous to class analysis. But if it is by this very interaction with specific material differences that we learn and form relationships and types of cognition, then the dismissal of its role and worth is catastrophic.

In May 2019, I watched a thesis presentation by my friend Sean Feiner. Their presentation interwove a history of the communities that produced house music and the way that community was shaped by the strategies it used to evade police and racist violence, observations about the reappropriation of industrialised spaces for the purposes of dancing, the way the references to work ('werk', 'work it', 'work your body', and 'make it work') permeate the music, the sense of collectivity that develops, and the way that dance as a kind of labour that 'makes us worse workers come Monday', among other things. I told them how much I enjoyed the presentation, and that I was sorry I hadn't seen or engaged with their work before. They told me, 'but you have – you've been with me at the rave'.[16]

I pause as I write, feel doubtful about the worth of anything that is not an analysis of someone or something else. Sean's ability to integrate their life and scholarship seemed an extraordinary thing. We do not adequately value or celebrate the lives of marginalised and oppressed people, or if we do they should be someone else's lives, and someone else's studies. And yet it is the processes that produce marginalisation, oppression, and exploitation that we wish to understand and transform. That transformation is not simply the production of a text or an analysis, but the living process of learning better ways of thinking and sharing the world.

This learning is not possible if we dissociate our living, working, feeling, and thinking into discrete categories. Our experiences are associative – that is, they are determined by relationships, by the inter-connectedness of environments and the people that inhabit them, mutually constituted and ever-changing. Attention to our own lives with the intent to grow our understanding and our critical and trans-formative capacities is valuable. We inhabit our own studies – they are for us, and they should belong to us all. In this interaction I am the writer, and you are the reader. We are also many other things, includ-ing time-travellers – my now and your now do not overlap. I am a transgender person of nebulous gender who identifies as a Marxist, and writes messy associative bits of theory. And you are presumably someone who reads things written by transgender Marxists. We are also both engaged in an activity that requires tools. I'm engaging these tools to justify and then make a somewhat complicated map of our new relationship, and to apply my experience to questions of teaching and learning, knowledge production, and materialism.

The object that you hold in your hand – a phone, laptop, e-reader, book – is populated with keystrokes registered and translated into binary and electronically parachuted from my lap to a server farm before they are translated again into whatever form you are reading now. The largest server farm in the world today is located at a tech campus called *The Citadel* in Tahoe Reno, Nevada. The recently completed and aptly-named Citadel is designed to house 7 million frigidly air-conditioned square feet of hot, busy machines.[17] In 2016, Berkeley lab estimated that server farms collectively utilise 70 billion kilowatt-hours of electricity annually. They generally employ fewer than 100 workers apiece, mostly engineers.[18]

Some of that server farm space is used to inefficiently house tran-scriptions of some of the most efficiently stored data in the world – DNA. A single gram of DNA can hold 215 million gigabytes of data.[19] It's a significantly more spacious medium for storage than, say, the smallish, encapsulated server farms that Microsoft intends to store on the bottom of the ocean.[20] More than 26 million people globally[21] have spat in a little tube, closed the cap, put the tube in a cardboard box, and left it in the mailbox where it is picked up and carried to a laboratory that retrieves that data and provides an admixture of useful medical information and a sort of ancestral horoscope of badly con-textualised positivist interpretations of social realities like race and mental illness. The tiniest archive housed in the largest.

I spit in a tube and mail it off. Among the reams of useless data that returns, from the revelation that I am red-haired and likely to sunburn to the intimation that I am marginally more likely to develop schizophrenia, I discover that I am 15 times as likely as the general population to develop pulmonary fibrosis and suffocate to death somewhere between the age of 50 and 70. A quick internet search tells me that there might be some edited genetic material piggybacked on a virus that they can inject into my body in another decade or so to turn the bad gene off. It also tells me that the most recent and astonishing gene therapy is the one produced for spinal muscular atrophy, a rare disease that is almost always fatal in early childhood. The price tag for the therapy is $2.1 million as a one-time treatment that, presumably but not definitely, lasts a lifetime and stops the unruly gene in its tracks.[22]

The drug manufacturer is offering payment plans to the insurance companies, with a money-back guarantee if the child dies anyway.

The test also informs me that I am female, though my insurance card says male, my name is Nathaniel, my pronouns are they/them/he/him, and I have spent some 100 hours on the process of convincing a variety of institutions to acknowledge my nebulous gender. What it is really describing is my karyotype – all those notorious X's and Y's – the combination of chromosomes that generally produces reproductive organs in all their variety.

Karyotypes are like books that nobody wants to read. Despite the overwhelming insistence on a biological basis for sex, the very word 'karyotype' isn't widely known and never enters the clinical discussion. The appeal to the materiality of gender is always a second-order appeal; we are meant to have a mystified relationship to material things, to understand spectral things as objective, and objectivity as a static thing removed from the activity of people. The screen re-presents the world, and the presumed materiality of the information provided there has substance only as evidence.

The absence of any visible trace of labour increases the authority of the test results. Nobody asks, whose test? What determines its content?

My gender and my identity are not constructed at the level of karyotype. They were constructed as the world entered me as language, food, chemicals, and other matter and organisms that interacted with the narrative possibilities that living things contain, from genetic material that copies itself generation after generation to the words we use to describe ourselves and others. They were constructed again after I had chest masculinisation surgery, when the silhouette of a doctor called Boris watched me gasp for breath, offered me a beer, and yanked at my bandages until I whimpered and cried out (not in that order). And again when a dear friend and trans woman came home from the ER traumatised because a doctor had pried open her infected jaw, after telling her to 'man up', rather than providing pain medicine. They were constructed by the insurance company that called to tell me I should change my gender to female. They could not figure out how to bill me for OBGYN care otherwise.

They are also constructed by my home, by sex, by work, by what I read, by whom I know – by my class identity, and all it entails. By the material love and labour of other revolutionary transgender and queer people. By the words that I am called tenderly and destructively. By the limits and potentialities of my body and the sensations these produce. By my roles in the lives of others, including parenthood. In other words, my material relation to the world brings me into being, sets me about my activities, and shapes the way that I think. Because the means of production are controlled by those that wish to exploit me, their design reflects the cognitive forms of exploitation. They will for so long as capitalism exists.

We are working in a world that is purpose built to exhaust and diminish our capacities to interpret, create, and transform. The process of transforming our world requires so many kinds of labour. How can we do that labour mindfully and in solidarity with others if we cannot imagine a world that could be otherwise? The process of imagining and realising a radically new relationship to oneself and to others is an integral part of gender transition. A liberatory trans epistemology is one that can help us to map the cognitive and relational possibilities that emerge as oppositional communities and individuals come into being, and as we transform through our relationships with one another and our strategies for survival.

Notes

1. Marx, K. & Engels, F. (1990). *Capital Volume I*. Fowkes, B. (Trans.). London, Penguin in association with *New Left Review*.
2. The law and scientific discourses have worked together to codify and construct oppressive definitions and practices. In the 1800's 'racial science'

relied on characteristics like hair texture to arbitrarily assign racial status to people brought before the court, as in the case of Abby Guy: Zackodnik, T. (2001). Fixing the Color Line: The Mulatto, Southern Courts, and Racial Identity. *American Quarterly*, 53(3), 420–451.

3. Shklovsky, V. (1917). *Art as Technique*. Archived December 2009 at the Wayback Machine.

4. Kai Green argues that 'the place of the demand' for inclusion and also reconstitution of the terms of gender is situated at the interstices of transness and blackness; 'I think Black feminists were asking for a reconstitution of the terms and the terrain (of gender), not simply for an assigned role or designated place on the already existing lands'. Particularly important is his description of the longstanding experiences of gender exclusion endured by cis Black women, who necessarily are always also negotiating an estranged experience of gender. See Green, K. M. & Bey, M. (2017). Where Black Feminist Thought and Trans* Feminism Meet: A Conversation. *Souls*, 19(4), 438–454.

5. 'Trans epistemology' and 'liberatory trans epistemology' are used somewhat interchangeably here. Not for any high theoretical reasons; I'm just waffling. It's totally possible to defeat the estranging and radicalising potential of transition (see the next endnote) with liberalism and use medicalist arguments to tidy up the cognitive dissonance. Happens all the time. Does that constitute an epistemically radical difference? Probably not. I don't think 'trans epistemology' necessarily needs a qualifier to reach for something beyond that … but sometimes I qualify it anyway.

6. I am a person for whom hormonal transition was important, and I reference medical access at many points throughout this chapter, so I want to affirm that 'transition' is used here in its broadest sense. I have no desire to replicate the WPATH and give either medicalising or lengthy legalistic definitions of what 'transition' means. If it feels to a trans person like a necessary activity in the process of becoming more fully themselves, it's transition.

7. Zazanis, N., Chapter 1 in this volume.

8. Gleeson, J. & Dickson, N.(2019). The Future of Trans Politics. *Verso Book Blog*. Accessed January 2020, https://www.versobooks.com/blogs/4269-the-future-of-trans-politics/.

9. Roberts, D. (2011). *Fatal Invention: How Science, Politics, and Big Business Re-Create Race in the Twenty-First Century*. New York, NY: New Press.

10. Cefalu, W. T. et al. (2018). Insulin Access and Affordability Working Group: Conclusions and Recommendations. *Diabetes Care*, 41(6), 1299–1311.

11. Metastasio, A., Negri, A., Martinotti, G., & Corazza, O. (2018). Transitioning Bodies. The Case of Self-Prescribing Sexual Hormones in Gender Affirmation in Individuals Attending Psychiatric Services. *Brain Sciences*, 8(5), 88, doi:10.3390/brainsci8050088.

12. Howes-Mischel, R. (2017). Stocking up on Fish Mox: a Systematic Analysis of Cultural Narratives about Self-medicating in Online Forums. *AIMS Public Health*, 4(5), 430–445, doi: 10.3934/publichealth.2017.5.430.

13. The three are now only one, as I finish my final revision of this chapter in the midst of the coronavirus, in a half-packed and mostly empty house.

14. Jules Gleeson describes many of the complexities of navigating legal, institutional, and social regulations – particularly in regards to trans women's experiences – in the introduction to Transition and Abolition. See Gleeson, J. (2017). Transition and Abolition: Notes on Marxism and Trans Politics. *Viewpoint Magazine*. Accessed November 2019, https://www.viewpointmag.com/2017/07/19/transition-and-abolition-notes-on-marxism-and-trans-politics/.

15. My thinking on difference here is drawing on Lorde; 'Advocating the mere tolerance of difference between women is the grossest reformism. It is a total denial of the creative function of difference in our lives. Difference must be not merely tolerated, but seen as a fund of necessary polarities between which our creativity can spark like a dialectic'. Lorde, A. (1984). The Master's Tools Will Never Dismantle the Master's House. In *Sister Outsider: Essays and Speeches*. Berkeley, CA: Crossing Press.

16. Feiner, S. (2019). A Rave at The End of World: The Politics of Queer Hauntology and Psychedelic Chronomancy. Accessed January 2020, https://ubir.buffalo.edu/xmlui/handle/10477/79988.

17. Hidalgo, J. (2017). Switch: Largest Data Center Building in World Opens Near Reno. *Reno Gazette Journal*. Accessed January 2020, https://www.rgj.com/story/money/business/2017/02/15/switch-largest-data-center-building-world-opens-near-reno/97925188/.

18. Shehabi, A., Smith, S.J., Horner, N., Azevedo, I., Brown, R., Koomey, J., Masanet, E., Sartor, D., Herrlin, M., & Lintner, W. (2016). *United States Data Center Energy Usage Report*. Berkeley, CA: Lawrence Berkeley National Laboratory, LBNL-1005775.

19. Service, R. (2017). DNA Could Store All of the World's Data in One Room. *Science Magazine*. Accessed January 2020, https://www.sciencemag.org/news/2017/03/dna-could-store-all-worlds-data-one-room.

20. Rutherford, S. (2018). Microsoft's Newest Data Center is a Giant Metal Can at the Bottom of the Sea. *Gizmodo*. Accessed December 2019, https://gizmodo.com/microsofts-newest-data-center-is-a-giant-metal-can-at-t-1826606291.

21. Regalado, A. (2019). More Than 26 Million People Have Taken An At-Home Ancestry Test. *MIT Technology Review*. Accessed December 2019, https://www.technologyreview.com/s/612880/more-than-26-million-people-have-taken-an-at-home-ancestry-test/.

22. Mahajan R. (2019). Onasemnogene Abeparvovec for Spinal Muscular Atrophy: The Costlier Drug Ever. *International Journal of Applied & Basic Medical Research*, 9(3), 127–128, accessed January 2020, doi: 10.4103/ijabmr.IJABMR_190_19.

13

'Why Are We Like This?': The Primacy of Transsexuality

Xandra Metcalfe

This chapter is a response to a trans friend, who some years ago asked me: 'Why are we like this? Why are we transgender?' Rather than immediately go searching for an answer to 'know thyself', it is important to pause and think about the implications of such a question. Who is asking? Why is the transsexual or transgender subject to be explained, rather than the cissexual or cisgender one? Why must we answer? Why did a trans woman ask another trans woman this question? Is the question different for non-binary, transmasc, and other transitioners? Here is an attempt to formulate a preliminary response to this most complex of questions.

The question usually comes from a curious cisgendered individual, which might be internalised by a transgender subject. Both forms of the question assume 'transness' is something that ought to be explained: that it is not only perplexing but demands a (quick) answer. Trans people are oppressed, so why live against the grain? With so many forces and several lively political movements militating *against* transition, why hold firm to this particular lived commitment? Why not just be cis? Is the impulse to transition an urge (something that must be done, a demand from the outside), or a desire (something the subject actively wants, and identifies with)?

That this question is asked at all is because the transgender subject is seen as an aberration from the cissexual subject, a swerve from an otherwise straight line. But perhaps we can teach ourselves to think in the opposite direction. This chapter views cisgenderism from the perspective of the transgender subject.

We will call the presupposition that trans is the aberration of cis normality *transnegativity*. It implies that being cis is *preferable* to being trans, that transness is 'lacking something'. A lack that the self-identical cis subject is supposed to possess.

So why do we exist then? We cannot ever presume there is one royal road to transition, a proper transitioning to the exclusion of all others. This is an unashamedly truscute viewpoint,[1] because our intention is to explain this 'aberrations of aberrations', the so-called 'false' transgender, not the 'true' transsexual. I will call the fact that there is no single road or essential way to be transgender the *overdetermination hypothesis*. What matters isn't whether you've felt this way all your life, or if it was a recent urge, nor whether you think, 'I am already a man', as opposed to, 'I want to be a man'. All that matters is a *rejection* of your assigned gender at birth, and more broadly your gendered facticity.

So if we are to take a *transpositive* viewpoint – theorising from the position of an assumed (and quite excarnate) transgender subject – what can we learn? The first thing to do is ask: why are *they* like *that*?

Setting aside the question of why *we* are as we are, at least for a moment, I will speculate as far in the other direction as possible. Why are there so many *cissexual* people?

The reproductive aberrations

It's nothing new that transgender people and transsexuality are considered – wrongly – as an aberration that needs to be explained in contradistinction to the self-evident naturalness of cisgender people. Transfeminism has often endeavoured to make transsexuality *as normal as* cissexuality. Here I will go further, arguing, from the Freudian account of polymorphous perversity, psychical hermaphroditism, and bisexuality that a more rigorously trans feminist account would begin from the observation that it is *cissexuality* itself that needs to be explained.

If we define cissexuality as a process of identification that actively reproduces itself in order to prevent a subject falling into transsexuality, then cissexuality begins to appear as in fact *less* 'natural' than transsexuality, as its aberration. Consider the cishetereosexual identification that is required for the Oedipal configuration which reproduces (mostly) heterosexual cissexuality: for Freud, it is *this* which is the unsolved, and perhaps unsolvable, 'problem' for psychoanalysis.[2] In other words, the real event here is not that trans people exist, and keep existing, but rather the surprising fact that we are so few in number.

Transsexuals do not constantly prevent themselves from 'falling into' cissexuality, contra the paranoiac claims of some transphobic individuals fearing transition as the ultimate countercultural 'fad' – a phobia voiced by those scaremongering against 'social contagion' or the 'transgender trend'. There is, in truth, nothing so novel about transsexuality. The trans social pathogen has been there from the start.

Rather, transsexuals likewise initially attempt to prevent their own falling away from cissexuality. We do this not thanks to cissexuality being truly 'natural', but primarily because we face so much social antagonism. In my experience, the realisation of my transsexuality was not merely the original joy of self-understanding, but also the original horror and anxiety at the upcoming difficulty I would face: 'Oh shit … I'm trans'. Cissexuality should be regarded in this instance as the true social pathogen, whereas *transsexuality is ontologically primary*. We could say the 'trans' signifies 'transcendental', a condition for the possibility of (cis)genderism.

Insofar as trans culture accumulates across time, it is through us each teaching one another *how not to lose a grip on ourselves*. How to revert to our original inversion.

To explain this position, we must delve into the nature of the drives and their reproduction. I will argue that even a cursory investigation will demonstrate the ontological primacy of transsexuality. But first we must start at the fact of the *forgetting* (and the forgetting of the forgetting) *of the primacy of transsexuality*.

Primordial transsexuality

Queer Marxist Mario Mieli deployed Freud's concept of polymorphous perversity and expanded it to gay ends. Here they offer their definition of transsexuality:

> I shall use the term transsexuality throughout this book to refer to the infantile polymorphous and 'undifferentiated' erotic disposition, which society surpasses and which, in adult life, every human carries within him in a latent state, or else confined to the depths of the unconscious via repression. 'Transsexuality' seems to me the best

word for expressing, at one and the same time, both the plurality of the erotic tendencies and the original and deep hermaphroditism of every individual.[3]

We need to play with this double meaning.

No longer can we conceive of polymorphous perversity as strictly directed at objects, as descriptive of sexual orientation. Rather, Mieli emphasises that polymorphous desire touches on something even more fundamental to the constitution of subjects. This sense of transsexuality refers not just to what Mieli calls the *manifest transsexual* – that is, 'adults who consciously live their own hermaphroditism, who recognise in themselves, in their body and mind, the presence of the "opposite" sex'[4] – but also to the causative factor behind manifest transsexuality. What we would today call either transgender or gender nonconforming people would be 'manifest transsexuals', while primordial transsexuality is a *universal notion* of how desire works for human, sexual subjects.[5]

Transsexuality in this sense attests to the simple fact that cissexual identification and heterosexual desire are not inborn, 'natural' functions of the subject. These structures of desire need to be *educated* into us through repression, like a cookie-cutter through dough. I will henceforth refer to this notion as 'primordial transsexuality' in order to distinguish this fundamental quality of sexed subjectivity from what we more commonly refer to as transsexuality or transgenderism according to the minimum definition of the conscious *identification* with a gender other than the one *assigned* at birth. It is both 'primordial' – our original, primary state – and 'trans-' (beyond, as in transcendent as well as across, between two poles) '-sexual' (of the sexual drives).

Primordial transsexuality isn't just a 'primordial bisexuality' – it isn't just before taking up sexual objects, but also prior to a fixed gender identification: the baby is not yet male or female as they simply cannot understand those concepts until it develops language (among other things).[6] Nothing could be further from the (essentialist) notion of 'gendered brains' existing in the wrong/right body – gender is essentially based on a non-binary origin.

So if primordial transsexuality is taken to be a fact of subjectivity, then the development of both heterosexuality and cissexuality (or indeed, 'binary' transsexuality) involves an act of violence upon an original polymorphous transsexuality – some desires stay, others go. However many transsexuals there are in the world, the most pressingly important feature we share is that we are a minority who are *not*. Our expendability is the trauma at the heart of the Oedipal conflict. Our consistent refusal of the demand that we not exist is a persistent irritant for those who were (through no fault of their own) much more tidily shorn of their primordial transsexualism.

For psychoanalysts, the Oedipal conflict installs the phallus as a central referent that men possess, or have 'it', and women merely are, or be 'it', the object of desire. Men own what women are resigned to merely being. It's this disparity which grounds the gender binary and heterosexual normalisation. But it is far from evident that Oedipus is universal, and our reflections on transsexuality have already revealed it to be a socially contingent phenomenon.[7] Prior to the installation of the phallus as the privileged signifier of sexual difference, no sexual, or gendered identification exists. In this sense, primordial transsexuality might be described as non-binary. Or inevitably *before* the binary.

The ferocious responses we inspire are therefore not imperfections of an ignorant society, but structural inevitabilities: clinging to the vestigial, we show up what (perhaps) never had to be lost at all.

Repressing manifestations of transsexuality

Thus we have set up the story as akin to a story of the Fall – there was an original 'free' state prior to repression, before humans enter heterosexual society. To become an acceptable heterosexual means to become cis: to have these original desires, urges, and identifications whittled away. Sometimes this process is subtle, but often enough with great violence. What matters is not the means, but instead the inevitable sacrifice. One must divide into two.

Insofar as the phallus is a contingency, not a natural state, it too needs to reproduce itself generation-to-generation. And it must do so imperially – any exception to the phallic norm must be eliminated, as it threatens its presumed naturalness with an exception. Much like why capitalist countries *must* enact imperialism on socialist ones, lest the threat of a good example. Reasons why come along the way.

The triumph of the phallus and the violence it enacts to repress or even eliminate those who do not conform to heterosexuality are a central mode of reproduction for patriarchal-capitalism as a whole. Eliminating alternatives, the phallus, along with the heterosexuality it engorges itself upon, sets itself up as natural, as having always-already been the case. The phallus must not only assert its dominance; it must render its reign eternal. Mieli lists schools, sport, family pressure, and employment among other types of 'fascism' that, in general, enact violence to those who do not conform to cissexist norms. Ideologically, this means setting up the transgender subject as abject, outside of the subject–object form of the man-woman dichotomy.

Hence why we need a gay communism (which also equally means a trans communism) – our aim is to liberate humanity from the phallocentric mode of reproduction. Post-capitalism will come only after the phallus. Gay communism will liberate humanity from the trappings of gender norms, abolish and dismantle institutions which exist through violently pruning away and suppressing primordial transsexuality. Gay communism will arise so we can liberate sexuality as a One that existed, before the Fall. In short, the aim of gay communism is to eliminate repression of the great id of primordial transsexuality. To put it more succinctly: gender abolitionism.

Many self-identified radicals tremble at this prospect, but through our lives being reduced to necessary expenditure, we have been left with no other choice.

To argue in these terms is to respond to civilisation's demand that we serve as its foundational sacrifice in kind. Understood through Freud's *Civilisation and its Discontents*, 'civilisation' is the phallic repressive mode on a primordial transsexual surface. It's this moment of entry, this civilising stripping away of our bisexual default, which gives rise to discontents when the repressed returns. Indeed, with the recent 'transgender tipping point', we might well posit this historical moment as precisely the return of the repressed of primordial transsexuality upon civilisation as a whole. Indeed, primordial transsexuality becomes a subject. Reactionaries have presented the rising tide of 'gender ideology' as threatening the very foundations of Western society. Perhaps they are not mistaken.

The Real of transsexuality

However, is Mieli's narrative of a Fall from primordial transsexuality entirely accurate? Is primordial transsexuality a pre-existing One of harmony and self-identity free from sexual difference? The problem is that sexuality isn't simply ever self-identical; it's a plethora of perversions and hermaphroditic identifications. Sex is problematic. Take the case of the transphobe – are they just abusing the trans subject because they are historically made abject by the phallus? Or rather is the abjection not merely an ideological move, but also saying something about primordial sexuality itself?

The move we are making here is not to reject primordial transsexuality, but to reject it as an original One or self-sameness. This is not where things exist in an ideal state of harmony, repressed by phallo-capitalism for its own reproductive purposes. We can call this, after Lacan, a fantasy.

There is no positive presence provided by the primordial state of transsexuality. Genders come into existence as a traumatic response to this *ex nihilo* origin.

One problem with 'psychical hermaphroditism' is that we need to explain how fixed identities come about from such chaos. My suspicion here is that what we call 'gender' is actually a *reaction* to primordial transsexuality. One could say every gender – including the lack of one – is a veil over the Real, an attempt to make sense of what is beyond sense. This leaves trans people sharing not a fundamental identity, but a fundamental *lack of identity*. Consider the dichotomy between primordial transsexuality and phallic civilisation with its repressive apparatuses. What is it that allows a gap between the two to arise?

Slavoj Žižek posits that 'one could even say that "man" (or "woman") is not a certain identity but more like a certain mode of avoiding an identity'.[8] Transgender people are not traumatic for heterosexuals merely because they pose a threat to the established binary of gender roles, but because they bring out the antagonistic tension which is constitutive of sexuality, of sexual difference itself. A transsexual is not a threat to sexual difference; rather, she is this difference in its pure, negative form, irreducible to a mere binary opposition (or unity) between positive gender identities.

Another way of articulating this concept is that the gender binary of the phallus provides a familiar and fundamental framework for how we relate to others. When we encounter the other, as a matter of custom we instantly try and figure out which side of the binary that other is on. This process often enough goes smoothly, setting an obvious limit to that which we know, and find familiar.

Gender ambiguity and transsexuality is a traumatic-Real for so many cis subjects as it is a *true unknown* to them. Ambiguity exists outside of them, which threatens to undermine their worldview where the phallic gender binary is primordial, and fundamental way of making sense of the world. The Real is precisely outside a place in the symbolic order; it isn't yet symbolised. The transsexual is a radical Other or Outside. Indeed one of the main aims of transitioning subject and the trans right movement/trans tipping point is a sort of symbolisation of what was considered a traumatic-Real. Symbolisation is the creation of a space, a name where the traumatic element of the Real has its radical alterity abolished – at least to a certain degree.

But at the same time, the task of symbolising is an asymptotic project. A huge battery of new (a)gender identifications (non-binary, agender, bi-gender, aporiagender etc.) are attempts at symbolisation. As Žižek has pointed out, the '+' of LGBT+ is the excessive element (the Real of sexual difference) that resists symbolisation. This means symbolisation is an eternal task, or as Butler would put it an unending performance. The Real must be symbolised, yet *fully* symbolising it is an impossibility.

So it must be said that transsexuality can never amount to a complete *escape* from sexual difference as an unconscious deadlock (not as 'a biological reality'). Rather, what makes transition traumatic for the transphobic cissexual is that their encounter with us exposes them to the reality of *sexual difference itself.* Transition attests to the conflict, which is the repressed core of *all* sexual relations. But that conflict is constantly repressed by fantasies of complementarity, whose primary symbolic referent is the *myth of heterosexuality itself.* Just as the notion of 'homosexual panic' represses or fails to capture its true concern, reactions to transition frame themselves as opposing delusions, when their true fear is our *reality.* That the trans subject is *Real* is the source of the 'panic' a cis subject might respond to us with; not merely a response to us as an object, but to the *pure negativity we embody.*

Trans people attempting to be conciliatory will often remark: this is just *me.* But these are no terms of peace! A transgender here is radically singular (hence Real). For us to be simply 'who we are' can only confront the heterosexual with *who they were.* Our moments of greatest ease are the stuff of complexes for those we pass by. And this fact many transphobes aim to repress or efface.

Let's end where we began when my trans woman friend asked me: 'why are we like this?'. In other words, what is the causation – if any – of transness? Regardless of one being transgender, transsexual, or a transvestite – there is an unsaid commonality of being 'across' and 'beyond' gender, sex, or mere clothing.

It struck me that trans people are the least likely to make a claim to know any causation of their transness. Our transness comes to us from the Real – not necessarily from history, from biology, nor society. But seemingly *all these things at once as an overdetermined heap*. If transness, like anything else, is indeed caused, then it must have causes in the plural. Yet even when the causes are tracked down, there is an element left unsaid. Some part of us is ultimately unintelligible for either trans people reflecting upon ourselves, and our analysts alike.

In many cases trans people attempt to paper over this question altogether: some assert our existence as *political* (sometimes crudely opposed to the pathological), a declaration to be celebrated and owned up to, rather than a neuro-developmental riddle to be dryly accounted for (and perhaps cured, at whatever cost). Others in pursuit of *deep stealth* seek to evade the question 'Why are we like this?' by attempting, as far as is possible, to avoid those around us noticing that we exist at all. To vanish without a trace can seem a much more practical fantasy than gay communism. However close we come to this mythical point, whether or not we even try to conceal ourselves, we are haunted by the stubborn fact of our continued existence. To exist in transition is to brush against the 'Why are you like that?' that the heterosexual world incessantly greets us with.

My answer isn't an answer, because the unanswerability of the question 'Why am I trans?' is not contingent, but essential to trans-ness. We reach the limits of speech, going beyond the outer reaches of intelligibility. We exist in this way as we have to, as the fact we must be *not* will never suffice to truly extinguish us. Transitions must be impossible, and yet they occur as a pure act. The bridge across gender is indeed built over an abyss.

Notes

1. In trans-centric internet slang, 'truscute', or 'tucute' refers to the view that one does not need to have gender dysphoria in order to be consid-

ered transgender. It is often used disparagingly by 'transmedicalists' (those who subscribe to the medical establishment's view that gender dysphoria, understood pathologically as discomfort with one's assigned sex at birth, is a necessary and defining condition for being trans*) as a counterpart to 'truscum'.

2. 'From the point of view of psycho-analysis the exclusive sexual interest felt by men for women is also a problem that needs elucidating and is not a self-evident fact based upon an attraction that is ultimately of a chemical nature' (Freud, S. (1905). *Three Essays on the Theory of Sexuality*. London: Hogarth, p. 12, n. 1). That the problem of *reproduction* is central to the psychoanalytic account of identification, specifically as it pertains to what the author has referred to here as 'cishetereosexual identification' as the normative outcome of the Oedipus complex is also presupposed in the work of Jacques Lacan, in whose work the repetitive function that attests to the 'beyond' of the pleasure principle is presented as a problem of repro- duction: 'What is this insistence on the part of the subject to reproduce? Reproduce what? Is it in his behaviour? Is it in his fantasies? Is it even in his ego? All kinds of things, from entirely different registers, can be used as material and as elements in this reproduction ... Freud asks himself what the inexhaustible nature of this reproduction means, from the point of view of the pleasure principle. Does it occur because of something unruly, or does it obey a different, more fundamental principle?' (Lacan, J. (1988). *The Seminar of Jacques Lacan Book II: The Ego in Freud's Theory and in the Technique of Psychoanalysis*. New York, NY: W. W. Norton, p. 63).

3. Mieli, M. (2018). *Towards a Gay Communism: Elements of a Homosexual Critique*. Fernbach, D. & Williams, E. C. (Trans.). London: Pluto Press, p. 6, emphasis in original.

4. Ibid., 7.

5. In part following the work of Catherine Malabou, some trans* theorists have in recent years taken to referring to this phenomenon as (sexual) plasticity. See, for instance, Malabou, C. (2005). *The Future of Hegel: Plasticity, Temporality and Dialectic*. London: Routledge; Gill Peterson, J. (2018). *Histories of the Transgender Child*. Minneapolis, MN: Minne- sota University Press; Gherovici, P. (2017). *Transgender Psychoanalysis*. London: Routledge.

6. It's worth noting that Freud's understanding of 'primordial bisexuality' isn't founded on a sex/gender distinction. In Freud and Lacan, polymor- phousness might be understood to refer to something like 'gender' as well, as this period of early childhood precedes the formation of object relations and the formation of the ego, or 'I-function'. This is in sharp distinction to Melanie Klein, who asserts that we have object relations from birth and gives priority to a more fundamental 'feminine position'.

7. 'When we study mythology, for example one that might perhaps appear with respect to a Sudanese population, we discover that for them the

Oedipus complex is just a rather thin joke' (Lacan, J. (1991). *Book I: Freud's Papers on Technique*. New York, NY: W. W. Norton, p. 86).

8. Žižek, S. (1 August 2016). The Sexual Is Political. *The Philosophical Salon*, thephilosophicalsalon.com/the-sexual-is-political/. The question of Žižek's theorisation of transsexuality more generally is a tangled one, which I will return to at least once, another time.

14

Cosmos Against Nature in the Class Struggle of Proletarian Trans Women

Anja Heisler Weiser Flower[1]

*Dedicated to the world proletariat's revolutionary potential,
which persists in the face of every defeat.*

Trans women appear on the world scene today as though we're brand new. Our political sympathisers offer us the equally unlikely stories that trans people in the modern sense have existed as an unvarying constant throughout human history, and that we are solely modern, having little or nothing to do with the gender minorities before and around us. Our most ridiculous opponents imagine that a conspiracy of doctors or pornographers invented us out of whole cloth. Our history in its fullness is buried and obscured. The social reality of our apparent novelty leaves us isolated and compelled to develop understandings of ourselves from the social cognition around us; these *ad hoc* under-standings fall far short of satisfying our needs. Over the long decades of our ascension to public presence, capital has more-or-less finished extending its domination across the planet, and has turned to intensi-fying its exploitation of the world proletariat. The social-democratic and Stalinist regimes that always defined themselves against us have slowly disappeared: we step out into a world of just-in-time produc-tion and 'flexible', insecure employment from firms hardly willing to hire us.

As the gap between proletarians and the political sphere contin-ually widens, the left, fragmented and confused, is mostly absent from the life at large of a disorganised US proletariat. The nature of the left as the left wing of capitalism's political sphere becomes more obvious. Conversely, identification with communism is normal among American transgender women: left/'progressive' activity of a distinctive character crops up easily among populations of the proletariat which social democracy, Stalinism, and much of the workers' movement defined themselves against.

This activity grows through nonprofits, the academy, and informal online channels. These are new forms for old activities: service provision, repressive population management, and ideological control, the traditional wheelhouse of the left wing of capitalist politics. The dominant politics in this trans left activity can be roughly split into liberalised, eclectic anarchism and various Stalinisms longing for states and father figures. Both streams take a crudely religious attitude. Both are obsessed with imposing their moral management on transgender social spaces. Neither can claim adherence from the majority of trans proletarians they claim to represent and serve. Tendencies with more fully communist abstract theoretical cores persist as sects, some still surviving five, seven, or more decades after the moments of resurgence that brought them into being. Their persistence is admirable, and they do attract some transgender recruits, but the isolation they're forced into in the absence of newly rising class power condemns their unfailing principles to hollow out into shells. This hollowing separation of theory from class practice forms a morbid pair with the trans-focused left's enshrinement of the separation of class practice from theory, as proletarian trans women are commanded to 'listen to' ourselves and get 'listened to' without systematising our insights on a class basis.

From the cycle of struggles of the 1960s and 1970s onward, the nominally revolutionary left has shifted focus from the disappearing 'worker's states' and social democracies to academia and NGOs, and has tended to break its loyal opposition to capital into segments in loyal opposition to the different forms of social oppression. Given this new terrain, these tendencies have found brilliant new ways to destroy and subvert the vital principles of communist thought and practice, for brief moments using that breakage to advance specific aspects of thought and practice into positions far ahead of tendencies with more fully communist abstract theoretical cores. At moments, their investigations even brought them to round out their positions and to start fusing into those older *formally* solid communist tendencies.[2] Thus we *almost* reached a great lurch forwards in the synthesis of communist praxis.

The cis-dominated gay and lesbian movements reacted to trans people's presence among them by splitting into sides for and against our existence. Younger Western trans people grew up caught politically between these sides. We gained political representation (or were cursed by it). We gained an easier life for some of us, while the rate of murders of proletarian Black trans women in the United States climbed ever-higher; we had little sense of trans proletarians' worldwide situation, despite an ongoing influx of trans people to Western urban centres from even more fatally hostile environments. A global morass and the feeling of impossibility surrounded us. Certain Marxists crafted useful new tools for struggle, though these didn't reach the level of weapons or find much audience. *TIME* magazine announced 'the transgender tipping point'.

We know now that we're moving.

A crop of young transgender Marxist intellectuals now appear in English-language circles, universities, nonprofits, and organisations oriented towards left-communism, communisation, anarchism, 'orthodox Marxist' paleo-Leninism, (post-)Trotskyism, and Maoism. Bisecting all of these is the abolitionist stream promoting the reduction or overcoming of police, of prisons, and of the oppression of Black people; abolitionism has its own transgender intellectuals.

That we trans Marxist intellectuals exist at all feels like a miracle. (Even academic 'transgender studies' is only 30 years old, defined generously.) Our orientation towards creating a genuinely communist world varies wildly, however. We are largely connected to other trans proletarians only within the English-speaking world; our insights are scattershot. This is to be expected given our newness, the uncertainty of the period we've arisen in, and the size of our task. Clear theorising is daunting, given the irregularity of concrete social cognition concerning the problems of transgender life. We face down the absence of any formally congealed global proletarian force, the thorny relationship of transgender proletarians to the political sphere, and the ever-intensifying estrangement of the worldwide proletariat from politics. We don't know how the coming brutal years of crisis in class society will hit trans proletarians, or what the dynamics of the coming class struggles will be. How many trans Marxist intellectuals will *seriously try* to defy the repressive inertia of the far left of capitalism's alienated political sphere, and merge with the swell of class force as it rushes around us?

The same above-ground capitalist world which walled us out now turns a 'human' face towards us in parts of its centre and semi-periphery, and clothes itself in our faces to sell magazines, razors, makeup, coffee, credit cards, luxury purses. Political formations from the Democrats to the tacitly pro-capitalist 'communists' found trans people dangerous or irrelevant. Now they too reach to awkwardly drape the banner 'transgender ally' over parties terrified of their own timid social-democratic wings. To sects with practices and programmes fundamentally friendly to the family which beats and disowns us. To the nation from which we have to flee to survive, and work for which no firm will hire us. Trans Marxist intellectuals will learn from and build on each other's work. Yet *how could there be any shared project* between those whose fundamental orientation is towards the discredited far-left political sphere, and those who insist on the absolute priority of the proletariat's own potential to realise and overcome itself by creating a communist world?

No existing tendency on the left has *fleshed out* a viable trajectory through which trans and cis proletarians can overcome their mutual estrangement and form a global revolutionary class. Partisans of a communist future are left to comb through our poorly mapped and bloodstained socialist history. We're left to pick out the cues orienting us to that viable trajectory of transgender liberation, orienting us towards the creation of a free communist world – a world in which the free-flowering of each person is the precondition for the free-flowering of all people. *The flight path to transgender liberation can only be the path to communism.*

Someone might want the best for trans proletarians, say 'protect trans women' with good intentions, call themselves a 'queer communist', be trans themselves, and act as a petty bureaucrat of social control *against* trans proletarians, a manager of our dissent. Someone else might not have thought of us at all, yet carry analysis and strategy that we cannot do without. It's not what a social force claims about itself but *where it's heading* that counts for our prospects.

The far left of the capitalist world's political sphere is basically as far out of proletarians' reach and as much of a block in our path as the rest of the political sphere, except that its history and materials are closer to the mark, more directly useful to our project, and so much easier to transform into what we need. The best materials of the last decades are there for us to use and transform out of their deadening frameworks. Even the doghouses of academic queer and trans studies have plenty of use to offer us. Why let anything useful go to waste? Finally, though, we need more than just an *intellectual revival* of even the truest communist analysis – as if that were possible in isolation from class struggle. *Marxism meets its purpose as a weapon of struggle.*

If it's true that we can't make our way into a communist world without theory, we can't *use* theory effectively without confronting our thought's immersion in the existing mode of production. Capitalism, like class societies before it, uses our intellectual labours in accumulation and in the discipline and control of the proletariat. Transgender proletarians can't understand and address our situation in an integrated way without starting to break down this division between intellectual labour and manual labour. Therefore, while a new crop of intellectuals may be exciting, it is not enough. Neither does the position of some of these intellectuals outside of the universities solve the problem. It is the *social relationship*, the division between mental and manual labour itself, that has to change.

* * *

Our world situation is extremely uncertain, and in some ways extremely novel. Until the contradictory dynamics of the capitalist mode of production are resolved, however (whether in the mutual destruction of bourgeoisie and proletariat or by the overcoming of capitalism into communism), those core dynamics will produce certain consistent and unvarying social features and trends. We can detect those features through historical and political-economic study. These give us solid intuitions to work with which can direct our further activity, and can be checked and refined in turn. I will give some of those intuitions here – without justifying them, which would take much more space and effort than I have to work with.

We can expect the field of class struggle to morph reciprocally with capital's desperate squeeze of proletariat and ecology, and with the resulting global crises. We can expect that shifting field to continually force our struggles to confront the realities of nation, family, and 'Nature' as these are wielded against us. We can expect, therefore, for dividing lines to continually appear around differing answers to the question of what the proletariat *is* in relations, internal composition, division of labour, and around the question of whether our responses to the coming disasters remain fixed on the national or regional terrain or begin to fuse across those boundaries. We can reasonably expect the development of practice and thought to remain tremendously jagged and uneven, coming into various foreshortened syntheses. This will continue until the proletariat has *congealed on a global stage as a class fighting independently for its own interests*, and in that process has formed its own properly global organism, its thinking body. We can expect the development of the independent global proletarian organism to initiate a complete transformation in the relationship of human activity to the ecology of which it is concretely a part, but which it is abstractly separated from and opposed to.

We can reasonably expect the proletariat at large who haven't been routed into the political sphere to hold an implicit understanding of their own situation – unsystematic and perhaps completely submerged, but in some ways outpacing the formal theories of the left – so that the emergence of the class organism is a process of reciprocal convergence rather than of specialists 'enlightening' the 'ignorant masses'. We can expect early manifestations of the nascent world proletarian organism to come from various locations, and various stations in life:

> When referring to the modern proletarian class, we must conceive of this process not in relationship to a trade category but to the class as a whole. It can then be realised how a more precise conscious-ness of the identity of interests gradually makes its appearance; this consciousness, however, results from such a complexity of experiences and ideas, that it can be found only in limited groups composed of elements selected from every category. Indeed only an advanced minority can have the clear vision of a collective action which is directed towards general ends that concern the whole class and which has at its core the project of changing the whole social regime.[3]

More accurately, a *diversity* of interests find their dialectical *unity* in the formation of the revolutionary proletarian class, its direction the real movement to abolish the present order, its purpose is the creation of a world of real freedom, a universal flowering.

We who want to fight for a communist world have everything to gain in fostering international connections between trans proletarians. In helping people to find each other and pushing our local struggles towards global connection wherever we can, we can take our part in developing accurate, grounded, and systematic collective understanding among trans proletarians of our own world situation. With the uncertainty hanging over us at present, we'd best get moving.

* * *

This is the first writing aimed at establishing a *way in* to the problem of transgender proletarian struggle and guide stars to sequence our further movement. It is rough and abstract, loose and partial, and provisional in many respects. We take on a problem that the scholars and Marxism-technicians have barely addressed. Meanwhile we fly ahead to find our own way, preferring the growth of our rough and partial understanding to any security we could find by clinging to intellectual and social fragmentation. In the technical dimension, as elsewhere, we have plenty of raw material to bring to the problem at hand. We have no need to build new frameworks out of whole cloth: Marx's framework, if properly understood, still provides by far the best foundation for a cohesive and *unified* analysis of the dynamics of societies resting on class modes of production. It can help us trace out our problem's fundamental directional thrust. Foreshortened thought and foreshortened feeling, sustained in mutual disconnection with each other, are wielded against trans people constantly. This makes it all the more urgent to set out now, to find coordinates for the path along which we will overcome the foreshortening of communist analysis, even if those coordinates are rough.

We start with a very thin cross-section of how one population – trans women, across class – relates to self and world. We follow one impulse out of that cross-section; gathering our resources, we move from there to the law of value. It shouldn't be a problem that the movement of our argument is episodic: our purpose here is not to make a complete study, but to rough out primary moves for further investigation, demonstrating the importance of investigative *method* along the way. That movements of argument between and within episodes

THE CLASS STRUGGLE OF PROLETARIAN TRANS WOMEN

remain abstract just encourages the research and practice towards concretion which we desperately need. In doing this we'll push against a number of false solutions to our problem: the promotion of reformed, 'diverse' class societies, 'crude communist' or pseudo-communist state regimes, localism, purportedly emancipatory segregation, and isolation of every kind.

> In reality it always happens that a phenomenon which later becomes universal originally emerges as an individual, particular, specific phenomenon, as an exception from the rule. It cannot actually emerge in any other way. Otherwise history would have a rather mysterious form.[4]

Stars: appearance, thought

> *Private property* is only the sensuous expression of the fact that man becomes *objective* for himself and at the same time becomes an alien and inhuman object for himself, that his expression of life is his alienation of life, and that his realization is a loss of reality ...[5]

The *concrete materials of a transgender woman's self* are estranged from her abstract inverted 'male' personhood as that personhood is realised at her expense. Any language thrown at this range of experiences to define it seems to slide off – this shearing effect and noisiness are among its general qualities. I experienced myself to be located some feet outside of my body for some stressful months in college, so that my 'I' would clip through walls while my body stood in the middle of a room. If the bank teller says my old name out loud, I'll get a medium-volume knot of revulsion in my stomach on the one hand, and on the other an ear-piercing intrusive thought announcing to me that this is in fact my name, as I am male and will be male forever. My sense of the size and location of my body parts has always been inaccurate and irregular. Of course senses of revulsion are as significant as senses of positive attraction, identification, and imprint. Some of us do have an affirmative internal beacon telling us that we definitely *are women*, some don't. The swirling mental-sensory clouds are fragmentary, but never random. They are as much social and impersonal as they are personal. They are induced in us, shape us, and are shaped by us.

The inverted personhood forced on us appears to us as an alien and inhuman object – and something more: evident Natural truth, an unmoving force. These materials also appear to us as objects, but – shreds, trash, excess bits of language and clusters of images, loops – they're obviously *moving*. The mutual constitution and movement of their force are much more visible. Weaving and making each other, they can lose their appearance of objecthood enough to join as walls of sense-feeling, mental-social-sensory-bodily noise. This noise can be quite painful. The shearing can cut our body-sense into ribbons. The sheer bareness of it can be impossible for our minds and bodies to inhabit. But then, we can identify this noise of the material of our selves with the image we see looking out to the cosmos: the microwave noise of the universe, the cosmic roar.

> For not only the five senses, but also the so-called spiritual senses, the practical senses (will, love, etc.), in a word, the *human* sense, the humanity of the senses – all these come into being only through the existence of *their* objects, through *humanized* nature. The *cultivation* of the five senses is the work of all previous history.[6]

* * *

The noise musician is an archetype among American trans women, alongside the uwu stripey-socked catgirl.

I wanted *very* badly to be a cat, wild dog, some kind of fox in my tween and teen years. Leiomy is of course the legendary Wonder Woman, falling on knifepoint so smoothly that dropping is already also getting up. SOPHIE's face appears in the video as a gelatinous bag, gooping this way and that, lips and eyes blobbing out:

> My face is the front of shop/My face is the real shop front/My shop is the face I front/I'm real when I shop my face.[7]

These counter-movements against the abstract reality of maleness aren't a 'celebration of artificiality' in any *obvious* sense – that's one-sided, a discount queer theorist's read. It's not that trans women hold the key to understanding all of this by virtue of our supposedly cohesive and distinct standpoint as trans women. Just that nothing much useful is *yet* said *directly* about it by anyone but ourselves.

The ideas at work in trans women's active self-fashioning far outstrip the appalling banalities applied to us by the bureaucratic LGBT+ NGO hand-wringers and good-natured concerned-parent conspiracy theorists who stalk us. The bureaucrats and bureaucrats-in-spirit can preach that trans people have an incredible variety of genders, reasons for transitioning, and transition experiences. Without knowing how to *historically trace* the concrete *unity* of that diversity, though, all they can do is write up typologies and make rather insulting explanatory diagrams for their corporate diversity seminars. The conspiracy theorists at least have the honesty to point out that trans women differ in a number of ways from the dominant *defining features* which are supposed to be common to all women, but they're aggressively uninterested in acknowledging that cis women also continually lack many of those features, or that the *selection and shaping* of the features that define a woman/female are determined by social relations of domination.

Because conspiracists deny that social domination determines the features that define sex, they can't explain how it is that those features are so heavily racialised, why transition is mashed together with questions of ability/disablement, or why transitions vary so much across time and space. Gender conspiracists will eagerly bring up the more painful aspects of trans women's social plight (which I don't discuss here) and tut about 'mental illness' while vigorously denying the social domination that cuts these features into us. Proletarian trans women grasping at tools for our liberation *cannot* afford to imitate our enemies' methods of analysis.

Ah-Mer-Ah-Su sings of 'space space space space space space space' among vampiric scenes against a night-time sky. Look to Juliana Huxtable: she's visualised herself as a bound, lactating, and shitting anthropomorphic cow, as a *Nuwaubian Princess* against colour spectrum sky and disco ball moon, in the stars shooting energy through her hands. Huxtable has worked with material from *Ghost in the Shell*, Raquel Welch films, and Octavia Butler novel covers. 'I think that, for me, science fiction is an alternative to theology'.[8] My last girlfriend often told me how much she'd like to be a ball of light. The programmer girls show up to a trans march in shirts advertising FULLY

AUTOMATED LUXURY GAY SPACE COMMUNISM with NASA/Star Trek/UN-derived rainbow hammer-and-sickle logos, and express allegiance to transhumanism for the sake of getting cat ears installed on their bodies. Marxist trans women I know are associated with a Marxist analysis website called Cosmonaut, a cybernetics podcast (*General Intellect Unit*), a Star Trek podcast (*Jumpsuit Utopia*). Walking down the street as a teenager I thought that passer-by must view me as an alien from another planet. My own teenage identification with *Ghost in the Shell* and adult *Sailor Moon* fandom is stereotypical.

This method of drawing a category by generality captures a still slice of contradictory or unrelated phenomena on the basis of similar qualities. It's served its purpose for us. We'll leave the strictly sociological and cultural study of these to the hacks of the academy, and run with this general cosmic and science-fictional subcategory, centre *one* of the contradictory tendencies flowing through it, and trace it to its root.

This tendency is *identification with space and the cosmos as an external image with which one would like to merge oneself*, so that one is no longer *with* the cosmos but *is* the cosmos: 'I would like to be *with* her, but I would like to *be* her'. This is, again, a cross-class feeling *in itself*, *as it stands* – but an unconscious, unrealised class impulse is submerged in its bones. We will find in it a hidden understanding of the possibility of breaking through the suffocation and starvation of daily proletarian life, something which most of us are currently divorced from the necessary tools to *systematically* grasp and *consciously* express.

* * *

The Soviet dialectician and activity theorist Evald Ilyenkov laid out a history of philosophers aligned to the ascendant European bourgeoisie reiterating a completely upside-down conception of the abstract and concrete.[9] According to this bourgeois worldview, what is concrete is the direct physical and sensible objects around us. The concrete is a set of individual objects with the same attributes, like redness or roundness, and it's these things which are most real. The abstract in this view is everything which isn't directly sensible and empirically graspable. The vague, that which lies beyond the reach of our senses, everything which is 'out there' in the ether, and is therefore understood as merely mental, ideal, or conceptual.

Marx could not have uncovered the origin of value as a concrete process, and its manifest expressions as part of a dialectically integrated social whole, by firstly listing the different uses of the term 'value' that we find in our everyday language and then abstracting away from the particular features of all in order to derive a 'universal' shared essence. He would have found himself with an empty formal abstraction rather than arriving at the *reality* of the value phenomenon.

Marx recognised that the universal features of reality can only be understood through – as – the *concrete in the true sense*. We'll advance our argument by taking for ourselves certain aspects of the thinking of one of the very finest New Left distorters of Marxism, the socialist lesbian-feminist Monique Wittig. Being correctly attuned to concerns of our analytical *method* will allow us to make-real the truth in Wittig's thinking beyond and against the major errors in her highly rhetorical general theoretical framework. This will give us a point from which to move further in our understanding of what gender/sex is.

For Wittig, gender manipulates sex into being, smoothing a social order into appearing 'natural'. Whatever 'clusters' of sexed bodies exist physically find their association with 'male' or 'female' *only ever* in the context of political ideology. Grouping together women as a 'natural kind' is work that cannot be done innocently. The work of what Wittig calls the *heterosexual regime* is far more insidious and contrived. That women are 'clustered' around the female is a bid to keep the social order intact. Gender is not simply a varied fabric to be draped over the stricter infrastructure of sex: sex is instead put together *post hoc*, to match the needs of gender. Female bodies appear female for the sake of sustaining an order that demands them to be so.[10] The subordination of women requires a physical defect, the 'mark of gender', that is fabricated in our apprehension.[11] The female is an ideology stitched up as an inevitability.

In the bourgeois schema, capital-W Woman is concrete, immediately empirically graspable, biologically apparent. The feminine, the social 'stuff' of being a woman, is abstract, unreal, 'out there'. You can't touch or taste it. By this schema, trans women are concretely, biologically males – males who transform ourselves physically and in affect and appearance by taking on the unreal, secondary abstract traits of femininity. This is of course entirely wrong.

Again stacking Ilyenkov with Wittig, the dialectical, Marxist view holds that the concrete is the totality of mutually-producing phenomena. The concrete is the whole grammatical relationship of elements strung together, unified in their mutually-produced difference. It is only with all the mutual aspects, all the sides in place, that we can grasp the fundamental indwelling dynamics of the organism. The *abstract* is when an *individual term or element is pulled out of place*. An abstract view appears when one aspect or part of things is isolated from the whole.

By this account, it is capital-W Woman that is abstract: it's a dominating abstraction, pressed down upon us and baked into the actions of our daily lives, in an incredibly oppressive way. The movement of the stuff of everyday life as a woman is the concrete: each element producing the other, the full sentence of phenomena hanging together, integrated in their unity-in-diversity.

This argument is quite powerful. Its rhetorical force – which Wittig is known for, as in her famous argument that lesbians are not women – encourages some looseness in interpretation, and may conceal problems. The kind and level of concretion engaged in here remains far too close to the *apparent social form* of Woman to provide for a full model of the subject at hand, and so one ends up restricted to extending the concretion in a linear way by drawing more and more sharply the dominating role of abstract *sex* over the concrete, which is rendered nearly unspeakable. The argument then falls into defining sex as a 'class'. Thus it pushes admirably hard against the social-ecological split between abstract, inverted Humanity and abstract, inverted Nature, but cannot concretise sex with capital accumulation, and so cannot really access the concrete that it gestures towards. The concrete is so hidden here that it even disappears from Wittig's conception of the abstract. She reduces the abstract to its representation, to ideology, a socially dominant idea: "'Woman' cannot be associated with writing because 'Woman' is an imaginary formation and not a concrete reality ..."[12] This cuts us off from the real political-economic natures of abstraction and social cognition. We're thus driven back to an exaggerated focus on what happens *within our own minds* and *in direct interpersonal interaction*. One has to stretch awfully hard to get this enticing but broken abstract-concrete modelling to explain the entire reality of gender/sex and gender/sex domination.

Wittig has gotten us close to "'that which calls for a hidden name", "that which dares not speak its name", "that which [minority writers] find everywhere although it is never written about'".[13] We cannot actually *understand* the concrete and its abstractions, however, without overcoming her serious mistakes and properly understanding class and production. We'll therefore proceed to our next sequence of stars by investigating what exactly a *social abstraction* actually is – but let's complete this sequence first.

* * *

Our dance with Ilyenkov and Wittig should sufficiently demonstrate the urgency of the question of *method of thinking* in crafting truth-seeking weapons for our class struggle. This importance carries over to the question of the importance of transgender proletarian struggle for communist praxis. From the majoritarian, democratic view, we proletarian trannies are insignificant, a tiny numerical minority with very specific needs that most proletarians don't share and probably shouldn't care about. This is a strictly quantitative view, though. *Qualitatively, human species-being carries a suppressed concrete potential*, which Mario Mieli names as 'trans-sexual' – although we need to concretise far beyond this framing. This potential pushes to be realised through class struggle, and most directly through the struggle of transgender proletarians. Either the potential of human species-being is realised and we attain full communism, or it is not, and we don't. A cisgender, heterosexual communism is absurd, impossible.

Some further notes on method

First, a renewed emphasis on method requires our dialectics to go beyond the limited dialectical materialism of the twentieth century left, which claimed to find the perfect formula through which thought would escape the straitjacket of formalisation. This form-against-form is a foreshortened dialectic. The straitjacket of formalism thought has proven an easier problem to identify than to escape. Equally formal inversions of form-against-form, such as those emphasising randomness, the unformed, and noise, don't escape this foreshortening pattern – yet dialectics has not been successfully superseded.

Second, discussion of *method of thought* simply cannot successfully seek truth without considering *activity as a whole*. Understanding the totality of activity means beginning to understand its extra-personal, social aspects, and how these practically congeal into the independent proletarian organism – our 'real party'. We begin to understand how thought and total activity will transform in the course of the formation of the proletarian organism; we begin thereby to understand the method of thought to be used here and now. Our victory will involve the realisation *and supersession* of Marxism as a tool and framework.

Thirdly, we make much discussion here of appearance – of abstract form and concrete content. We should clarify that we're not talking about *true essences and false appearances*. Appearance is truncated and partial, yes, but it is a component of the totality which it is the appearance of, and dialectically co-develops with. Neither is abstraction nor form the same as appearance, as we'll see.

* * *

There's no better completion to this sequence than to reproduce in near-full the *Economic and Philosophical Manuscripts of 1844* passage quoted above:

Just as *private property* is only the sensuous expression of the fact that man becomes *objective* for himself and at the same time becomes an alien and inhuman object for himself, that his expression of life [*Lebensäusserung*] is his alienation of life [*Lebensentäusserung*], and that his realisation is a loss of reality, an *alien* reality, so the positive supersession of private property, i.e. the *sensuous* appropriation of the human essence and human life, of objective man and of human *works* by and for man, should not be understood only in the sense of *direct*, one-sided *consumption*, of *possession*, of *having*. Man appropriates his integral essence in an integral way, as a total man. All his *human* relations to the world – seeing, hearing, smelling, tasting, feeling, thinking, contemplating, sensing, wanting, acting, loving – in short, all the organs of his individuality, like the organs which are directly communal in form, are in their *objective* approach or in their *approach to the object* the appropriation of that object. This appropriation of *human* reality, their approach to the object, is therefore the *confirmation of human reality.*[14] It is human *effectiveness* and human *suffering*, for suffering, humanly conceived, is an enjoyment of the self for man.

Private property has made us so stupid and one-sided that an object is *ours* only when we have it, when it exists for us as capital or when we directly possess, eat, drink, wear, inhabit it, etc., in short, when we *use* it. Although private property conceives all these immediate realizations of possession only as *means of life*; and the life they serve is the *life* of *private property*, labour and capitalization.

Therefore *all* the physical and intellectual senses have been replaced by the simple estrangement of *all* these senses – the sense of *having*. So that it might give birth to its inner wealth, human nature had to be reduced to this absolute poverty. (On the category of *having* see Hess in *Einundzwanzig Bogen*.)[15]

The supersession of private property is therefore the complete *emancipation* of all human senses and attributes; but it is this emancipation precisely because these senses and attributes have become *human*, subjectively as well as objectively. The eye has become a *human* eye, just as its *object* has become a social, *human* object, made by man for man. The *senses* have therefore become *theoreticians* in their immediate praxis. They relate to the *thing* for its own sake, but the thing itself is an *objective human* relation to itself and to man,[16] and vice-versa. Need or enjoyment have therefore lost their *egoistic* nature, and nature has lost its mere *utility* in the sense that its use has become *human* use.

Similarly, the senses and enjoyment of other men have become my *own* appropriation. Apart from these direct organs, *social* organs are therefore created in the *form* of society; for example, activity in direct association with others, etc. has become an organ of my *life expression* and a mode of appropriation of *human* life.[17]

Of course, the *partial suppression* of private property within 'socialist' states has done no such thing. Although this historical disaster fell far short of private property's full *supersession* (*aufhebung*), it points us beyond the *form of property* to the part played by the social effects of *value* in moulding our world and personhood. We'll take this up soon.

* * *

Stars: abstract realities

What are these real social categories, and how are they produced? They are *abstract realities* in human society: they are *abstractions*.

In speaking of an *abstraction* as a *reality*, we mean it is *not* primarily a cognitive phenomenon. It emerges *behind our backs* out of the dynamics of the capitalist process, as one of the mediations of class. It goes as deep as production. Consider Marx describing abstract labour in the *Grundrisse*:

> Indifference towards any specific kind of labour presupposes a very developed totality of real kinds of labour, of which no single one is any longer predominant. As a rule, the most general abstractions arise only in the midst of the richest possible concrete development, where one thing appears as common to many, to all. Then it ceases to be thinkable in a particular form alone. On the other side, this abstraction of labour as such is not merely the mental product of a concrete totality of labours. Indifference towards specific labours corresponds to a form of society in which individuals can with ease transfer from one labour to another, and where the specific kind is a matter of chance for them, hence of indifference. Not only the category, labour, but labour in reality has here become the means of creating wealth in general, and has ceased to be organically linked with particular individuals in any specific form. Such a state of affairs is at its most developed in the most modern form of existence of bourgeois society – in the United States. Here, then, for the first time, the point of departure of modern economics, namely the abstraction of the category 'labour', 'labour as such', labour pure and simple, becomes true in practice.[18]

This abstract domination is intimately woven into the fabric of our lives as proletarians. It is inextricable from our experience of dispossession, alienation, and exploitation. Our labours are no longer just theoretically abstract but, in practice, actually so[19] – 'individuals are now ruled by *abstractions*, whereas earlier they depended on one another'.[20]

This means that describing gender/sex as *an idea treated as though it were real*, as *reification*,[21] is quite off the mark. Analysis of reification certainly holds for the *cognitive-linguistic aspects* of the sex/gender abstraction, but cognition doesn't happen only via language,[22] and the sex/gender abstraction is *not* primarily an identity or name. To describe the politics of such abstractions as 'identity politics' thus makes the mistake of buying into the reification that the advocates of seeing sex/gender as reification critique – although such politics of course inevitably does *involve* identity. The identity is not the main thing; rather, identity is a *representation* of the abstraction.

A criticism of how the capitalist mode of production moulds social phenomena after the form of the commodity is indispensable, but for our needs it does not go far enough. Say as György Lukács had it:

> At this stage in the history of mankind there is no problem that does not ultimately lead back to that question [of the fundamental nature of capitalist society] and there is no solution that could not be found in the solution to the riddle of commodity-structure … That is to say, the problem of commodities must not be considered in isolation or even regarded as the central problem in economics, but as the central, structural problem of capitalist society in all its aspects.[23]

If this is true, we're presented with an analysis that's stuck at the level of circulation of commodities, rather than understanding production[24] and the totality of human activity. How are we to understand the severe degree to which the sex/gender abstraction *shapes and modifies* the constitution, including the *physical constitution*, of human bodies/minds, human organisation, human infrastructure? These are dynamics which the analysis of reification mostly points at only secondarily or indirectly.

It has been argued to me that understanding gender/sex as real abstraction is inaccurate, as it overstates the likeness between sex/gender, race, disablement, etc., and value. We might grant that value is a real abstraction of a distinctive type, with no direct parallel. However, we *cannot* confine or centre sex/gender in cognition and language – *especially* not in personal or directly interpersonal psychology. This is a dangerous concession with liberal and transphobic consequences.[25]

* * *

We turn now to Jeanne Neton and Maya Andrea Gonzalez's majestic and pivotal essay *The Logic of Gender* to consider an integrated political-economic model of gender/sex as a real abstraction.[26] Investigating their model will allow us to tentatively feel out its limits.

It is obvious to observant communists that gender/sex has a lot to do with the division of labour in class modes of production, yet division of labour remains under-theorised in Marxism. This under-theorisation foreshortens even the most advanced theories of gender/sex. Thus transgender proletarians are deprived of fundamental analytical tools.

Neton and Gonzalez criticise the dominant divisions used by the 'Marxist feminist' analytical currents: productive and reproductive labour, paid and unpaid labour, public and private. They obliterate the usual public/private distinction, pointing out that under capitalism and its states, the private is 'the totality of activities, inside and outside the home'. The public is *only* the meeting of abstract citizens with abstract rights in the abstract 'public square'. They correctly contextualise reproductive *labour* in the *total* process of capitalist production/reproduction, quoting *Capital Vol. 1* to point out that Marx concerns himself not with the reproduction of the commodity labour power in particular but the reproduction of the social totality:

> Whatever the form of the process of production in a society, it must be a continuous process, must continue to go periodically through the same phases. A society can no more cease to produce than it can cease to consume. When viewed, therefore, as a connected whole, and as flowing on with incessant renewal, every social process of production is, at the same time, a process of reproduction.[27]

Most crucially, they refuse to link the gender/sex abstraction directly with the household and reproductive labour, linking it instead to a distinction between *directly market-mediated* (DMM) activities and *indirectly market-mediated* (IMM) activities, as this intersects with the distinction between *waged and unwaged* (rather than paid and unpaid). This gives *much* more analytical space for analysing the struggles of proletarian trans women. The proletarian trans woman is frequently expelled entirely from her family of origin, leaving her dependent for survival on the support of vital but internally fractious and abusive queer/trans alternative family. She is routinely locked out of legal employment and professional training. This leaves her to survive via sex work, in which she sells her ability to deliver highly gendered sexual experiences in brutally close proximity to the market. From here the social relations through which proletarian trans women are produced and produce ourselves start to come into view, and we're freed from the conceptual division between society and economy that previously dogged our thinking. As before, though, *The Logic of Gender* points to the concrete without fully entering into it. Its modelling of gender/sex as an abstract reality remains too thin for our needs.

Neton and Gonzalez assert that value and the inverted abstract 'citizen' are each secured by an outside. They perceptively cite white reactionaries' racial defence of 'the purity of white womanhood' against perceived threats from Black people as an example of this. They situate sex/gender in terms of a price differential in the cost of labour power, which is a result of association with indispensable but *cast-off, abjected* activity. This should give us pause. Neton and Gonzalez come close to equating sex/gender with disablement, yet they never *once* directly mention the subject. The woman worker is marked as coming with distracting housework, with having to suddenly leave work for months to give birth, and so on. Likewise, the disabled worker is marked as coming with all sorts of extra costs: physical and social accommodations; loss of customers who recoil from the disabled worker socially and aesthetically; their suddenly having to leave work for health reasons. Two severely under-theorised mediations of class share fundamental features in the production process, and we're left unsure how to tell one from the other. An unsurprising problem.

While naming the cast-off remainder of activity as *abject*, Neton and Gonzalez assert that this remainder is *not* socially necessary labour – that in fact this activity is *not labour at all*, because it is not abstracted as such or treated as such. The nature of labour is a substantial problem, and we can't puzzle through it here. In completely rejecting any description of labour as physiological, though, and asserting their assumption 'from the outset that one can talk about gender without any reference to biology' (which in fact they themselves end up doing), don't they end up accepting the abstract reality which splits abstract inverted Humanity from abstract inverted Nature, even while they press against it? The problem we had with Wittig hasn't been fully solved.

We're stuck if we can't see beyond the Nature abstraction in our thinking, and this has especially dire consequences for trans proletarians. Of course, the argument that abstract labour is trans-historically physiologically real seems to accept and positively endorse abstract Nature, so it doesn't offer a particularly enticing alternative. We've got to go further, to a cosmic-ecological view.

Stars: 'Humanity' and 'Nature'

The abstract and formal inverted Human Citizen is turned inward, relating to his self and the phenomena of his world as objects in a world which in fact *makes* them objects *on the level of abstract form*. He appears to himself to be living not as part of a breathing, changing cosmos, but by himself, in a void. In the public sphere, he sees around him other Citizen-objects. *Outside* of his public Citizenship he sees non-human beings: non-entities, nothing.

Capitalist production, abstracting our labours, drives a metabolic rift between them and the ecology of which we are concretely a part, dis-coordinating our inputs and outputs. It shapes the technical and infrastructural apparatus in a manner to progressively deepen this rift. It is not hard to trace the rise of ecological disaster to the rise of modern world colonial extraction, and of world capital.

The 'black void' outside of the abstract anti-human Human must be extracted from and formed for use.[28] Here is the realm of timeless, formless Nature.

Concretely, human beings are completely ecologically interwoven into a cosmos which brought us into being, and without which we could not exist. Our life is natural life; our history is natural history. When we speak of alienation, *what we are alienated from is our concrete metabolism, interchange, with the world of which we're a part* – a metabolic interaction in which the world shapes us, we shape the world, and we shape ourselves by shaping the world. But on that alienated, abstract level, pressed into the abstract form of Humanity by the relations of everyday capitalist life, we face Nature as something completely separate from and opposed to us. Nature thus becomes a mere object of limitless extraction; the catastrophic consequences of this relationship are continually obscured.

Being forcibly naturalised as Man/Male while formed *against* Man/Male and barred from naturalisation as Woman/Female defines the experience of trans women. Forcibly disciplined as Male in the public sphere and barred from the private sphere – from work and family alike – the proletarian trans woman is trapped. We have plenty to learn about the family and abstract Nature by studying this predicament.

Stars: our inverted personhood

Because we're constituted in and constitute ourselves in *social relations anchored in value*, we're crushed – crushed by the nature of our forcible exclusion in the public sphere. And crushed by our exclusion from the private sphere. We're thus deprived of a liveable life and find ourselves clipping in and out of the abstract realities of human life, deprived of any sense of our own historical presence. This births the tendency towards science-fictional and cosmic themes in our consciousness. It is, at present, a consciousness characteristic of a population *across class*, not yet shaped by the formation of a proletarian class-for-itself. This consciousness is important as a site to see *among various contradictory strands* a *pro-ecological desire which is against the abstract inverted Human and against abstract inverted Nature*.

These science-fictional and cosmic themes are differentiated across race and other aspects of class composition. We can't expect the positive content of a communist social organism to come entirely from any one location. We *can*, however, expect *more* of our positive content to come from Afrofuturism streams than from white transhumanist streams heavily weighted with eugenic undertones. Whiteness has little or nothing in the way of positive content.

The (highly varied) currently existing consciousness of transgender proletarians is certainly *not* the revolutionary standpoint from which to attain truth. There can't be one 'transgender standpoint' in a class society; transgender people are *certainly* not a substitute for the proletariat as revolutionary subject.

We *can* expect the *realised class standpoint* – the standpoint of the proletariat at the moment of its victory and self-abolition – to seem *more trans than trans, more Black than Black, more disabled than disabled,* while being in the process of escaping from the disciplinary functions of those abstractions.

*   *   *

The various capitals, states, and non-governmental bodies work at cross purposes with each other, caught in a 'war of all against all'. They're capable of coordinating with each other only in narrow ways and narrow circumstances. Capital is generally incapable of truly coordinating itself as a single integrated body. Its processes continually manifest unexpected side effects, results contrary to its goals, and results favourable to one capital and harmful to another. The production and reproduction processes of capital and the human species generate a constant remainder of 'inhuman human beings'. Those of us who have a Male sex imposed and develop our personhood *against* Maleness are counted in that number. This inhuman generation may be out of line with the rational collective interests of capital, but capital *necessarily* expresses its interests in a foreshortened manner.

Gender changes with the changes in the mode of production and its various phases. As capital accumulation has long since passed from its *extensive* phase to its *intensive* phase, we see a collapse in the predominantly white working-class family form of single cis male breadwinner and stay-at-home wife. Among proles there has been a rise in 'alternative' family forms.[29] States now excuse themselves from organising indirectly market-mediated activity, and capital moves towards the use of 'feminised' labour – cheap, short-term, just-in-time, 'de-skilled', agile, flexible. These are the circumstances in which trans women in the global cores of capital accumulation have made our gradual gains.

Our concrete personhood is kept cut into fragments – isn't allowed to properly concretise – by remaining under the domain of the abstraction Male. We are crushed under an abstraction which we have developed *against*. This fate makes us miserable, can even kill us. Our development *against* the Male is an unnamed, unspoken condition. It becomes extremely urgent that we name that condition; however, the naming is ultimately just a tool secondary to what it *does*. Naming our condition facilitates our living under the abstraction Woman/Female, which allows us to concretise our personhood more fully. (The naming *represents* the abstraction; the abstraction itself is not a *name*. It is instead a *process* emergent from the dynamics of capital accumulation, which goes on behind our backs.) It's common to hear 'I was not a person until I transitioned'. A trans woman's move to solidify her life under the abstraction Woman, and demand that the world cooperates in her doing so, is a move from the abstract to the concrete. This is not, however, a final overcoming of her domination via abstraction. Such an overcoming can't happen individually. She is making a vital move towards a liveable life, yes – but she's forcing her way in to *renegotiate* her alienation, not abolishing it. This is inevitable until capitalism and value are overcome, and remains true of all transitions: the assertion of non-binary genders is a demand to be captured in a new and more liveable way.

*   *   *

Gender/sex is one of the mediations of class. Nascent class pressure routes itself through transness into changing and lightening the boundaries of gender/sex abstractions, and easing travel between them. This pressure needn't be conscious: one necessarily channels and develops incredible social-organismic creativity under fire simply to make it through life caught between the double-sided transphobic crush of public and private spheres. It's no coincidence that trans people tend to be so fully formed compared to our cis counterparts. We create our own personhood, though not under conditions of our own choosing. Particularly inhospitable conditions of self-development bring out particularly vigorous self-creation.[30] Cis or trans, we create ourselves and our conditions, while our conditions create us; only *then* is the individual abstracted inverted pseudo-person registered. This fact neatly does away with the idea that trans women are specially guilty of living out regressive stereotypes of womanhood – doubly so in that our abstract human personhood is registered in an especially shaky and inconstant fashion. Many of us cannot even live as ourselves full-time. Those forced not to transition at all may have to scratch by in barely survivable conditions.

We create ourselves and our conditions, while our conditions create us: this means that we are *transforming social capacities, technical capacities, infrastructure, transforming the shaping of human bodies*. Only *then* do names and language come into play, as weapons of this process. Is there a positive use of transness for capital? – to secure an outside against which cisgender life poses itself? Or is the gradual granting of provisional recognition to transness *just* a concession made to contain class pressure via the abstract mediations of class?

It might be reasonable to see in the gains for trans people a double-sided concession, akin to unions. Do these benefits apply evenly across race and disability? Absolutely not. Racialisation modifies and displaces gender, hence the figures of the 'masculine, hypersexual' Black woman, the role of the figure of the endangered white woman, the atypical concealment of the family among Black proletarians, and all the rest. There is always a danger of solidifying whiteness, abledness, etc. in those who get the most benefit from concessions to trans people.

We *must* side with the *positive content* in transness rather than with the *form* of transness. The form isn't all bad, and the content isn't all good; regardless, an inversion of form and content has to occur. Our liberation is incompatible with the abstract inverted Human, and incompatible with abstract Nature. Our liberation *requires* a view from full ecological concreteness. Our liberation requires a view from the point at which there is no 'Human' and 'Nature', but a single concrete unity-in-difference. It requires the overcoming of the metabolic rift between human activity and non-human ecology – *and this requires communism.*

Opening to the world, turning to the cosmos

This thinking is speculative, provisional, quite loosely rationalist – a character made necessary by the current abysmal state of communist analysis on the transgender mediation of class struggle. We're made to think in the course of our activity. That fact doesn't in any way consti-tute an invitation to snub evidence or granular analysis – it calls instead for contestation and expansive development, in a manner interested neither in abandoning proven principles to run after opportunities nor in clinging to forms inappropriate for the present situation. Shoehorn-ing evidence into these arguments in order to preserve them would therefore be deeply counter to their thrust.

* * *

Again: the present-day orientation brought up here is an *orientation towards the cosmos as an external object with which one identifies oneself and with which one wishes to merge.* This is a contemplative attitude which seeks to become an active and concretising attitude. The cosmos is simply *the total interrelation – or totality – of what exists*. Through truly opening ourselves to integrating thoroughly with the totality, we could realise our concrete reality as the thinking-feeling-doing matter of the cosmos. This would demand that we overcome the division of labour between head and hand; that we supersede the social relations of disembodied social abstractions – such as Woman – that facilitate our subjugation. In other words, that we attain communism.

This explains why the orientation towards space and the future among trans women is frequently not posed *in opposition to* 'organic' things, to divinity, to images of animals and flowers; why we do not typically set up an opposition between 'natural' things and 'artificial', technological or machine phenomena.

Thinking on transgender life and struggle has been helped along by social-constructionist, anti-naturalist streams. It has, however, continually hit that thinking's limits: its reification of the abstract reality of the *split between the inverted Human and inverted Nature stemming from the metabolic rift between human activity and non-human ecology.* This shows us that successful praxis in class struggle requires *practical movement* towards a point of view that realises the positive concrete content of both abstractions while being directed at the abolition of both abstractions in the realisation of human species-being: communism. This thrust is *profoundly* at odds with the contemplative and reactive bourgeois environmentalist 'conservationism' on the one hand, and the technophilic and eugenic attitude of transhumanism on the other. It means taking seriously *nature as the external body of man*, to such a severe degree that we take our classically Marxist opposition to the mind-body split, and apply it in turn to the split between internal and external mind, between internal and external body.

This thrust proposes a consciously regulated ecological metabolism which is profoundly coordinated and capacitating. A metabolism carried out by a human organism who transforms themselves in a manner at total odds with the eugenic, quantitative competitiveness of the abstract person developed by capitalism. A human organism self-preserving in a way that today's nature-conservationist would hardly recognise: this profoundly prosthetic, human and interspecies society is the total realisation of the best aims of both disability liberation and transgender liberation in one stroke. *It is first a society in*

*which social–ecological concreteness rules over social abstraction and qual-
itative social development rules over quantity. Then, finally, it is a society
that completely dialectically fuses its abstract elements and its concretising
process, its quantities and its qualities, its forms and its contents.*

Notes

1. Thank you to my editors and community readers: Emrys, Charlie
   Powell, Amy De'Ath, Maya Andrea Gonzalez. Thank you so, so much
   to everyone who took the time to work with me in discussion to disen-
   tangle and build these concepts – Amy, Maya, Daniel Spaulding, Justin
   Lieberman, Sam – and above all to my co-thinker and closest comrade,
   who has shaped my orientation towards the world more deeply than they
   realise, a friend who also prefers to remain nameless: 'The revolution will
   rise again, and will be terrible, but anonymous'.
2. As in the cases of James Carr, an American former Black Panther and
   compatriot of George Jackson who aligned himself with adherents of
   the council communist Situationist International, and Mario Mieli, the
   London Gay Liberation Front and Fronte Unitario Omosessuale Rivoluz-
   ionario Italiano (FUORI) leader whose work was informed by theoretical
   dialogue with Jacques Camatte of the formerly Bordigist *Invariance*
   journal; along a slightly different timeline was Ngô Văn Xuyết, the Vietnamese former *La Lutte* Trotskyist and anticolonial/worker's movement
   militant who survived a mass assassination campaign by Ho Chi Minh's
   forces to flee to France, join with the council communist forces circle of
   Maximilien Rubel, and take part as a factory worker in the uprising of
   May 1968. See Carr, J. (2016). *Bad: the Autobiography of James Carr.* New
   York, NY: Three Rooms Press; Mieli, M. (2018). *Towards a Gay Communism: Elements of a Homosexual Critique.* Fernbach, D. (Trans.). London:
   Pluto Press; Văn, N. (2010). *In the Crossfire: Adventures of a Vietnamese
   Revolutionary.* Knabb, K. (Trans.). Chicago, CA: AK Press.
3. Bordiga, A. (1921). Party and Class. First published in *Rassegna Comuni-
   sta*, 2 & 4, translated by the International Communist Party, https://www.
   international-communist-party.org/BasicTexts/English/21PartyC.htm.
4. Ilyenkov, E. (1960). *The Dialectics of the Abstract and the Concrete in Marx's
   Capital*, Chapter 1, Section 'The Concrete and the Dialectics of the Universal and the Individual'. Kuzyakov, Sergei (Trans.). Moscow: Progress
   Publishers edition, 1982, https://www.marxists.org/archive/ilyenkov/
   works/abstract/abstra1f.htm.
5. Marx, K. (1844). *Economic and Philosophical Manuscripts of 1844.* In *Karl
   Marx: Early Writings*, Livingstone, R. & Benton, G. (Trans.). London:
   Vintage Books, 1975, p. 351. I have left out untranslated German terminology which is inserted in brackets in the Vintage edition.

6. Ibid., p. 353.

7. SOPHIE, lyrics from Faceshopping, on the album *OIL OF EVERY PEARL'S UN-INSIDES*, 2018, Transgressive Records.

8. LMCA (n.d.). Introducing: Lorraine O'Grady and Juliana Huxtable, Part 2. *Los Angeles Museum of Contemporary Art MOCA Stream Blog*. Discussion organised by Dean, A.; Dean. A. and Wildenhaus, K. (Eds.), https://www.moca.org/stream/post/introducing-lorraine-ogrady-and-juliana-huxtable-part-2

9. Ilyenkov, *The Dialectics of the Abstract* , Chapter 1, Section 'From the History of the Concepts of the Abstract and the Concrete'.

10. Wittig, M. (1976/1982 [1992]). The Category of Sex. In Wittig, M. (1992). *The Straight Mind and Other Essays*. Boston, MA: Beacon Press, pp. 1–8.

11. Wittig, M. (1985 [1992]). The Mark of Gender. In *The Straight Mind and Other Essays*, pp. 76–89.

12. Wittig, M. (1983 [1992]). The Point of View: Universal or Particular? In *The Straight Mind and Other Essays*, p. 59.

13. Ibid., p. 62.

14. It is therefore just as varied as the *determinations* of the *human essence* and *activities*. [Marx's note].

15. Cf. Hess, M. (1843). Philosophie der Tat. In *Einundzwanzig Bogen aus der Schweiz*. Teil, E. (Trans.). Zürich: Verlag des Literarischen Comptoirs, p. 329. [translator's note].

16. In practice I can only relate myself to a thing in a human way if the thing is related in a human way to man. [Marx's note].

17. Marx, *Economic and Philosophical Manuscripts of 1844*, pp. 351–352.

18. Marx, K. (1957–1961 [1973]). *Grundrisse: Foundations of the Critique of Political Economy* (Rough Draft). Nicolaus, M. (Trans.). London: Penguin, p. 104.

19. In Alfred Sohn-Rethel's account, it is not just the direct domination of one class over another, but the fact that this domination, our entire social metabolism, is now mediated through the commodity form and its general equivalent, money. We are forced to labour as private, indirectly social labourers creating surplus value for capitalists in return for money wages, which produces, through the sale of these products on the market – given their exchangeability with one another as commodities for money – the realisation of this concrete abstraction. This account seems quite contestible, however, not least for its intense focus on the exchange nexus. See Sohn-Rethel, A. (1978). *Intellectual and Manual Labor: a Critique of Epistemology*. London: Macmillan.

20. Ibid., p. 164.

21. As is done with gender/sex in Gabriel, K. (13 April 2020). Gender as Accumulation Strategy, *Invert*, https://invertjournal.org.uk/posts?view=articles&post=7106265#gender-as-accumulation-strategy; and in Floyd,

K. (2009). *The Reification of Desire: Towards a Queer Marxism*. Minneapolis, MA: University of Minnesota Press.

22. Ilyenkov, E. (1974). The Universal. In *Philosophical Investigations in the USSR*. Frederick J. Adelmann (Ed.). Marxists Internet Archive, pp. 26–51, https://www.marxists.org/archive/ilyenkov/works/articles/universal.htm.

23. Lukács, G. (1973). *History and Class Consciousness: Studies in Marxist Dialectics*. Livingstone, R. (Trans.) Cambridge, MA: MIT Press, pp. 83.

24. This following the analysis of De'Ath, A. (2018). Gender and Social Reproduction. In Best, B., Bonefeld, W., & O'Kane, C. (Eds.), *The SAGE Handbook of Frankfurt School Critical Theory*. London: SAGE Publications, pp. 1534–1549.

25. Although, in fairness, its advocates may not think of it as such.

26. Neton, J. & Gonzalez, M. A. (2013). The Logic of Gender. *Endnotes*, 3 (Gender, Race, Class, and Other Misfortunes), 56–90.

27. Marx, *Capital Vol. 1*, p. 585, as quoted in Neton and Gonzalez, The Logic of Gender, p. 58.

28. For which see Franklin, S. (2016). The Contexts of Forms. *World Picture*, 11 (Context), http://worldpicturejournal.com/WP_11/Franklin_11.html.

29. On the collapse see Cooper, M. (2017). *Family Values: Between Neoliberalism and the New Social Conservatism*. London: Zone Books; on the queer family and the limits of the working class family see O'Brien, M. (2019). To Abolish the Family: The Working-Class Family and Gender Liberation in Capitalist Development. *Endnotes*, 5 (The Passions and the Interests), 360–417.

30. Here we converge with Kay Gabriel in spirit.

Afterword
One Utopia, One Dystopia

Jordy Rosenberg[1]

There is a path into Marx that proceeds through transness. More specifically, there is a path into the increasingly prominent Marxian interest in the metabolic relation with nature that proceeds through transness. This is so, I wish to propose, because the concept of metabolism has functioned, since at least the mid-twentieth century, as a concrete abstraction that is lived dialectically by trans people. I will extrapolate this argument, in my Afterword, by way of a reading of Leslie Feinberg's Afterword to hir iconic *Stone Butch Blues*, as well as by situating both that book and some of the concerns of *Transgender Marxism* – particularly those around the usefulness of social reproduction theory – in the context of a broader historical cycle of colonialism and capitalism.

I will begin this argument more properly in the next section, but it is first necessary to acknowledge something of the specificity of our historical moment. To every trans Marxist and communist who has dredged language and thought out of themselves during this time, I imagine I speak for a collective readership when I thank you. Needless to say, 2020 has given those in power a vicious weapon, and the punishment of Black and Indigenous people, the poor, working people, incarcerated people, migrants, teachers, children, the unhoused, the indebted, renters, and disabled people has been relentless. Yet the largest uprisings we have known in decades are in play: the massive, nationwide abolitionist rebellions against the police murders of George Floyd and Breonna Taylor this past summer; the union strike and victory at the country's largest wholesale produce market in the winter of 2021 at Hunts Point; the farmers' strikes in India, possibly the largest strike in human history;[2] worldwide rent, sanitation, distribution, and logistics strikes, to name a few. We are spinning in a storm, but we are strategising and organising, too. The Romantic tradition does not quite capture the immensity of this landscape, but Muriel Rukeyser's mega-engineering sublime gets at something concerning the epic battles being waged: the blasted rock and destoppered river at Hawk's Nest – the fatal labour of coaxing this tumult into tunnels of profit:

> the crest leans under/concrete arches and the channelled hills/turns in the gorge towards its release;/kinetic and controlled, the sluice/ urging the hollow, the thunder,/energy.

Those tasked with shaping the course of this water by hand and brow will carry the scars of that labour in their bodies, as Rukeyser documented in her 1938 *Book of the Dead*.[3] Poetic and critical labour congeals in these landscapes too, but any fantasies cultural workers may have once had about that creative work as an unalienated rind circling the rotten core of capitalist extraction are no longer possible. No labour escapes the ravages of the commodity form. Or, as Ernst Bloch said of life under fascism, 'But no one gets used to living here'.[4] Not when they come for people the way they do, and not when our social reproduction – childcare, eldercare, community care – has been pressed to an impossible limit by the sadistic flood unleashed through the virus. And yet somehow the thinkers collected in *Transgender Marxism* have written into the wreck of the now. We must celebrate this. I am also talking about the poets in Andrea Abi-Karam, and Kay Gabriel's recently released *We Want It All: An Anthology of Radical Trans Poetics*, which I've been reading together with this manuscript, and which feels like a companion volume.[5] Let it be a fellow traveller, as a provocation, to begin.

Stretching social reproduction

We Want It All is a magnificent collection in general, but I want to draw attention to one aspect in particular: Abi-Karam and Gabriel's inclusion of Leslie Feinberg's infamous Letter to Teresa (from *Stone Butch Blues*) in this poetics collection. What might this inclusion mean for us? What might it mean for Transgender Marxism?

I had already been writing about *Stone Butch Blues*, but I'd been focusing on a section that I now see as the verso side of the 'Letter': forged of the same pulp, but facing outward. In the Afterword to the book's 10th anniversary edition, Feinberg declares ze is encountering *Stone Butch Blues* for 'the first time'. Perhaps it is true that no author can ever experience their own book as a reader, but this seems a notable phenomenon when that book is one's own 'very thinly veiled autobiography'. Nonetheless, Feinberg is disoriented by the very path ze has carved:

> By the time I held the [book] ... in my hands the inked words seemed like faint animal tracks on a smooth landscape, a cold trail I couldn't follow.[6]

Stone Butch Blues has served for many as an important early work of trans literature. But I wish to propose that the addition of the Afterword fundamentally changes *Stone Butch Blues* in ways that are relevant to Marxism and transgender thought. It does so because the addition brings into view the question of genre, and – as such – the collective dynamics and aesthetic secretions of history. The history in question is that particular stretch of time understood variously as deindustrialisation, the onset of neoliberalism, and the intensification of service work. And the question of genre? Framed by the new paratextual apparatus, the book takes on something of the character of a cold case file. An untraceable trail – noirish and baroque – registers uncannily the function Fredric Jameson ascribes to detective fiction, connecting seemingly disparate aspects of the social world through the libidinal attention of a detective-character who serves as an 'organ of perception, a membrane which, irritated, serves to indicate in its sensitivity the nature of the world around it'.[7]

Perhaps it is ironic for stone butchness to serve as such a sensitive 'organ', but then again (as anyone who has met a stone butch might object), perhaps it is not. And so Feinberg's novel begins with an epistolary moan to a former lover, written from within the cold antiheroic night of her absence. Teresa, Jess's once co-worker at a cannery, union comrade, partner, and communist, is the addressee of *Stone Butch Blues* – current whereabouts and occupation unknown. 'For more than twenty years I have lived on this lonely shore', says Jess, on that infamous first page, 'wondering what became of you ... Are you turning tricks today? Are you waiting tables or learning Word Perfect 5.1?' The catalogue of service work periodises the moment of the text's writing across a chasm of love lost and industrialisation off-shored, from the perspective of an unknowable neoliberal landscape across which a collection of possible Teresas transit. The litany of rhetorically interchangeable jobs – turning tricks, waiting tables, learning Word Perfect 5.1 – anticipates what Jules Gleeson and Elle O'Rourke, in their introduction to this volume, periodise as the moment in which 'the supposed sureties of Fordist employment ... have been superseded by casualisation ... and a growing demand for the feminised skills of caring and service labour'. This periodisation, furthermore, presents a very specific set of contradictions for trans workers:

> On the one hand, the casualisation of labour has made it less likely that any given trans person will require a singular 'professional persona', to last their whole working lifetime. On the other, this same process also guts the institutions which might previously have been called upon to offer some semblance of protection from employer prejudices.

If the Afterword speaks to the context of casualisation, much of the first half of *Stone Butch Blues* is about the labour of securing protections: love, community, and especially a union job. Perhaps the apex of this quest unfolds in the gripping rendering of a softball game played between union butches and union cis men for the practically Hegelian stakes of mutual recognition. But *Stone Butch Blues* begins somewhere in the *après-coup* of all this, the vertiginous afterwardness of deindustrialisation, when everything has been lost to anomie, urban dating, and the ongoing primitive accumulation that separates workers from union jobs, 'freeing' them into a roster of service work.

In 1993, when *Stone Butch Blues* was originally published, the US was in the midst of a massive process of labour market transformation, notably the decline of manufacturing jobs and the rise of low-wage service work.[8] While many historians begin their analyses somewhere between the 1970s and the 1990s, recently scholars have taken much longer views. Gabriel Winant, for example, complicates the too-easy narrative of simple transposition, arguing that the rise of service work does not supplant manufacturing, but rather develops alongside it out of a schema articulated in the New Deal Era. 'We

might think of the New Deal as … enacting dual decommodifica-
tions', Winant argues.

> [O]ne positive and one negative. On the one hand, industrial labour
> (largely racialised as white and overwhelmingly gendered male)
> was partially decommodified by the securing of working-class
> life through the welfare state … On the other hand, the labor of
> social reproduction was also decommodified but not in the same
> way. Rather than regulate reproductive labor through public policy
> – as with productive labor – the institutions of the New Deal state
> instead decommodified reproductive labor by pushing it to the
> margins of the economy.[9]

For Winant, the rise of service work develops out of these
dually-decommodified tracks, and from the forces unleashed by the
disintegration of manufacture, which re-commodifies a reproductive labour force into the ranks of the expanding health care industry.
'These two processes – the expulsion of working-class men from
industrial labour and the absorption of women into the bottom ranks
of the care industries – are one … As they hemorrhaged factory jobs,
American cities came to need more care labour to tend to their wors-
ening socioeconomic injuries'.[10] The intimacy of deindustrialisation,
incarceration, and the recommodified care work sector has come to
an extreme crisis in 2020–2021, as we know. Contextualising this, in
a recent interview with SEIU steward Shantonia Jackson about the
experience of organising care workers in a nursing home facility on
lockdown during COVID-19, Winant explains:

> The category that the Census calls 'health care and social assis-
> tance' is the largest sector of employment in the country, accounting
> for about one in seven jobs nationwide. It encompasses hospitals,
> clinics, labs, long-term care facilities, home care, and social work
> agencies … [I]n the bottom quintile of the wage structure, accord-
> ing to sociologist Rachel Dwyer, a majority of new jobs since the
> 1980s have been care jobs of some kind.[11]

Moreover, the proximity of care work to the 'racialised and punished'[12]
subjects means that the incarcerated and those caring for them are

drawn from 'the most economically marginal sections of the working class. For example, the Bronx commits one-quarter of its entire work-force to healthcare and social assistance, making that dispossessed borough the leader among the most populous counties in the United States on this measure'.[13]

The carceral state forms the context, the lens, and the complex hinge between industrial and service work. Any political-economic account of neoliberalism that lacks an understanding of this will necessarily be partial, for the relationship between such analysis and abolition as a political commitment is vital. As Ruth Wilson Gilmore has recently noted regarding the inextricable relationship under carceral capitalism between economic abandonment and policing/criminalisation:

> [O]rganized abandonment has to do with the way that people ... do not have equal levels of support and protection against the pandemic, and that the response to people trying to figure out how to shelter themselves and save themselves ... is to use policing and criminalisation ... to resolve the problems of abandonment. Now, organised abandonment is not only abandonment by the state, but it's also abandonment by capital, whether it's abandonment by real estate capital, that produces more and more luxury apartments but not affordable housing, as we can see in struggles throughout the city of New York and around the United States, or tourism capital, that pushes certain kinds of people out of certain areas of the city and only welcomes them in if they work as workers in the service industry, delivering, serving, taking care of and cleaning.[14]

Treva Ellison has articulated vital dimensions of this relation at the mid-twentieth-century intersection of 'Black trans reproductive labor', geographies of gentrification and surveillance, and policing in Los Angeles.[15] Such work is critical, and – as Doyle Griffiths, Zazanis, Raha, and O'Brien indicate in this volume – social reproduction theory (SRT) is overdue for – to invoke Fanon – a stretching.[16]

In their work on Black trans reproductive labour, Ellison conceptu-alises reproduction beyond the sphere of the home, extending an SRT analysis to the broader 'life-making capacities'[17] of the social world. For Ellison, reproductive labour is not simply about the production and gendering of domestic space, but also how 'gender as a mutable category' names a 'relationship between people and the environment'. For example, what are the 'economic networks of support' that Black trans people have used to navigate what (citing David Stein), Ellison describes as 'racial Keynesianism'? And how does and did the state seek to destroy those networks through policing as a tool not *just* for direct surveillance and punishment, but for the transformation of the labour market? Here, Ellison points to the intensification of laws against 'masquerade' as an effort to 'de-wage or unwage drag performance'. This queer and trans archival work specifies in crucial ways the field of neoliberal decommodification that Winant sketches. A queer and trans carcerally-oriented perspective on neoliberalism allows an inimitable analytic subtlety and acuity. Indeed, queer and trans subjects, argues Ellison, 'come into archival view at the nexus of the carceral state and urban geopolitics', because the 'criminalisation of gender and sexual deviance developed as a part of the transition from a war on labour that was crucial to the growth and development of the city's infrastructure'.[18]

Navigating the landscape of police violence is part of the life-making labour of queer and gender non-conforming Black subjects. One of the strongest versions of this formulation was made during the uprisings, in the summer of 2020, when Angela Davis said: '[T]he trans community taught us that it is possible to effectively challenge that which is considered the very foundation of our sense of normalcy. So if it is possible to challenge the gender binary, then we can certainly, effectively, resist prisons, and jails, and police'. '*Taught us*': the language of pedagogy opens the question of organising, politicisation, and struggle. It seems to me that Davis is not talking about transness as a *figure* for resistance;[19] rather, for Davis, the path to revolution appears to be cleared by transness in a dialectical relation, materially lived. Building, perhaps, off the implications of her own 2003 argument that 'gender structures the prison system', transgender life, in its historical struggles against the carceral state, is a necessary though surely not sufficient condition for the work of abolition.[20] Davis's reflections from the rebellions of 2020, taken together with Ellison's archival matrix, describe a dialectics of social reproduction: the ways in which life is both made and makes other life possible, and the ways in which that life is stalked and subjected to violence. What does a broader left owe to the labour of those who live this dialectic? That is, I think, in part Davis's question.

Chokepoints/demand upon pleasure

The violent combination of surveillance and abandonment to which trans people have historically been subjected expresses itself in struggles over social reproduction in ways that might not be immediately apparent. Obscuring the work of trans social reproduction produces what the historian Morgan M. Page describes as the phenomenon by which 'trans people [seem to be] in a constant state of being discovered'.[21] Documenting, narrating, archiving not just our existence, but the labours of our social reproduction falls to us, as does the conceptual and theoretical work of linking seemingly disparate struggles.[22]

As Michelle O'Brien notes of Doyle Griffith's work on the West Virginia teachers' strikes of 2018:

> Kate Doyle Griffiths documents ... the central concern of many workers over a new healthcare monitoring practice of forcing them to wear Fitbits and be subject to regular medical testing, and to fine them if they fail to exercise sufficiently or don't lose weight or meet other health targets.[23] Teachers understandably found this level of coercive surveillance and disciplining of their bodies to be outrageous and unacceptable, in ways remarkably close to why trans people are willing to be fired rather than not transition on the job.[24]

The shared limit point of the body generates an organisational lever, a location of resistant power. As Doyle Griffiths elaborates in this volume, 'trans and queer experiences can be seen as offering us additional access to an often neglected aspect of the fragility of capitalist relations. Namely, choke points of social reproduction'.[25] Doyle Griffiths's argument has only become inexpressibly more relevant as the COVID-19 pandemic makes clear both that zones of social reproduction (whether in the home, the school, the nursing home, the care centre, etc.), will be forcibly compelled to take up the failures of the state, and – as such – are alive with the potential to asphyxiate sources of capital accumulation and profit. Writing even before the pandemic hit, Doyle Griffiths notes:

The teacher strike wave demonstrates that social reproduction choke points are now central to a new wave of struggle; workers who are paid to do the work of the daily remaking of the working class-in-itself play a central role in expanding and politicising workplace struggles.[26]

When it is the body itself that forms a chokepoint, it is not simply a question of withholding, but also – as per Kay Gabriel's powerful recent argument in *Invert Journal* – of making a demand upon our own pleasure. Beginning – then departing – from Maya Andrea Gonzalez's argument in *Endnotes* around the abjection associated with 'indirectly market mediated' feminised labour,[27] Gabriel argues that:

Th[e] impact of phobic abjection extends beyond the wage relationship into the reproductive sphere, variously constraining the ability of transsexuals to reproduce ourselves. Considering the critical role of the family in regulating social reproduction – a role that, following Mohandesi and Teitelman, has only expanded in the 'crisis of social reproduction' in the post-1980s global north – the uneven alienation of trans people from the family unit further exacerbates our social precarity.[28]

Part of revolutionary work is to transform these vulnerabilities into pressure points to build power through the articulation of a demand: 'transsexual demands to exercise autonomy, however, enabled by social or medical interventions, over our configurations of embodiment and sexuality pertain to a category of high-stakes desires and pleasures, whose utopian core is the demand for the body to be a site of affirmation over and against routine abjection'. This demand – as for Doyle Griffiths – is far from only relevant to transsexuals:

A specifically transsexual standpoint then discloses for a liberatory gender politics the critical insight that the body, *including its capacities within the signification of sexual difference,* is an indispensable site of struggle over the creation of a disalienated life-world available to all. Where Bhattacharya urges that the 'demand by [working-class] communities to extend their sphere of pleasure is a vital class demand, "the foregrounding of the body as a mediation between desire and the social appears as the intensive side of this extensive demand'".[29]

The indispensability of pleasure returns us to *Stone Butch Blues*, and to the (ultimately irreparable) fissure that develops between Jess and Teresa as Jess articulates a desire to begin taking exogenous hormones. Jess's Letter to Teresa is penned in the aftermath of a break between how Jess and Teresa inhabit social worlds, their workplace, and politics, and how they endure assaults by the police. None of these questions can be separated from the question of their shared – and unshared, or unshareable – pleasures.[30]

> Teresa sighed. 'I'm a femme, Jess. I want to be with a butch. And I'm starting to feel like part of the women's movement, even though I can't be all the parts of who I am at the same time. My world's expanding.' 'Great,' I snorted. 'Mine's shrinking. But the hormones are like the looking glass for me. If I pass through it, my world could open up, too.' Theresa shook her head. 'I don't want to be with a man, Jess. I won't do it.'

A certain kind of medicalised transness produces the rift that lands Jess on 'this lonely shore' years later, wondering what kind of casualised labour Teresa is doing now. Around their romantic shattering, the rise of service work ripples out. Annie McClanahan has developed a powerful long durée account of this period as the generalisation of a racialised hierarchy of tipped vs wage work that extends a plantation logic through the twentieth and twenty-first centuries.

> One of the leading proponents of tip wages in the early twentieth century was the Pullman Company, which exclusively hired black men from the South because, in the words of one executive, 'the southern negro is more pleasing to the travelling public. He is more adapted to wait on people and serve with a smile'.[31]

The characterological, eugenicist basis of service work, for McClanhahn 'registers the sense that there was a deep connection between the non-waged work of in-person service and the non-waged work of chattel slavery'. The twentieth-century twist of all this was that

Pullman exploited its ability to make customers complicit in its schema. As a *St. Louis Republic* editorial in 1915 reads, 'Other corporations before now have underpaid their employees, but it remained for the Pullman Corporation to discover how to ... induce [the] public to make up, by gratuities, for its failure to pay its employees a living wage'. This practice of relying on customers to make up for the absence of a living wage, says McClanahan,

> was legalised and codified by the 1966 FLSA [Fair Labor Standards Act] amendment ... [T]he setting of a subminimum wage for the restaurant and hospitality sector was a massive labour-cost subsidy for the restaurant, hotel, and leisure industry, one that arguably contributed to the transformation of the US economy from a manufacturing to a service economy.[32]

Stone Butch Blues does not, itself, articulate this long view of the rise of the service industry. Nor – as several critics have pointed out – does it account for the ways in which it itself relies on Black and indigenous figures to 'teach' Jess something either about race politics or – as Mark Rifkin has pointed out – about accepting hir own gender nonconformativity.[33] Something like the dialectic of Black trans reproductive labour described by Ellison and Davis is both figured in the book as central to Jess's development, and then figuratively elided in the event of the break-up, which becomes, in many ways, the emotional turning point that organises the narration of history thereafter such that the transit from a post-war world of union jobs to a chaos of gig work becomes figured as an apostrophic address from a butch to a femme. The schism of history is allegorised as a schism between lovers, one that is violently introduced in the diegesis of the book by Jess's ambivalent but ultimately realised desire to take exogenous hormones toward a more phenotypically organised trans identity.

In other words, the catachresis between the rift caused by medicalised transness and the historical rift of deindustrialisation is the inverted form of appearance of the book's real historical context in which the racialised hierarchy of labour, both in terms of Black and Indigenous people caring labour and the historical context of plantation labour and post-Reconstruction Jim Crow codes, feeds into the twentieth-century explosion of service work which leaves Jess wondering where and at what occupation Teresa is at now. Of course, *Stone Butch Blues* is not a work of historical scholarship. And I'm not able to adjudicate whether and how it might have been able to produce a different account of its own context; I am, however, interested in how the narrative trope of the medicalised transition and break up both figures and elides a question about 'politics'. It is here that the inclusion of the Letter to Teresa within *We Want It All* opens a framework for analysis.

Trans auto-apostrophic

Jess's lament to Teresa bears some similarity both in its non-specificity and its sentimentality, to the trope of poetic apostrophe – or, as Jonathan Culler famously had it, the 'embarrassment' of address. In addition to being an embarrassment (or perhaps because of it), apostrophe, as Anahid Nersessian has recently argued, creates the 'common ground of an artificial space'; it summons – per Rosalind Krauss – a 'phenomenological vector' between subject and world.[34]

'I had coffee in Greenwich Village earlier with a woman', Jess continues, plinking a pebble into the well of Teresalessness. 'A mutual friend fixed us up, since we're both "into politics." Well, we sat in a coffee shop, and she talked about Democratic politics and seminars and photography and problems with her co-op and how she's so opposed to rent control. Small wonder – Daddy is a real estate developer'. The expanse between an erstwhile communist partnership and the bathetic and tragic equation of 'politics' to the Democratic party yawns wide. How is it that Jess has gone from being lovers with a comrade and co-worker and sharing a political horizon, to coffee with the daughter of a real estate developer? This could be the dystopian verso facet of interclass contact to which Samuel Delany writes a paean in *Times Square Red, Times Square Blue*. Delany eulogises the Times Square porn theatres as spaces where people of different classes forged a connection, while Feinberg recoils at the ersatz forms of contact that neoliberalism makes possible in our simultaneously highly atomised and massively contracted field of the social.[35] In *Stone Butch Blues*'s Manhattan, class contact is a horror story in which gentrification prises open a miserable portal through which a working-class butch might find herself on a terrible date with the daughter of a developer.

Let us remember that Feinberg's last reported words were 'Remember me as a revolutionary communist'. Maybe the apostrophic yearning for a lost object is not just Jess's, but the book's – and the object is not (or not only) Teresa, but politics.

If we hadn't already read *Stone Butch Blues* as autofiction, we might be tempted to do so when we put the Letter to Teresa together with the Afterword. The vexations of trans memoir and trans self-reflexivity are of course dusty old questions that continue to dog us – a seemingly ineradicable refrain. The critic Vivian Namaste some time ago generated the highly quotable objection that 'autobiography is the only genre in which transgender people' would be permitted to speak. In other words, we are only allowed to write creatively when we are attesting to the authenticity of our own subjectivity. This longstanding problem has recently taken the form of what we might see as the auto-fictive question. Although published before autofiction became the genre du jour, *Stone Butch Blues* is not immune from this retroactive generic assignation. Recently Juliet Jacques has wrestled with this problem, describing *Stone Butch Blues* as, on the one hand, 'not quite autofiction, as it doesn't use Feinberg's own name', but nonetheless 'end[s] up ... blur[ing] the boundaries between Feinberg's own life and fiction'. The demand for an auto-fictive impulse from trans people – and the tacit enforcement of this norm by publishers – has produced a host of really wonderful subversions and detournements from queer and trans authors, playing with and against this genre restriction, often leaning towards auto-fictional wink. Kai Cheng Thom, McKenzie Wark, T. Clutch Flesichmann, Renee Gladman, to name a few.

But I want to suggest – following Abi-Karam and Gabriel's curation of the Letter to Teresa – we can read the text not so much as autofiction, but rather as a poetics. Doing so changes not only our interpretation of the work, but also has implications for a Marxist study of contemporary literature more broadly, which I will get to in a moment.

'I am typing these words as June 2003 surges with Pride', writes Feinberg in the Afterword. 'What year is it now, as you read', Feinberg asks. We know ze wrote this Afterword after a lengthy court battle to re-secure the copyright for the novel after Alyson Press, the original publisher, declared bankruptcy. Having won, Feinberg makes the book available for free on hir website, as it still is today, where you can read it as a sort of Teresa yourself. Like Teresa, we are asked: where are you and what are you doing? 'What has been won; what has been lost? I can't see from here', Feinberg continues. We know that ze was ill as ze wrote these words, and they strike with an enormity more than uncanniness when we encounter them now.

The apostrophe is slipping. Where are we? And, when we read this Afterword now, where is the 'here' from which Feinberg is speaking, as it seems to recede perspectivally into the distance? It is hard not to absorb this Afterword as an aleatory apostrophe from Feinberg to Feinberg hirself – a noirish, meta, and auto-fictional supplement to the body text. In his truly wonderful book, *Contemporary Drift*, Theodore Martin spends some time with the 'acousmatic and nondiegetic' quality of noir voiceover. 'To listen to voice-over is to be haunted by the often unanswerable question of where the voice that's talking to us is talking to us from. [B]ecause they aren't located in the diegesis of the films, they have no source for us to discover'.[36] This is the case, exemplarily, with Sunset Boulevard, the famous opening shots of which show police and paparazzi gathered around a scandal of Hollywood death: Gillies – our narrator – face down in the pool. The shot is from the bottom of the pool. The viewer is beneath the scene, looking up at Gillies' dead eyes unseeing them, then through the rippling surface at the cops and the paparazzi. Cameras flash like solar flares – a galaxy of light blinks above; the viewer is buried at the bottom of a pool, and the dead narrator lives on in a voiceover from beyond the grave.

Noir voiceover in general stages a paradox. A neutral tone, clinical and precise about location and context – retracing steps to show the way things have proceeded inexorably to their fatal conclusion. But the 'acousmatic' and 'nondiegetic' fact of voiceover showcases the asynchronicity of picture and sound; the media that make up the genre are coming from two different locations. In this way, the voiceover's placelessness:

> Points to the here-and-now of the speaking subject; it describes -
> and circumscribes...how an individual is situated in social space by
> depicting the institutional forces that have compelled him to speak
> in the first place ... Registering the call of the acousmatic voice ...
> the noir voice-over points us to its underlying source, which turns
> out to be its overarching social situation.[37]

Feinberg's Afterword marshals the conventions of noir voiceover as a kind of poetic apostrophe and, in so doing, dramatises hir projected 'situation' after death as a kind of utopian de-alienation of cultural worker from hir labour. Alienation gives way onto an affective, intensive contraction of space, an imagined unmediated intimacy between author and reader that exceeds both the reign of the commodity form and the death of the author. The Afterword makes palpable the eventfulness of having regained the rights to the work through an apostrophic address, now not to Teresa – though echoing that earlier address – but to the vastness and absolute contingency of the audience reading the work after Feinberg's passing, once copyright has been lifted. If the noir voiceover, as per Martin, points ultimately to the situational context of the speaker, in the case of Feinberg's paratextual Afterword, the dramatising of escape from corporate ownership and the positing of the manuscript as a gift to incalculable numbers of readers stages the opening of history itself to the absolute contingency of situation. 'What year is it now, as you read? What has been won … I can't see from here'. The unknowable 'here' from which Feinberg is speaking becomes the unknowable constellation of situations – with all their political opportunities – from which ze is, and will be, read.

This generalisation of address is the realisation of apostrophe's most utopian modality as the 'common ground of an artificial space', a 'phenomenological vector' that, finally, voices – or *voiceovers* – the real question of situation, which is the question of politics. Not politics as the Democratic party, but politics as the openness of the conjuncture towards the abolition of alienation, a horizon resolved not in the diegesis of the novel, but in the poetics of its paratext. Not politics as a platform, but politics as the enjambment of temporal markers ('what year is it now?') with the material question of how that year is lived – 'what has been won?' Not politics as stagism, but rather as the utter contingency of a heterogeneity of readers, with all their wins and losses.

There's a utopian and a dystopian version of what transness – or a version of transness that has to do with hormones and medicalised technique – is doing here. On the one hand, transness is the precipitating cataclysm that generates the temporal and spatial chasm across which deindustrialisation and the rise of service work unfolds, even as the emotional fulcrum of the transition narrative makes a great deal of the historical context of that transition to neoliberalism invisible. Transness in this dystopian sense becomes a narrative fixation that occludes its own real historical context.

At the same time, the chasm created by the event of medicalised transness furnishes the landscape for an apostrophe to the political – an opportunity for exhortative speech, a zone or dimension of agitprop which makes possible the question of the necessity and the contingency of *intervening* in a situation. The issue thus becomes to ask how the self-reflexivity of transness functions as the vehicle through which these utopian and dystopian modalities get actualised. Reading Feinberg as a poetics, from a Marxist perspective and after Abi-Karam and Gabriel, allows us unique purchase on the ambivalent relationship between literary reflexivity and trans utopias/dystopias.

Trans Marxist hermeneutics: a preliminary sketch

Gabriel and Abi-Karam clarify how a revolutionary poetics might work:

> Poetry isn't revolutionary practice; poetry provides a way to inhabit revolutionary practice, to ground ourselves in our relations to ourselves and each other, to think about an unevenly miserable world and to spit in its face. We believe that poetry can do things that theory can't, that poetry leaps into what theory tends towards. We think that poetry conjoins and extends the interventions that trans people make into our lives and bodily presence in the world, which always have an aesthetic dimension. We assert that poetry should be an activity by and for everybody.

If we understand the resistance to the demand for trans authenticity as a kind of poetics, Feinberg's 'Letter' – together with the Afterword – seem less a self-reflexive auto-fictive loop, and rather more a different kind of reflexivity and contraction of distance: an inhabitation of revolutionariness – figured here as the utopian-apostrophic drawing close of reader and author.

The implications of a trans Marxist literary hermeneutic are, to my mind, broad. The prevalence of reflexivity as a literary-critical frame extends beyond trans writing. Indeed, it could be said to be one of the central ways in which post-war US literature has been periodised, in large part due to Mark McGurl's field-defining *Program Era*, which centralises metafiction and self-referentiality in the periodisation of Post-War and contemporary literature: 'In recognition of the fundamental importance of self-reference ... I will call the act of authorship in the Program Era the "autopoetic process," and here designate as two of its most basic interacting elements the values of creativity and experience ... [and the] act of authorship that it records ...'[38]

For McGurl, the aesthetic aetiology of self-management is the 'intensification' of 'modernist reflexivity'; this self-reflexivity, via the institution of the creative writing programme, becomes what McGurl sees as a generalised or dominant mode of creative expression:

[T]he metafictional impulse in postwar writing ... suggest[s] that literary practices might partake in a larger, multivalent social dynamic of self-observation. This would extend from the self-observation of society as a whole in the social sciences, media, and the arts, to the 'reflexive accumulation' of corporations which pay more and more attention to their own management practices and organizational structures, down to the self-monitoring of individuals who understand themselves to be living, not lives simply, but life stories of which they are the protagonists.[39]

Compulsive self-performance is the literary expression of what McGurl describes as the information economy, which doesn't consume experience directly, but rather the product of transformative labour that is conducted upon experience.

There is certainly something to the post-war explosion of literary reflexivity, but is the relationship between this figural matrix and the self-regulation of aesthetic value the kind of mirroring that McGurl seems to suggest? Alison Shonkwiler's recent identification of a point of intersection between the explosion of memoir and 'neohomesteaderism' clarifies some of the stakes of my hesitation about this point in McGurl's analysis. Though written before the COVID-19 pandemic, Shonkwiler's essay is a helpful framing of the pandemic's unleashing of a seemingly bottomless petit-bourgeois rage for land, fantastical self-sufficiency, and the hysterical intensification of the romance of the nuclear family. For Shonkwiler, neohomesteading needs to be situated within a long tradition of 'early twentieth-century back-to-the-land models ... In an era before Social Security, food stamps, or Medicaid ... The goal of homesteading was not necessarily to preserve an artisanal way of life...but to achieve 'security, independence, and autonomy'. After WWII, Shonkwiler argues, liberals turned 'away from homesteading as a guarantee of security, and instead concentrate[d] on public spending programmes and the development of a full-employment economy'.[40] The return of neohomesteading today, for Shonkwiler, registers the instability of waged labour in the present, and takes a wide variety of forms, from far-right petit-bourgeois prepperism to liberal fetishes of artisanal and ultimately 'conservative ethics of production', to 'new leftist "peasantism"' sceptical that 'the industrial or even the post-industrial working class is somehow going to deliver humanity into an abundant and egalitarian socialism'.[41]

Noting the proliferation of memoirs in general, and memoirs *about* homesteading in particular, Shonkwiler argues that this vortex of literary attestations to self-reliance registers various neoliberal adaptations in the white-collar and professional job economy. 'Trying to combine waged work with unwaged producerism (including but not limited to selling memoirs)', argues Shonkwiler, 'is fundamentally an effort to compensate for declining real wages and job security, the loss of the family wage, and all the other ways that post-Fordist flexibility defines conditions of employment'.[42]

Shonkwiler's argument refines an important point of difference, for me, from McGurl's account of the relative weight of *reflexivity* in describing the dynamics of late capitalism. More specifically, the tropes of neohomesteading that Shonkwiler uncovers reveals the extent to which 'reflexivity', self-performance, and self-management are not direct reflections of a mode of production, but rather *fantasies* that capital tells about itself – fantasies that are not fully explained by a *Zeitgeist* of entrepreneurial neoliberalism, and rather more by the question of what Marx called primitive accumulation, or what David Harvey calls accumulation by dispossession, or what Rosa Luxemburg calls extended accumulation. The uneven distribution of violence domestically and globally as the ongoing condition of late capitalism's so-called 'self-management' – whether it is through police violence as a key arm of the transformation of the New Deal Era labour market and the autonomisation of the police unions (Ellison), the valorisation of the value of whiteness (Singh), violence as the organising rubric of the uneven development of debt (Wang), the subjection to violence and the 'affectability' of the subject as the foundation of the racial hierarchisation of persons (da Silva), or violence to the body as itself a commodity (Valencia), self-management is both a form of accumulation by dispossession, and the *fiction* that is produced *by* this violence. Self-management is the fiction capitalism tells about itself and, as such, I am not sure how much hermeneutic force we can derive from also claiming that this is the fiction that fiction tells. What I am making, then, is a different point and it has to do with the implications for a hermeneutic of Western literature if we understand this violence as primary and constitutive rather than as exceptional. Surely the concepts of 'experience' and 'creativity' – not to mention self-referentiality – shift when our point of reference is not the information economy as such, but rather the uneven distribution of violence as the means by which value – informational or whatever – is valorised.

A trans Marxist hermeneutic presses us to revise our understanding of the role and meaning of metafiction and autofiction, including the auto-fictive demand on transness and our responses to it. What if for 'autofiction' or 'memoir' (or narrative self-referentiaity), we instead regard contemporary tropes of self-reflexivity as *auto-apostrophic*? As, in other words, poetic? *We Want It All* has done just this. Can we generalise this impulse? And how would it allow us to more accurately name the violence of ongoing primitive accumulation as the underlying condition for tropes of self-referentiality.

Moreover, if poetics is how we are meant to understand trans self-reflexivity, then should self-reflexivity be more properly understood less as 'auto-fictive' and more broadly as an attenuation of the allegorical? We might then understand this attenuation of the allegorical – the giving way of allegory to self-referentiality – as a certain post-war coming into prominence of aesthetics' anti-figural supplement (what Benjamin might have called history's 'trash'[43]). This anti-figuralness, in as much as it is 'auto-fictional', is, beyond a waning of allegory, also – and more specifically – a poetic revaluation of abjection (per Gabriel, above) and surplus. The other name for this abjected excess, of course, is the body.[44] This is what Jameson understands as contemporary fiction's 'reduction to the body' – something like the making of fiction into a sixth sense: 'waves of generalised sensations'[45] burrowed into a perpetual present in which allegory, or the naming-function, has lost its stature, and the haptic has taken its place. There are utopian and dystopian versions of this, of course. And the utopian vein is not really visible unless one understands it from the perspective of a poetics – and this is something Jameson does not do, because of his legendary allergy to poetry – as an apostrophic-phenomenological vector.[46]

As for self-reflexive *dystopias*, an interesting companion text to Shonkwiler's would be Phil Neel's *Hinterland*, which wages a many-genred effort (memoir, travel narrative, political-economic treatise, manifesto, etc.) – itself a kind of autofiction – to delineate the post-industrial US as a landscape of intensifying hinterland. Zones of dispossession – neither urban nor rural – ranged around the maintenance of massive infrastructures. For Neel, 'Economic activity shapes itself into sharper and sharper peaks, centred on palatial urban cores which then splay out into megacities'.[47] These hubs are then encircled by 'megaregions' (in Sarah Brouillette's useful redaction):

> industrial farms, power generation sites, and logistics hubs ... Neel describes [this] as a 'disavowed, distributed core' – a sort of hidden abode, where the service sector and the 'FIRE' industries (of finance, insurance, and real estate) that define the urban centre find their integral foundations in massive operations of highly automated food and energy production.[48]

In *Hinterland*, Neel argues, forms of ultra-right 'self-reliant networks' develop, bound by xenophobia and white supremacy. To this we are summoned to proliferate left and ultraleft similar form of self-reliance. This is not the place for a tactical discussion, but reading *Hinterland* now, one is acutely aware of how necessary it is to include an abolitionist epidemiological ethos in the ambit of such imagined, large-scale leftist self-reliance, lest such projects contract into reiterations of nuclearism at worst, or coterie culture at medium-worst. An ethos, perhaps, of which Du Bois took particular note in his biography of John Brown. Ill with a bout of scarlet fever, Brown responds by protecting those *outside* the perimeter of the family home: 'When his children were ill he took care of us himself, and if he saw persons coming to the house he would go to the gate to meet them not wishing them to come in, for fear of spreading the disease'.[49]

The lavish narrative attention Du Bois pays to this interlude – but one example of the countless times he extols Brown's life-reproducing labour and care work[50] – suggests a glimpse of a people's epidemiology that is the near obverse of the petit-bourgeois neohomesteading of the COVID-19 period. For Du Bois's Brown, disease doesn't trigger a sequestering/'saving' of the white family from the world. Rather, the white family *is* the pathogen from which the world must be protected.

But I've gotten off topic.

Rift lit

Or perhaps not, because the pathologies of the white family are not only critical to our current moment, but reconnect both to the question of abjection raised by Gabriel, and to the matrix of cultivation, reflexivity, neoliberalism, and literary value raised – but not really satisfactorily addressed – by McGurl. Returning to our discussion of violence above, I'd submit that self-cultivation as a literary aesthetic dynamises when we take a longer view, specifically when we look to its potential pre-history in the early modern travel narrative. There we will find an origin story of sorts for the fantasy of white settler bodies as anti-pathological, indeed as vital elements of colonial ecosystems and agriculture. As such, these texts figurally veil the actual historical plantation and proto-plantation systems of labour on which the cultivation of these lands depended. Exemplary in this regard is Richard Ligon's 1657 *True & Exact History of Barbadoes*, in which fantasies of settler cultivation and family life attain an uncanny, indeed Oedipal, precision. In the course of the typical colonialist description of the flora of the island, Ligon inserts a strange theatrical tangent in the form of an eavesdropped conversation between settler father and daughter: Ligon describes a kind of tree, the Gnaver, which

holds within a pulpie substance, full of small seeds, like a fig ... These seeds have this property, that when they have past through the body, wheresoever they are laid down, they grow. A Planter, & an eminent man in the Iland, seeing his Daughter by chance about her naturall businesse, call'd to her: Plant even, Daughter, plant even. She answered: If you do not like 'em, remove 'em, Father, remove 'em.[51]

What the *Barbadoes* document burps up from its baleful depths is cultivation as the imagined capacity of settler bodies – and indeed settler familial reproductive units – to repair the problems produced by settler bodies in their capacities as agents of primitive accumulation. I'm thinking in particular here of the phenomenon known to Marxists as 'metabolic rift',[52] or the increasing distance between the sites of consumption and the sites of production, which results in the non-return of waste products to the site at which they are produced, and the resulting impoverishment of the soil. Metabolic rift is a crisis of cultivation, and we can read the triply voyeuristic scene of the settler daughter's fecund excrescence in Ligon, then, as articulating with some unnerving exactitude an ideological drive to both encode and exceed this crisis. The settler body is idealised as magically able to repair/fertilise/make productive the contradictions it itself produces through its seemingly perfect metabolic integration with the land. Moreover, it is the white family and white primogeniture that deploys these energy reserves in the form of the settler daughter's anal productivity.

Ligon's text evinces, in other words, an anxiety about primitive accumulation and its ever-present threat in the form of metabolic rift and ongoing separations between persons and environment that it puts into play. The fact that historical conditions had to converge to set capitalism in motion raises the spectre of contingency. A collision of historical forces thus haunts capitalism as the 'threat of its dissolution'. If metabolic rift continues unbridled, this dissolution will take the form of total environmental destruction. To this threat – which even the bourgeoisie and the colonists knew (and *know*) was a problem that would extinguish them too – comes its ideological 'answer' in the fantasy of the perfect metabolicism of settler bodies. This metabolicism, I wager, itself haunts the contemporary self-reflexivity of literary form – a form which is inextricable from its fantasy of not only the body's but also fiction's perfect metabolicism (is not the *mise-en-abyme* of bad autofiction the spectre of a book which refers only to itself?). This white settler imaginary resolution of the real social contradiction of primitive accumulation constitutes, I want to say, the pre-history of the self-reflexive and the anti-aesthetic, which is insufficiently described as self-management, and would be better understood as the *longue durée* of a violent reverie of the West. Settler bodies as the metabolic 'solution' to the separations wrought by those bodies itself. Missiles sent from the metropole.

To close, I want to make three polemical points about metabolic rift.

1. If the white family is the inauthentic (but frenetically propped up) 'solution' to the metabolic rift, a people's epidemiology, *pace* Du Bois's Brown, offers the horizon of repairing that rift. Not repair as a return to some pre-rift fantasy, and not repair as some suture. Rather, repair of the rift as a kind of family abolition: the refusal to sacralise the reproduction of whiteness. Protection is offered outward, rather than hoarded.[53]

2. The next, related, point follows from Ryan Jobson's excellent recent essay, Dead Labor: On Racial Capital and Fossil Capital.[54] Here, Jobson offers a long-overdue and much needed corrective to contemporary work around metabolic rift – in particular, Andreas Malm's argument, in Fossil Capital, that the development of carbon-based energy forms such as coal form the origin point for metabolic rift writ large. For Malm, once energy is not a property of nature specific to the location where it manifests (wind, water), but can be stored (as in coal), the ability to transport energy vast distances intensifies metabolic rift for the industrial age. These conditions are responsible for 'liberat[ing] [capital] from the strictures of absolute space'.[55]

   Jobson argues that the fascination with 'fossils' as the focal point for understanding metabolic rift

   > necessarily departs from an earlier moment in which human labour was first rendered in thermodynamic terms as labour *power* – a productive machine fated to compete with nonhuman machines. The slave is the original expression of human labour as labour power ... [In this way], race supplies the premise on which certain select classes of labour are appraised from their thermodynamic capacity for work, rather than their material needs and creative potential.[56]

Enslaved persons, in other words, constitute the originary 'energy reserves' and thus the *sine qua non* of any theorisation of metabolic rift.

3. The final points I want to make have to do with the sexed and gendered dimensions of this thermodynamic frame. My proposition is that *how* we understand metabolic rift is conditioned on 20th-century transformations in the sex/gender matrix.

We might begin here by situating Jobson's claims around enslaved persons as the originary model of energy reserves, in relation to Hortense Spillers's account of the contradictory status of Black matriarchal 'power' – both the 'patholog[isation]' of Black matriarchal 'strength' as an 'instrument of castration' (i.e., in the Freudian schematic, the ungendering threat/cut that itself produces binary gender), and the 'misnaming' of the 'power of the [enslaved] female', because 'the female could not, in fact, claim her child'.[57] Spillers describes captive female bodies as 'translat[ing] into a potential for pornotroping and embod[ying] sheer physical powerlessness that slides into a modern general powerlessness'.[58] What are the implications of Spillers's argument for Jobson's matrix, and how can we include the 'storage' of 'powerlessness' as a particular kind of thermodynamics within racial capitalism? Moreover, C. Riley Snorton expands on Spillers's account to argue that, given

> that the capacity for gender differentiation was lost in the outcome of the New World, ordered by the violent theft of body and land ... captive flesh figures a critical genealogy for modern transness, as chattel persons gave rise to an understanding of gender as mutable and as an amendable form of being.[59]

Spillers's, Snorton's, and Jobson's arguments, taken together, suggest that trans studies has the potential for a significant intervention into current discussions of metabolic rift; indeed, they suggest that a certain racialised matrix of sex is at the root of all such metabolicisms. Though I don't have nearly enough space to explore these questions at greater length here, we can gesture toward the implications through a quick review of Marxian metabolics.

We know from Marx's notebooks, as well as from Kohei Saito's important new book[60] on the topic, that Marx was studying soil science extensively while preparing to write *Capital*, as well as afterwards. Marx's first major undertaking in this area was the work of Justus von Liebig who was at the vanguard of a counter-tendency within agricultural science in arguing that soil functioned through the operation of metabolism, or 'Stoffwechsel'. This was a field-changing argument; the orthodoxy of agricultural chemistry had understood soil as having a kind of limitless value-producing capacity in and of itself. The productiveness of soil was a property of soil. For von Liebig, soil could not replenish itself, but rather existed metabolically with the world, which for Marx also implied the people who laboured upon it and the particular mode of production to which it was subjected. For Liebig, the soil needed to be fed with the waste products of its own production, otherwise it would become increasingly exhausted, as the split between country and city that marked the onset of capitalist production itself increased. Liebig's answer to soil exhaustion was focused largely on the manufacture of artificial fertiliser to stave off the impending crisis of fertiliser scarcity, as '[i]n a few years, the guano reserves [which were being expropriated and imported as a source of fertiliser] will be depleted'. Despite the superexploitation of largely Chinese indentured labour and the large-scale colonial project of sourcing guano from Peru, for Liebig, the unrelenting 'law of replenishment' required an even readier-to-hand supply than the most brutal colonial processes could produce. He devoted himself to figuring out how to produce artificial fertiliser, in particular how to isolate the key element of nitrogen from the air.

Liebig's work was very influential for Marx, in particular because it ran directly against bourgeois progressivist conceptions of history and agricultural advancement.[61] The importance of the metabolic schematic for Marx's entire project cannot be overstated. For one, it grounds the idea that 'rent' does not name the autonomous value of soil and land; rather, the exchange value of rent is an abstraction which more often than not functions at odds with nourishing the land's use value in a sustainable way. Moreover, Marx began to generalise the principle of 'Stoffwechsel' beyond the agricultural scene proper; 'Stoffwechsel' is also the term Marx used to describe the mode of production and commodity exchange. For Marx, 'The exchange of commodities is the process, in which the social metabolism takes place, i.e. the exchange of the particular products of private individuals, as well as the creation of definite social relations of production through which the individuals enter into this metabolism'. For Alfred Schmidt, this means that 'metabolism' broadly describes the exchange process:

> In the process of exchange, the use value, which is the direct product of the relation between man and nature, 'takes on an existence as an exchange value ... cut loose from any connection with its natural existence.' Then, through the mediation of this social metabolism, the exchange value returns to its former immediacy, i.e. again becomes a use value.[62]

Marx's concept of metabolic rift has become increasingly prominent of late. From John Bellamy Foster to Malm and Saito, metabolic rift has come to the fore in Marxist thought in ways not previously articulated, at least in the English-speaking West. The recent uptick in metabolic analysis has led some to ask why Marx's concept of metabolic rift wasn't recognised more extensively until recently. Ian Angus, for example, offers a recent account, arguing that because there was no equivalent word for 'Stoffwechsel' in English, it did not appear in Aveling's translation. Indeed, it wasn't until Fowkes's 1976 version, that 'Stoffwechsel' was translated as 'metabolism': 'In the French translation of Tiedemann's book', says Angus, 'Stoffwechsel was rendered as le renouvellement du Matériel – renewal of material. In English, the word was commonly translated as some variant of "exchange of material", which was literally correct, but didn't express the complexity of the German word'.[63]

Angus's proposition regarding the translation of 'Stoffwechsel' may address why 'metabolism' did *not* appear in Aveling's translation, but it does not address why 'metabolism' *did* appear in Fowkes's. Indeed, this question needs to be pursued in relation to the broader social conditions that would have made it possible for Fowkes to translate 'Stoffwechsel' *as* metabolism in the first place. I propose that those social conditions share a common root in certain notions of sexuality and gender that became both concrete and abstract in the US and England in the 1950s and onwards. In other words, the later twentieth century is the period in which 'metabolism' itself came to function as a concrete abstraction. This was a process that was tied intimately to a metabolic theory of the body in general – and of *embodied sex* in particular.

More precisely: to the question of why it took so long for metabolism to take on a central role in Marxist work in English, my sense is that the term made itself available as a concrete abstraction (naming an axiomatic of capitalism) in large part only after it had transited through sexology, and in particular the sexology of mid-century clinics.

This claim is undergirded in large part by Jules Gill Peterson's pivotal book, *Histories of the Transgender Child*, in which she studies the archives of the Johns Hopkins Hospital, in particular case records of patients with congenital adrenal hyperplasia (CAH), a metabolic variation which can produce so-called virilising secondary sex characteristics (enlarged clitoris and body hair) in subjects usually assigned female at birth, as well as potentially life-threatening adrenal crises. Gill Peterson finds in the archive traces of anxiety on the part of clinicians and researchers about the impossibility of sequestering adrenal systems from secondary sex characteristics – either in CAH itself, or in therapeutic approaches to it. As there is no way to address metabolic regulation without also having effects on sex characteristics, researchers and doctors found themselves forced to conclude that biological sex is far less stable and fixed than they might have liked to presume. Sex, in other words, is not an autonomous property of the body; rather, it – and the body – exist in a tangled metabolic flux.

Gill Peterson effects a complete inversion of the sex/gender model as understood by mid-century bourgeois feminism (for which sex is understood as fixed and biological, and gender its malleable cultural counterpart). But also something of a departure from the queer-theoretical Butlerian tradition that derives some of its force in the so-called startling revelation that 'sex' is as culturally coded as gender, and both are performative. Queer theory's primal 'aha' thus loses much of its force when we realise, by way of Gill Peterson, that dominant medical models at the mid-century did not conceive sex to be fixed, but rather unnervingly capricious. In response, physicians and researchers began to construct 'gender' as a way to stabilise the instability of sex: 'The ongoing intersex-trans dialogues led in the 1950s to the invention of gender ...'

Reassigning the sex of intersex infants led to a theory of gender that coordinated the development of the biological body with the psychological acquisition of an ineradicable identity, 'installing a new difference between sex and gender ... that ... had very little intelligibility over the preceding fifty years'.[64] Medical transition becomes a way to align the plasticity of sex with the intractability of gender.[65] Here, gender is a kind of characterological predisposition that – unlike the plasticity of sex – is immovable. Trans character is a fixation; trans embodiment is malleable.[66] So essentially, for the clinics, an understanding of the metabolic nature of the body – and the non-separability of sex phenotype from any other of the body's functions – meant that biology was plastic, whereas gender identity was fixed. 'Gender' then became the concept that made binary sex coherent. The medicalisation of transness secured this binarisation of sex through a *libidinalisation of metabolism*. Metabolism served not only an ontological ground of human life, but as an expression of character and desire. As the so-called primary foundation of relationality and social life. This matrix is a profoundly racialised formation:

> By limiting trans children's value to an abstract biological force through which medicine aimed to alter sex and gender as phenotypes, those children became living laboratories, proxies for working out broader questions about human sex and gender that had little investment in their personhood. Children became the incarnation and aetiology of sex's plasticity as an abstract form of whiteness, the capacity to take on a new form and be transformed by medical scientific intervention early on in life.[67]

Following Gill Peterson, along with Spillers and Snorton, we might say that the concept of metabolism only began to function as a concrete abstraction insofar as it became attached to the *whiteness* of plasticity, and – by extension – the whiteness of an idealised form of clinic-based transsexuality.

But did the researchers at Johns Hopkins simply devise this idea of a fixed 'character' to gender identity, or might this formulation be mediating a pre-existing cultural condition? Drawing on the work of Emma Heaney, we might speculate that the doctors find themselves *able* to conceptualise gender in the ways that they do because

of the Modernist literary heritage. For Heaney, fiction of this era nat-
uralises the 'transfeminine allegory' as a single, fixed characterisation
of transfeminine experience: being 'born into the wrong body'. For
Heaney, the Modernists abstract from the variability of transfeminine
experience to produce the transfeminine as an allegory for modernity
more broadly.[68] Historical shifts in the nature of work – including the
increasing entry of women into the labour force – as well as the rise
of the bourgeois family (theorised by Freud as a formation hinging on
the phobia and fetishisation of castration) impel and empower this
allegorisation. In some contrast, Heaney delivers a materialist account
of the transfeminine:

> Build[ing] on the Marxist feminist theorisation of woman as the
> social category that emerges through a historical relation to repro-
> ductive labor, noting that the category of trans woman emerges at
> the intersection of this reproductive material basis and an a priori
> association with sex work, a form of criminalised labor.[69]

The relationship between transfeminine experience and the transfeminine allegory takes the form of a difference between 'expert' and
'vernacular' forms.

The challenge to cis-presumptions around the binary logic of sex,
if we follow Heaney, thus would pre-exist the work at Johns Hopkins,
since it is 'trans feminine life in its great diversity ... [that] presents
[a] singular challenge to cis logic and not the Modernist period's technological innovations in endocrinology and genital surgery'. In other
words, Hopkins finds at its ready disposal a pre-existing allegory of
trans femininity as a gendered 'solution' to the constitutive instability of sex.[70]

Following Ellison, Heaney, and Gill Peterson, I think there's work
to be done here to investigate how intersections of metabolism – particularly the whiteness of sexual plasticity as Gill Peterson has outlined
it – the racialisation and criminalisation of labour, and social reproduction not only contributed to the articulation of gender as such, but also
thereby composed, in part, a context and set of preconditions for Ben
Fowkes's (1971) and David Fernbach's (1981) editions of *Capital* – in
both of which 'Stoffwechsel' is translated for the first time in English
as 'metabolism'.[71] To what extent, in other words, do the articulation

of medicalised forms of transgender subjectivity and our most recent translations of *Capital* share a common discursive origin?[72] And, following this, to what extent do texts of trans studies and Marxism thus need to be read in relation to one another? The material conditions of trans life furnish the terrain in which the seeds of abstract concepts come to fruition. What I hope to have offered here is simply one face of a larger point that there is indeed a path to Marx that proceeds through transness.

This path has both to do with the specific conditions of trans life, and with the sociogeny of sexual difference itself, which is largely unthought within Marx's own works – but which overcodes the sexual division of labour, the abstraction of metabolics, and the question of social reproduction alike. The dystopian facet of this matrix is that trans people have long been a fixation, scapegoat, and target for convulsions in the mode of production, the organisation of space, and the social world.[73] The utopian facet of this matrix is written, as Marx had it, in the 'letters of blood and fire' (and, as Marx did not quite have it, in the embodied life) of our struggle.

Notes

1. With many thanks to Jasbir Puar for her many conversations about this work with me. And to Kay Gabriel for her acumen as an editor and interlocutor. This piece surely retains many flaws, but it would have many more without Jasbir and Kay's thoughtful attention and expertise.

2. This is a claim that has been made widely. See, for example, Vijay Prashad's account of a single day of the strike, India's One-Day Strike Largest in History, https://consortiumnews.com/2020/12/04/indias-one-day-general-strike-largest-in-history/. See also the media and statements collected at the Panth-Punjab Project: https://www.panth punjab.org/media/siege-of-delhi.

3. Rukeyser, M. (1938). *The Book of the Dead*. New York, NY: Covici-Friede.

4. Bloch, E. (2009). *Heritage of Our Times*. London: Polity.

5. Abi-Karam, A. and Gabriel, K. (2020). *We Want It All: An Anthology of Radical Trans Poetics*. Brooklyn, NY: Nightboat Books.

6. Feinberg, L. (1993). *Stone Butch Blues*, https://www.lesliefeinberg.net/.

7. Jameson, F. (2016). *Raymond Chandler: The Detections of Totality*. New York, NY: Verso, p. 10.

8. Since 1993, as Annie McClanahan has charted, 'nearly half of job growth [in the US] has been in low-paid service work, and as of 2016, the combination of retail, leisure, hospitality, and "personal" service makes up around

23% of all employment'. McClanahan, A. (2019). Tipwork and Tipwork-ification. *Post45*, https://post45.org/2019/01/tv-and-tipworkification/.

9. Winant, G. (2019). 'Hard Times Make for Hard Arteries and Hard Livers': Deindustrialization, Biopolitics, and the Making of a New Working Class. *Journal of Social History*, 53(1).

10. Ibid.

11. Winant, G. (2020). 'What's Actually Going on in Our Nursing Homes': An Interview with Shantonia Jackson. *Dissent*, Fall.

12. Winant, Hard Times. Abolitionist organizers frequently consider nursing homes, together with psychiatric facilities as 'institutional care settings'. See the archives of Critical Resistance, e.g. http://criticalresistance.org/los-angeles-32-organizations-submit-letter-against-jail-construction/. Needless to say, the COVID-19 pandemic has clarified at a wide scale the extent to which 'prisons, nursing homes, psychiatric wards and halfway houses become recognized as sites of both confinement and infection'. Boodman, E. (8 May 2020) Covid, Biopolitics and Abolitionist Care Beyond Security and Containment. *Abolition Journal*, https://abolitionjournal.org/covid-19-biopolitics-and-abolitionist-care-beyond-security-and-containment/.

13. Winant, What's Actually Going on.

14. Wilson Gilmore, R. (5 May 2020). Interview with Amy Goodman, 'The Case for Prison Abolition: Ruth Wilson Gilmore on Covid-19, Decarceration and Abolition'. *Democracy Now*.

15. Ellison, T. (19 October 2017). Black Trans Reproductive Labor. New York, NY: Barnard Center for Research on Women, https://bcrw.barnard.edu/videos/treva-ellison-black-trans-reproductive-labor/

16. Fanon, F. (1963). *The Wretched of the Earth*. New York: Grove Press.

17. See Bhattacharya, T. (2017). Introduction to *Social Reproduction Theory: Remapping Class, Recentering Oppression*. London: Pluto Press.

18. 'Containing sexual deviance', argues Ellison, 'was taken up by the LAPD as one avenue of boosting its own autonomy and organizational capacity'.

19. See Heaney, E. (2017). *The New Woman*. Evanston, IL: Northwestern University Press, and Namaste, V. (2000). *Invisible Lives: The Erasure of Transsexual and Transgendered People*. Chicago, IL: University of Chicago Press, for the use of trans women as figures for, as Kay Gabriel has it, 'social dynamics more broadly' (Kay Gabriel, private communication). Davis, needless to say, is not engaging in this kind of figural exploitation.

20. See Davis, A. (2003). *Are Prisons Obsolete?* New York, NY: Seven Stories Press. This question of the relation of transness and abolition opens 'the critical problem of self-determination' (Kay Gabriel, private communica-tion). This is a very rich area of inquiry and debate within trans studies specifically, and for the left more broadly. See, for example, Kadji Amin's critique of 'self-determination' as inextricable from a national project (Amin, K. (2017). *Disturbing Attachments: Genet, Modern Pederasty and Queer History*. Durham, NC: Duke University Press). Gabriel sources

self-determination in a very different historical trajectory: 'I think that doctrine (created by Lenin and M.N. Roy) is an important legacy of communist internationalism, rather than liberal statecraft'.

21. https://valleyofthed.substack.com/p/never-be-new-again.

22. As Jules Gleeson has explained, 'the seemingly spontaneous resurgence of trans politics in the 2010s follows from the ceaseless social reproductive work trans women have committed to establishing their own new gender order. Trans women, like drag queens and transvestites before them, have not come from nowhere. Indeed, an enormous amount of labor is required to bring each of us into being, and to keep us alive' (Gleeson, J. (2017). Transition and Abolition. V*iewpoint Magazine*, https://viewpointmag.com/2017/07/19/transition-and-abolition-notes-on-marxism-and-trans-politics/). Or as Noah Zazanis comments, in this volume, 'So far, most writing available on transformative practices of reproduction has come directly from queer and trans scholars writing on their own conditions of daily living'.

23. Doyle Griffiths, K. (2018). Crossroads and Country Roads: Wildcat West Virginia and the Possibilities of a Working Class Offensive. *Viewpoint Magazine*, https://www.viewpointmag.com/2018/03/13/crossroads-and-country-roads-wildcat-west-virginia-and-the-possibilities-of-a-working-class-offensive/.

24. See Chapter 2 in this volume.

25. Needless to say, as Jin Haritaworn, Adi Kuntsman, and Sylvia Posocco note, it is working class, Black, and 'people of color' who bear the brunt of the assaults of the 'liberal democratic state'. Citing Eric Stanley, they extrapolate the ways in which this 'exceptional violence' or 'overkill' is 'central to the reproduction' of the state. See, Haritaworn, J., Kuntsman, A., and Posocco, S. (2014). *Queer Necropolitics*. London: Routledge. See also, Stanley, E. (2011) Near Life, Queer Death: Overkill and Ontological Capture. *Social Text*.

26. We have been looking for chokepoints for a long time. As Nat Raha notes in her work on the London chapter of Wages Due Lesbians, which, in 1986 'published a three and a half page list of forms of emotional labour expected of lesbians ... where they argued for the recognition, counting of, and pay for "the particular physical and emotional housework of surviving as lesbian women in a hostile and prejudiced society ... The document highlights many facets of the emotional work demanded of lesbian or bisexual women within Thatcher's Britain'. Identifying what we do as labour enables us to strategize on how to withhold it.

27. '[W]e can say that, if many of our mothers and grandmothers were caught in the sphere of IMM activities, the problem we face today is different. It is not that we will have to "go back to the kitchen", if only because *we cannot afford it*. Our fate, rather, is *having to deal with the abject*. Contrary to the IMM activities of the past, this abject has already been to a large extent denaturalised. It does not appear to those performing it as some

unfortunate natural fate, but more like an extra burden that one must deal with alongside wage-labour. Being left to deal with it is the ugly face of gender today, and this helps us to see gender as it is: a powerful constraint'. Gonzales, M. A. and Neton, J. (2013). The Logic of Gender. *Endnotes*, 3, https://endnotes.org.uk/issues/3/en/endnotes-the-logic-of-gender.

28. Gabriel, K. (2020). Gender as Accumulation Strategy. *Invert Journal*, https://invertjournal.org.uk/posts?view=articles&post=7106265 #gender-as-accumulation-strategy.

29. Ibid.

30. Jess does not explicitly describe medical transition in terms of an embodied desire to inhabit passing maleness per se. However, *Stone Butch Blues* represents several exchanges of intimacy between Jess and hir femme lovers and chosen kin taking place just after ze has been released from jail. The connection between intimate repair and excarceration is worthy of a much longer examination. I will simply say here that the book has already established this connection, so that when Jess articulates a need for more safety from police violence, this need also registers effects in the realm of the erotic, broadly speaking. Beyond the question of erotics as such, the structural layering of love story and transition story is something I will speak to shortly in the body text.

31. McClanahan, Tipwork and Tipworkification.

32. Ibid.

33. Rifkin, M. (2011). *When Did Indians Become Straight? Kinship, the History of Sexuality and Native Sovereignty*. Oxford: Oxford University Press.

34. Lyric poetry and detective stories, then, share a function, if not a form: an obsessive melancholy that is ultimately less about solving the mystery of a lost object, than evoking a set of affects around it.

35. Delany, S. (1999). *Times Square Red, Times Square Blue*. New York, NY: New York University Press.

36. Martin T. (2017). *Contemporary Drift: Genre, Historicism, and the Problem of the Present*. New York, NY: Columbia University Press, p. 61.

37. Ibid.

38. McGurl, M. (2011). *The Program Era: Postwar Fiction and the Rise of Creative Writing*. Cambridge, MA: Harvard University Press, p. 19.

39. Ibid., p. 12.

40. Shonkwiler, A. (2020). Neo-homesteading: Domestic Production and the Limits of the Postwage Imagination. *Public Culture*, https://read.dukeupress.edu/public-culture/article-abstract/32/3%20(92)/465/167180/Neo-homesteadingDomestic-Production-and-the-Limits?redirectedFrom=PDF.

41. Ibid.

42. Ibid.

43. Benjamin, W. (2002). *The Arcades Project*. Eiland, H. (Trans.). Cambridge, MA: Harvard University Press.

44. In private conversation, Kay Gabriel rephrased my claim this way: 'base materialism, as the abject, attenuates the force of allegory'.

45. Jameson, F. (2015). *The Antinomies of Realism. London:* Verso, p. 28.

46. 'The other side of this argument, also, is that the self-reflexivity that, I agree, Andrea and I are interested in, is one that points outward towards modes of collective being: so it's both particular and deindividuated. The way we like to put this is: how does a particular poetic experiment make it possible to speak in a collective voice? And that turn from individual self-creation to the replenishing and reproduction of movement work is maybe where this self-reflexivity really gets its utopian heft' (Kay Gabriel, private communication).

47. Neel, P. (2018). *Hinterland: America's New Landscape of Class and Conflict.* Chicago, IL: University of Chicago Press, p. 2.

48. Brouillette, S. (27 October 2018). Wageless Life. *Los Angeles Review of Books.*

49. Chandler, N. D. (2003). The Souls of an Ex-White Man: W.E.B. Du Bois and the Biography of John Brown. *CR: The New Centennial Review*, 3, Spring. Chandler spends some time on the significance of Du Bois basing his biography, not in archival research, but rather the rearranging of extant texts. This refusal of the archive is crucial, according to Chandler, for it precipitates a 'dissolution of whiteness' as the figure of Brown gives way to the *perspective* of Du Bois that inhabits the material. The 'originality of [Brown's] story' is not derived from archival discovery, but rather 'the orientation of an interpretation' – specifically, Du Bois's interpretation of the life of Brown – 'from the point of view of the Negro'. 'Du Bois delivers John Brown to us, and to the future, by situating the meaning of John Brown as a figure arising within or through the meaning of the Negro, the African, in the history of America and, by implication, the modern world'. The importance of this refusal of archives in favor of reconstellating extant materials is not something I can explore further here, but might represent an important avenue to a *longue durée* understanding of reflexivity as something other than a reflection of entrepreneurialism and creative self-management.

50. This work is often described in traditionally feminized ways; Brown is many times described as an excellent 'nurse'.

51. Ligon, R. (2011). *A True and Exact History of the Island of Barbadoes.* Indianapolis, IN: Hackett Classics, p. 127.

52. See Bellamy Foster, J. (2000). *Marx's Ecology: Materialism and Nature.* New York, NY: Monthly Review Press.

53. See, e.g. Lethabo King, T. (January 2019). Black 'Feminisms' and Pessimism: Abolishing Moynihan's Negro Family. *Theory &Event*, and Lewis, S. (2019). *Full Surrogacy Now: Feminism Against Family.* London: Verso.

54. Jobson, R. (2012). Dead Labor: On Racial Capital and Fossil Capital. In Jenkins, D. and Leroy, J. (Eds.). *Histories of Racial Capitalism*. New York, NY: Columbia University Press.

55. Ibid., p. 222.

56. Ibid., pp. 220–221.

57. Ibid., p. 80.

58. Spillers, H. J. (1987). Mama's Baby, Papa's Maybe: An American Grammar Book. *Diacritics*, 17(2), 64-81. I am very grateful to Jasbir Puar for extrapolating this argument with me.

59. Snorton, C. R. (2017). *Black on Both Sides: A Racial History of Trans Identity*. Minneapolis, MN: University of Minnesota Press, http://ebook-central.proquest.com/lib/uma/detail.action?docID=5118045.

60. Saito, K. (2017). *Karl Marx's Ecosocialism: Capital, Nature, and the Unfinished Business of Political Economy*. New York, NY: Monthly Review Press.

61. However, Liebig's conclusions did not lead in a naturally revolutionary direction. Rather, his reliance on concepts of what political economic Henry Charles Carey dubbed 'robbery agriculture' lead to a highly pessimistic and Mathusian worldview of degeneration, overpopulation, scarcity and impending chaos. 'In other words', argues Saito, 'Liebig's historicization of modern agriculture provided Marx with a useful scientific basis for rejecting abstract and linear treatments of agricultural development'. But it did not provide a totalizing enough account of agriculture and indeed of 'Stoffwechsel' itself, for Marx to be satisfied with this perspective. So although Marx cites Liebig approvingly in *Capital* – 'To have developed from the point of view of natural science, the negative, i.e., destructive side of modern agriculture, is one of Liebig's immortal merits', after publishing the first edition, Marx went on to read some of Liebig's critics. This further work cannot be addressed here.

62. Schmidt, A. (2014). *The Concept of Nature in Marx*. Fowkes, B. (1971, Trans.). London: Verso). I don't have the space here to explore the significance of Fowkes' translation of Schmidt in 1971, just before his work on the translation of *Capital* in 1976 – although one would imagine there is a direct connection here in Fowkes' attention to the concept of 'Stoffwechsel'. For reasons that should become clear, I don't believe the adjacency of these translations can sufficiently account for the availability of the concept of "metabolism" for translation in the 1970s.

63. Angus, I. (August 2019). The Discovery and Rediscovery of Metabolic Rift. *Monthly Review*, https://mronline.org/2019/07/30/the-discovery-and-rediscovery-of-metabolic-rift/.

64. Gill Peterson J. (2018). *Histories of the Transgender Child*. Minneapolis, MN: University of Minnesota Press, p. 17.

65. As Gill Peterson, C. Riley Snorton, and others have noted, the gendering of sex is – and has been – a racial formation in the West since the inception of the plantation system. See Snorton, *Black on Both Sides*. Aren Aizura, in a recent issue of *Social Text*, summarizes the context of the emergence

of trans in the twentieth century: 'Across the twentieth century, trans emerged as a category; synthetic hormones and body modifying surgeries became available to particular, mainly white middle-class populations. But twentieth-century trans medicine itself produced a transgender whiteness we contend with now as a racialized biopolitical sorting of populations into recognizable and invisible, life to be fostered and life that is disposable'. Aizura, A. (2021). Introduction to 'Thinking with Trans Now' roundtable. *Social Text*, 38(4 (145)), 125–147.

66. The implications of this for a theory of *literary* character are too extensive to explore here – but include the traditional presumption that what novels do is showcase the formation and change of character over time (see, for example, Bender, J. (1989). *Imagining the Penitentiary: Fiction and the Architecture of Mind in Eighteenth-Century England.* Chicago, IL: Chicago University Press).

67. Gill Peterson, *Histories of the Transgender Child*, p. 4.

68. Here, too, the whiteness of this universal is critical to note.

69. Heaney, The New Woman, p. 20.

70. See, in particular, the oeuvre of Hannah Landecker. Landecher's work is essential to a social history of metabolism, especially as it tracks the term through its agricultural, industrial, and embodied applications. But I aim to complicate her apparently progressive model of the historical development of this concept, e.g. 'Through examination of four examples from contemporary metabolic sciences, this article characterizes the rise of a postindustrial metabolism. Concerned with regulation, timing, and information, this emergent metabolism is analyzed as a shift away from the factory or motor model of classic metabolism, in which food was fuel, providing energy and building blocks to the body. Accordingly, metabolic disorders – treatments for which are the explicit aim of much of this research – are increasingly explained and intervened in as regulatory crises, asynchronies, or instances of misinformation. Close examination of the explanatory frameworks and experimental design of the contemporary metabolic sciences answers, with some specificity, the question of the knowledge effects of obesity and diabetes research, or *fat knowledge*'. Landecker, H. (2013). Postindustrial Metabolism: Fat Knowledge. *Public Culture.*

71. I do not have the space here to offer a reading of Kay Gabriel's extremely relevant poem, STOFFWECHSEL. I will just bookmark that Gabriel's poem adds a number of crucial poetic qualifications to contemporary discussions of metabolic rift, having to do with the *unevenness* of humans' metabolic interaction with nature, as well as a reminder – by way of transness – that nature itself is not 'natural,' but is always, as Neil Smith had it, 'second nature'. For more on this poem, and for the poem itself, see, Pleasure and Provocation: Kay Gabriel Interview with Jordy Rosenberg. *Salvage Quarterly* (2018), https://salvage.zone/online-exclusive/

never-not-a-matter-of-taking-sides-kay-gabriel-interview-with-jordy-rosenberg/.

72. See Ertürk, N. and Serin, Ö. (2016). Marxism, Communism and Translation. *Boundary*, 2. 'Translation is not an afterlife of Marxist-communist texts but a constitutive force that impels them from the start ... The communist translations of the revolutionary period ought not to be considered as mere secondary reproductions but rather as fulfillments of the original Russian documents themselves. Insofar as the original gift message marks a hollow state to come and a temporal gap, it calls for translation to realize its content. Equally important, the practice of Leninist translation offers a displacement of the tension between the universal and the particular, by imagining a dual birth'.

73. Referencing Stuart Hall's *Policing the Crisis*, Ellison draws connections between the criminalization of British Blackness and the contradictory coming-into-popular-visibility of trans life: 'Hall shows how the articulation of the mugger was a driver of authoritarian populism that cathected anxieties about political, economic, and social instabilities occurring at multiple spatial scales onto working-class Black migrants. We are in a similar moment where there is a lot of conversation around transgender identity and studies and the transgender experience: what is essential about it, what is not, who is it for?' Ellison, T. (2021) Thinking with Trans Now roundtable. *Social Text*.

Notes on the Contributors

Noah Zazanis is a Marxist feminist, epidemiological researcher, and unrepentant transsexual. He lives in Queens and writes and organizes when he can.

Michelle Esther O'Brien is a militant and practicing psychoanalyst living in New York City. She recently graduated from New York University, with a doctoral thesis addressing how political economy and class politics shape LGBTQ organising in post-austerity NYC. Michelle is a co-editor of *Pinko* magazine, and was previously a social worker in HIV and AIDS services, and the long-time coordinator of the NYC Trans Oral History Project. She is a queer, a mom, and a communist.

Rosa Lee is an editor at *Viewpoint Magazine*, a graduate from UC Santa Cruz and an active gabber producer.

Nat Raha is a poet based in Edinburgh, who completed a PhD at the University of Sussex entitled 'Queer Capital: Marxism in queer theory and post-1950 poetics'. Her current research investigates radical trans-feminism, and race in UK poetry and poetics. She has performed her work internationally, and is the author of three collections and numerous pamphlets of poetry. Nat is co-editor of the *Radical Transfeminism* zine.

Farah Thompson is a Black, bisexual trans woman who lives in San Diego. She advocates for anti-imperialism, LGBT rights, decriminalisation of drug use and sex work, and self-determination of Black and colonized peoples. Her writing is found on longpaleroad.com.

Kate Doyle Griffiths is an anthropologist at City University of New York's Graduate Center, a lecturer at Brooklyn College, and co-chair Red Bloom in New York City. Kate is an editor of *Spectre*. They are an ethnographer who writes about Southern Africa and the USA, workers, strikes, health and medicine, gender, Queers, race, class, Marxism and what is to be done.

Virgínia Guitzel is a working-class philosophy student at the Federal University of ABC, and a Member of the Movimento Revolucionário de Trabalhadores (MRT), which is the Brazilian section of the Fração Trotskista – Quarta Internacional. She is a participant in the Women's group Pão e Rosas, which worked in the front line struggling for legal abortion in Argentina.

JN Hoad is a femme de lettres, carer and communist in the North West of England. They are concerned with trans and queer care practices, and how these come to make change in the world. Their work has appeared in *Salvage* magazine, *Blind Field* and *New Socialist*.

Zoe Belinsky received her Master's in the study of Philosophy from Villanova University, where she studied in the PhD program. She has since left the program, and now works in Jewish education and local organising.

CAACD is a collective name for dialogue encouraging lines of flight, and shaking of the habitual.

Nathaniel Dickson is a queer writer, communist and graduate student in the University at Buffalo's English Department where he is dissertating on collective desire, futurity, and apocalypse.

Xandra Metcalfe is a psychoanalytic communist and noise artist based in Melbourne, Australia.

Anja Heisler Weiser Flower is an internationalist communist and artist living in San Francisco, California. Theoretically, she focuses on picking up the dropped threads of the left-communist and heretical tendencies of the twentieth century, to understand class and domination of oppressed groups in a capacious, unitary manner, and to confront the possibilities of a revolutionary proletariat. She eagerly awaits the end of gender, private automobiles and inaccessible buildings.

Jordy Rosenberg is a professor of literature at University of Massachusetts Amherst, and the author of the monograph *Critical Enthusiasm: Capital Accumulation and the Transformation of Religious Passion* (2011) and the novel *Confessions of the Fox* (2018). Jordy's hybrid work, *The Day Unravels What the Night has Woven*, is forthcoming from Random House/One World.

Editors

Jules Joanne Gleeson is a Londoner living in Vienna. She has performed lectures and stand-up comedy internationally. Her essays have been published widely, including by *Viewpoint Magazine*, *Invert*, *TSQ*, *Homintern*, *VICE*, *Oxford Art Journal* and *Salvage*. Jules co-founded the Leftovers communist discussion group, has copyedited several Marxist monographs, and is writing a book about logic and hermaphrodites. She enjoys pop music, mystical texts and kettlebells.

Elle O'Rourke is a political economist and gender theorist living in Manchester. She has been involved in trans activism for many years, and is currently a carer and advocate with QueerCare. She is a founding editor of *New Socialist*, a magazine of left thought and commentary, where she serves as Economics editor. Elle is currently working on a project on critical macro-finance, household debt, and the reproduction of gendered and racial inequalities.

Index